Hiking

Kentucky

Michael H. Brown

FALCON®

GUILFORD, CONNECTICUT

An imprint of The Globe Pequot Press

*A*FALCONGUIDE ®

Front cover photo by Brian Maslar/Index Stock
Back cover photo by Kathy Heister/Index Stock
All other photos by the author
Maps by Moore Creative Designs
Excerpt from *Kentucky is My Land* reprinted with permission from the Jesse Stuart Foundation.

Library of Congress Cataloging-in-Publication Data

Brown, Michael H. (Michael Hunt), 1942-
   Hiking Kentucky / Michael H. Brown.—1st ed.
      p. cm.—(A Falcon guide)
   ISBN-13: 978-0-7627-1116-1
   ISBN-10: 0-7627-1116-7
      1. Hiking—Kentucky—Guidebooks. 2. Kentucky—Guidebooks. I. Title. II. Series.

GV199.42.K4 B76 2001
917.6904′44—dc21   2001040722

Manufactured in the United States of America
First Edition/Fourth Printing

To buy books in quantity for corporate use
or incentives, call **(800) 962–0973, ext. 4551,**
or e-mail **premiums@GlobePequot.com.**

Contents

Acknowledgments

In putting together this collection of hikes, I had valuable help from the people who look after the public lands and trails of Kentucky. To all of these rangers, administrators, receptionists, and others of whatever title, thanks for your pointers and patience.

Thanks also to the men and women of Kentucky—paid and volunteer, public and private—who do the hellishly hard work of building and maintaining the state's footpaths.

Hike Locator Map

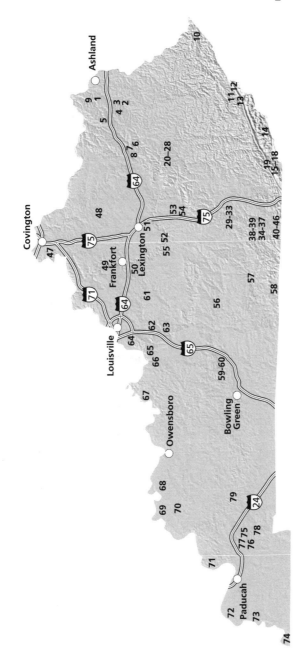

Map Legend

Interstate		Trailhead		
US Highway		Main Trail		
State Highway		Secondary Trail		
County Road		National Forest/ Park/Wilderness Boundary		
Forest Road				
Paved Road		State Boundary	KY TN	
Gravel Road		Lake		
Unimproved Road		Meadow/Marsh		
Gate		Spring		
Ranger Station		River		
Campground		Stream		
Cabins/Structures		Intermittent Stream		
Point of Interest		Waterfalls		
Picnic Area				
Cemetery		Map Orientation	N	
Parking				
Church		Scale	0 0.5 1 Mile	

Introduction

Kentucky is neither southern, northern, eastern or western,
It is the core of America.
If these United States can be called a body,
Kentucky can be called its heart.

—Jesse Stuart, *Kentucky is My Land*

Yes, it's a bit Kentucky-centric, but this verse by the state's late poet laureate has a lot of truth to it. Kentucky is a widely varied land that, despite the colorful stereotypes—racehorses, whiskey, hillbillies, and the like—fits no convenient classification, geographic or otherwise. Stretching from the jagged Appalachians to the flat Mississippi valley, from industrial plants on the Ohio River to magnolia trees in the Old Confederacy, Kentucky belongs to no one section of the country but is, rather, an intriguing mix. Of northern, southern, and midwestern. Of rural and urban. Of mountains and plains. It is an irony of history but an understandable one that Kentucky was the birthplace of both Abraham Lincoln and Jefferson Davis, the opposing leaders in the great conflict between two views of America. Today Kentuckians living on the state's western edge can drive to St. Louis or Memphis in less than half the time it takes them to visit their fellow Kentuckians in Ashland. Southern Kentuckians who can get to Nashville in less than an hour need more than three to get to the northern Kentucky suburbs of Cincinnati. The purpose of this book is to help hikers and would-be hikers explore this diverse collection of mountains and hollows, ridges and bottomlands, rolling fields and thick forests known as the Bluegrass State.

From the Big Sandy in the east to the Mississippi, from the Ohio on the north to the Tennessee line, Kentucky encompasses 40,395 square miles of land and water. Within these borders are:

- Two national parks, two major federal recreation areas, the Daniel Boone National Forest stretching almost the width of the state, and more than a dozen large Corps of Engineers reservoirs with significant amounts of adjacent land.

- More than 160 state parks, forests, wildlife areas, and nature preserves.

- Scores of additional parcels owned by private groups and local governments and opened to public use.

This book is a guide to the most appealing of these areas and to seventy-nine specific hikes within them. Kentucky is said to have 1,500 miles of maintained, marked trails. I certainly haven't been on all 1,500 of them, and so will resist the temptation to pronounce these seventy-nine hikes the best in the state. But after walking every foot of the seventy-nine, I do guarantee that each offers a rewarding experience.

Multitiered Tioga Falls cascades down the rocks after a heavy rain.

These hikes cover all sections of Kentucky and, hopefully, offer a variety to satisfy people of all ages, experience, and stamina. They range in length from short loops of less than 2 miles to overnight backpacking trips, the longest a 31.2-mile excursion through the Land Between the Lakes National Recreation Area. In my travels across Kentucky, I found that local knowledge of hiking opportunities often extends only to the county line. My hope is that this guide will be as useful to the state's lifelong residents as it is to first-time visitors.

Kentucky Briefly

THE LAND

Simply put, the eastern edge of Kentucky is covered with sharp ridges and narrow valleys; the western edge of the state is low and level; and the vast middle is a moderate mix. Kentucky's highest point is 4,145-foot Black Mountain in Harlan County in the southeast corner near Virginia. The low point—257 feet—is in the state's southwest corner on the Mississippi River across from Missouri.

For the hiker, the upshot is that the eastern part of the state, especially the southeast, involves steeper climbs and more of them; as you go west, the terrain generally becomes less demanding. This book includes several western Kentucky hikes along the Mississippi and Ohio Rivers that are literally flat as a pancake. On the other hand, if you like to hike to high overlooks with dramatic vistas, the eastern third of the state is your best bet.

Eastern Kentucky is on the edge of the long Appalachian mountain system that extends from the Canadian province of Quebec all the way into Alabama. The eastern Kentucky surface is Pennsylvanian-era rock formed 325 to 290 million years ago and composed of shale, sandstone, conglomerates, and coal. The coal deposits in this and a smaller Pennsylvanian outcrop in western Kentucky make the state a leading coal producer—once first in the nation, now number three, behind Wyoming and West Virginia. One of the constants of Kentucky history has been the struggle, particularly amid the steep slopes of Appalachia, between those who want to reap the financial

A quiet stream provides a cool spot along Gibson Gap Trail.

3

rewards of this resource and those more interested in protecting the land and streams underlying it. Though muted by federal reclamation requirements enacted in the late 1970s, it is a struggle that continues today.

The western edge of the plateau across eastern Kentucky (called the Appalachian or Cumberland Plateau) is lined with a wall of rock known as the Pottsville Escarpment. This escarpment includes hard sandstones able to withstand nature's weathering process better than the surrounding materials. The result is an uneven erosion process that has produced one of the state's most noteworthy physical attributes: the arches and rock houses in the Red River Gorge and other areas along the western side of eastern Kentucky.

In north-central Kentucky, ringed by a series of steep but small hills called the Knobs, is the Bluegrass region. The underlying rock is the oldest in the state (510 to 440 million years) and contains limestones that naturally fertilize the soil, making this a rich agricultural area and center of the state's thoroughbred horse industry. Bluegrass, which thrives here and accounts for the state's nickname, is green but has buds that give a field of it a bluish tint. The rolling area immediately around Lexington is known as the Inner Bluegrass; the sharper-ridged, outlying counties as the Outer Bluegrass.

South-central Kentucky and the area south of the western coalfields are covered by a younger rock (from the Mississippian age, 360 to 325 million years ago) that is rich in soluble limestones and conducive to erosion by underground water flow. Mammoth Cave, the largest-known cave system in the world, is a product of this process. Named for the pennyroyal, a mint-family plant that grows in the region, this part of the state is called the Pennyroyal or Pennyrile, also the Mississippian Plateau.

The southwestern tip of the state is named the Jackson Purchase, because Andrew Jackson of neighboring Tennessee helped negotiate its acquisition from the Chickasaw Indians. It is at the end of the coastal plain that extends north from the Gulf of Mexico, and consists of relatively young, easily eroded sediment. This part of Kentucky is flat and full of marshy areas called sloughs, many of them with beautiful bald cypress trees.

The Ohio River flows 664 miles along the northern border and the state is intersected by several major west-flowing rivers that empty into the Ohio: most significantly, from east to west, the Licking, Kentucky, Green, Cumberland, and Tennessee Rivers. Altogether, Kentucky has 1,100 miles of commercially navigable waterways, and claims to be second only to Alaska in total water mileage.

Water travel was an important impetus to Kentucky commerce and development; Louisville, the biggest city, started as an Ohio River port. But the flip side was a state long plagued by flooding. Flood control was a major reason (along with hydropower and navigation) behind the construction of the extensive system of reservoirs that now runs through the state. Together with federally funded floodwalls for endangered cities, these man-made lakes have curtailed the flooding threat, though not eliminated it. The lakes are also a main source of recreation.

Almost half the state is covered by forest, mainly hardwoods. The predominant species include white and red oak, walnut, yellow poplar, beech,

Nearly 11,000 acres along the Ohio River ooze with flooded fields and woods.

sugar maple, white ash, and hickory. Kentucky is among the top five states in producing hardwood-lumber, and over the years it has been heavily logged—all of it at least once. But while there are no truly virgin forests, there are several patches of old-growth trees (Hike 11 takes you through one of them) and many beautiful wooded spots with tall trees, leafy rhododendron shrubs, ferns, and wildflowers. In springtime, for a rundown on what wildflowers are blooming where, telephone the state Department of Travel at (800) 225-8747. The official state tree is the tulip, sometimes called the tulip poplar—though it's actually a magnolia, not a poplar. Goldenrod is the state flower.

For more information about the geology and regions of Kentucky, see the Kentucky Geological Survey Web site: www.uky.edu/KGS.

HISTORY

In 1902, in the midst of the bitter partisan battle, Kentuckian James H. Mulligan penned a poem ending:

> *The mountains tower proudest,*
> *Thunder peals the loudest,*
> *The landscape is the grandest,*
> *And politics the damnedest,*
> *In Kentucky.*

If it weren't for its lighthearted nature, this piece of doggerel would be an apt description of Kentucky's Civil War role, the most significant chapter in the state's history.

Kentucky was a slave state but badly split over the question of secession. As a result, it remained in the Union but declared itself neutral in the hostilities. In their readable *A New History of Kentucky,* historians Lowell H. Harrison and James C. Klotter explain how this attempt to stay above the fray failed to protect the state or its families from division and tragedy. They cite estimates that 90,000 to 100,000 Kentuckians fought for the Union, 25,000 to 40,000 for the Confederacy; nearly one out of every five men who went off to the war did not return. There were a number of battles on Kentucky soil, but the government in Frankfort, the capital, kept the state in the Union throughout the war. That, however, did not stop Southern sympathizers from setting up their own state government in Bowling Green and securing Kentucky's admission to the Confederacy. Thus, along with neighboring Missouri, Kentucky was on both sides. That's why the flag of the eleven-state Confederacy had thirteen stars.

Several of the seventy-nine hikes in this guide involve the state's Civil War history. Others visit sites linked to the earliest Kentuckians. The first people are believed to have arrived in what is now Kentucky about 12,000 years ago, probably in search of game. Over the centuries these hunting groups became less nomadic. By the time the Europeans arrived in the New World, the early Kentuckians we call Indians were growing corn and beans and building large settlements.

Even before whites moved into the state, the Native population was in decline, in part because the Indians had no immunity against European diseases that made their way inland from the East Coast settlements. White men began entering Kentucky, then a part of Virginia, in the late 1700s. First came

A trailhead sign for Chadwell Gap Trail greets visitors in the parking lot.

hunters, the best known of whom was Daniel Boone, and then settlers seeking land. Their entry was through Cumberland Gap, a mountain notch that is now a national park with some of the best hiking in the state. In 1792 Kentucky was admitted to the Union as the fifteenth state.

Those who have followed Daniel Boone into Kentucky's pantheon of the famous (in addition to Lincoln and Davis) include:

- Nineteenth-century statesman Henry Clay

- President Zachary Taylor

- Naturalist John James Audubon

- Supreme Court Justices Louis Brandeis and John Marshall Harlan

- Vice President Alben Barkley

- Author Robert Penn Warren

- Boxer Muhammed Ali

THE PEOPLE

Kentucky today has a population of just under four million, ranking twenty-fifth in the nation. In many respects the state retains the flavor of its frontier origins. With about half the people living outside urban areas, it's one of the most rural states in the country. Notwithstanding the handsome horse-breeding estates that line the shaded lanes of the Bluegrass, small farms are mainly what you find across the countryside. The state has some 90,000 farms, the fifth-highest number in the country. But they average only 154 acres, the seventh-smallest average.

For all of the death and destruction it causes, tobacco has an attribute important to small farming: Thanks to production controls and price supports, it's a cash crop that's profitable even when grown in small amounts—which is the only way anything can be grown on some of the little plots in steep-slope Appalachia. So it's no accident that only North Carolina farmers grow more tobacco than us. Kentucky is the top producer of burley, one of the two main types of tobacco used in cigarettes.

Kentuckians seem to excel in controversial products. The central part of the state is a major producer of bourbon whiskey, in part because the limestone provides good water for the distilling process. Thoroughbred horses bred and raised on Lexington-area farms are a multimillion-dollar business, and the Kentucky Derby run at Louisville's Churchill Downs the first Saturday in May is the nation's premier horserace.

Despite the importance of farms and farm products, manufacturing accounts for the largest share of the state's economy. Automobile-related plants have become increasingly important. Toyota has a large facility near Georgetown north of Lexington, and Ford is a major employer in Louisville. About 18 percent of the state's nonfarm employees work in manufacturing jobs, one of the highest percentages in the country. Louisville, the state's largest urban area, has almost 700,000 residents counting surrounding Jefferson County. Lexington and Fayette County are second with about 240,000.

Kentucky is not an affluent state. It has a high poverty rate (eleventh highest in the nation) and ranks thirty-ninth in per capita personal income, according to recent figures. In 1999, 10 percent of its residents were on food stamps, the sixth-highest percentage among the fifty states.

One economic fact hikers should be aware of is that a large amount of marijuana is grown—illegally—in the state, much of it in eastern Kentucky, including the Daniel Boone National Forest. To protect their crop from theft, growers have been known to booby-trap their marijuana fields with everything from explosives to fishhooks. While none of the routes in this book should entail danger of this kind, eastern Kentucky rangers and park administrators advise hikers to stay on sanctioned trails and be careful not to wander into untrod territory.

A more benign fact of Kentucky life is that the state has two time zones. While the division is not a straight line, basically the eastern half, including Louisville, is on Eastern Time; the western half is on Central.

WEATHER

An aunt of mine who used to escape her Louisville home in the summer for the cool of Michigan liked to lead her fellow vacationers in an evening chorus of the state song, "My Old Kentucky Home." After the last words—"We will sing one song for the old Kentucky home / For the old Kentucky home far away"—she would yell, "Thank goodness." That heretical outburst was not

An old wagon remains at Hensley Settlement.

directed at the state itself, which she surely loved, but at its brutal summer weather. She was delighted to be far away.

Which is to say that in the dog days of summer, you should think long and hard about taking a hike in Kentucky and certainly about a long and hard hike. In August the average high is 85 degrees, but that doesn't tell the whole story. In addition to the heat, it's usually humid—the sticky, horribly uncomfortable kind of humid that makes you think it's 20 degrees hotter than it really is. Caution is also in order for the dead of winter. January, the coldest month, has an average low of 23 degrees, but the thermometer can easily drop below that. Although snowstorms are not an everyday occurrence, you can expect one or two a winter. Annual snowfall ranges from 40 inches in the southeastern mountains to 5 to 10 inches in the southwest.

That said, the Kentucky climate is generally temperate. The normal daily mean temperature—56.1 degrees—is eighteenth highest among the states, number one being sunny Hawaii. The one certainty about Kentucky weather is that it's unpredictable. One March day I was hiking in shorts and T-shirt, and even took a dip—a quick one, to be sure—in Kentucky Lake. Two days later I was bundled up in a sweater and long pants. One fairly safe statement is that spring, especially early spring, and fall are the most pleasant hiking periods.

However, tornadoes cause significant destruction—and many fatalities—in Kentucky, and although they can and do strike any time of year, they are most frequent in spring. In April 1974 a storm packing twenty-eight twisters killed seventy-six Kentuckians, thirty-one in the Ohio River town of Brandenburg. The state's weather-warning system has improved since then, but Kentucky still ranks high in tornado victims. If you are stranded in a tornado without secure shelter nearby, experts say the best course is to lie flat in a ditch or culvert—assuming that flash flooding or lightning is not a threat. If you are in a car and a tornado approaches, the experts advise getting out. Twisters can easily fling an automobile.

Flash flooding is another potential danger, especially on the slopes of eastern Kentucky, where a heavy rain can send what is normally a lazy stream suddenly raging out of its narrow banks. Be careful camping in low-lying areas, and if you come to a swollen stream, don't be afraid to turn around and go back the way you came. When done correctly and carefully, fording a big stream can be safe. But you must know your limits and the limits of your hiking party, especially children.

The first defense against bad weather, of course, is to check the forecast before setting out. Once on your way, watch cloud formations closely so you aren't caught in an exposed setting. In a lightning storm, which is the most common weather threat in Kentucky, you don't want to be on a ridgetop, under a large, solitary tree, in the open, or near standing water. Also take these other precautions:

- Lightning can travel ahead of a storm, so take cover before the storm hits.

- Don't try to make it back to your vehicle; it's not worth the risk. Instead, seek shelter in a low-lying area, ideally in a stand of small, uniformly sized trees.

Clouds obscure the westward view from the ridge at Breaks Interstate Park.

- Avoid anything that attracts lightning, such as metal tent poles, graphite fishing rods, or pack frames.

- Crouch with both feet firmly on the ground. If you have a sleeping bag or a pack without a metal frame, put your feet on it for extra insulation.

- Don't walk or huddle together with your hiking partners. Instead, stay 50 feet apart so that if one is hit, others can give first aid.

- If you are in a tent, stay in your sleeping bag with your feet on your pad.

WILDLIFE

"The biggest thing people have to watch out for in Kentucky is themselves," says state park naturalist Carey Tichenor. He's right. You don't have to worry about grizzlies, mountain lions, or other four-footed predators in Kentucky. There aren't any. A few black bears are spotted each year in the far eastern part of the state, but there have been no reports of danger to humans. Most of the bears probably wander in from Virginia and West Virginia, though there have been experimental efforts to reintroduce black bears into Land Between the Lakes. Bears were once plentiful throughout the state, but today your chances of seeing one are less than slim.

The largest wild animal you are likely to encounter is the elk. A program to reestablish elk in the state is proving successful; currently there are believed to be almost 800, all in the southeastern corner. White-tailed deer, of course, are plentiful, and a small, nonaggressive member of the cat family, the bobcat, lives throughout the state. Beavers, foxes, muskrats, opossums, raccoons, woodchucks, coyotes, and wild hogs are also in residence. The state bird is the Kentucky cardinal. Believe it or not, there's also a state wild animal, the gray squirrel, and even a state fish, the Kentucky bass. The list goes on (can you believe a state fossil?), but I won't.

One of the most exciting creatures you are apt to see is the wild turkey, the largest game bird in North America; an adult male can approach thirty pounds. Kentucky's wild turkey population had been all but eliminated a few decades ago. Restoration efforts, however, have now brought it back to well over 100,000, and it's not at all uncommon for one of the birds to blast out of its wooded hiding spot as you traipse by.

There are poisonous snakes in Kentucky—primarily the timber rattlesnake and copperhead, found in most parts of the state, and the water moccasin in the west only. Carey Tichenor, the naturalist, says there are occasional snakebite reports but no fatalities that he knows of in recent years.

Snakes strike humans only in self-defense, or when startled or otherwise afraid. The solution is to avoid scaring them. Look where you place your feet, especially in tall grass, and don't reach under or over rocks or logs without looking first. If you do encounter a snake, slowly back away and give it a chance to slither off—an opportunity it will invariably take. Don't throw rocks and sticks at it. If bitten, try not to panic. Running or otherwise speeding up your circulation increases the speed with which the venom travels through your bloodstream. Keep the bite site lower than your heart to decrease the venom spread, and seek medical attention.

Unlike poisonous snakes, ticks are common in Kentucky—and a real pest for the hiker. In the Beaver Creek Wilderness, after sitting on the ground while eating dinner, I retired to my tent for what I expected to be a good night's sleep. It never came. Instead, I spent the night battling what felt like an army of the little crawlies.

In addition to being a nuisance, ticks can cause serious health problems. Lyme disease, a flu-like sickness whose symptoms include nausea, fever, fatigue, and muscle and joint aches, is spread by the bite of infected deer ticks. Most ticks are not infected, and Kentucky reports few cases of the disease. However, if a red inflammation develops at the site of a tick bite, it should be checked by a doctor; it may signal infection. Another disease, Rocky Mountain spotted fever, is spread by infected American dog ticks; each year the disease strikes about 800 people across the country, though mainly in the southeastern states.

To prevent tick bites and the possibility of disease, follow this advice from officials at Land Between the Lakes, where ticks are out in force much of the year:

- Wear long pants and tuck the legs into your socks or boots, or else tape your pant legs closed.

- Spray your clothes with a tick repellent.

- Periodically check your clothes and body for ticks, and remove any you find with tweezers or fingers, taking care not to crush the body of an attached tick.

HUNTING SEASONS

While animals are not much of a danger in Kentucky, the same cannot be said of the humans trying to kill the animals. Hunting is a major activity in the state, and it's a good bet that no matter what time of year you take a hike, there is some kind of officially sanctioned hunting season under way. The wild hog season is literally year-round. It's widely agreed, however, that two seasons are by far the most dangerous for hikers—or anyone else in the woods. First is Kentucky's modern-gun deer season, which generally runs for ten days starting the second Saturday in November. Additional days in November and December for special hunts are likely. Second is the spring wild turkey season, which starts in early April and lasts three weeks. There is also a short fall turkey season around the first of December. To learn the exact dates for a particular year, call the state Department of Fish and Wildlife Resources at (800) 858–1549.

My personal rule is to stay out of the woods during deer and turkey seasons, especially deer season. If you do go hiking at those times, be sure to wear hunter orange clothing. Also, be aware that in Kentucky hunting is allowed on a wide variety of public lands, including the Daniel Boone National Forest and the two national recreation areas—Big South Fork and Land Between the Lakes. And don't be misled by the term *wildlife management area;* most of the seventy-seven state-administered parcels with that name allow some kind of hunting. Even some state parks hold special deer hunts.

How to Use This Guide

TYPE OF HIKE

The seventy-nine hikes outlined in this book are split into the following categories:

- **Day hike:** Best for short excursions due to the shortness of the trail, lack of water, or unsuitable camping opportunities.

- **Backpack:** Best for backpacking one or more nights, although many can also be completed as day hikes.

- **Loop:** Starts and finishes at the same spot with little or no retracing of steps. Sometimes the definition of *loop* is stretched to include more creative shapes, like a figure-eight or lollipop.

- **Out-and-back:** Travels the same route going and returning.

- **Shuttle:** A point-to-point trip that requires two vehicles (one at each end of the trail), or a prearranged pickup, or some other strategy for getting back to your car. One possibility is to arrange for a second party to start at the other end of the trail; the two of you trade car keys when you meet up in the middle, and at the end of the hike you drive each other's vehicle to a rendezvous point.

DISTANCE

I carried a pedometer and a global positioning system (GPS) as I hiked each trail, and most of the mileage figures in this book are based on a combination of the readings from these two instruments, distance figures shown on hiking maps and trail signs, and conversations with local rangers and others familiar with that particular area. After each hike I laid out my route on a topographic map and used a map-measuring device to check the mileage. The most accurate way to determine a trail's length is to roll a measuring wheel over it. When agency personnel overseeing a trail gave assurance that this had been done, I relied on that measurement if it differed from my own.

While I have done my best to make the distances in this book accurate, measuring trails is an inexact science however it's done. You should be sufficiently skeptical of distance figures—my own included, and certainly those you see on trail signs. Trails are dynamic creatures, continually rerouted, added to, and closed down. Years can pass before the signs catch up.

Also, keep in mind that distance is often less important than difficulty. A steep 2-mile climb on rocky tread can take longer than a 4-mile stroll through a gentle river valley. For planning, it may be helpful to know that most hikers average 2 miles an hour.

DIFFICULTY RATINGS

Difficulty ratings are inherently flawed: What's easy for you might be hard for me. Still, they are a useful approximation of a hike's challenge. In this book the ratings are based primarily on the difficulty of the terrain, and to a lesser extent on the hike's length. The general guidelines for the ratings are:

- **Easy:** Suitable for any hiker, young or old. Expect no serious elevation gain, trail hazards, or navigation problems.

- **Moderate:** Suitable for hikers who have some experience and average fitness level. Includes some elevation change and possibly places where the trail is faint.

- **Strenuous:** Suitable only for experienced hikers with above-average fitness. Includes hazardous trail sections, navigation problems, or serious elevation change. Only one hike in this book —Hike 79—is rated strenuous.

BEST MONTHS

As noted earlier, hiking can be miserable at the height of a Kentucky summer. That's a given, and so this guide is generally geared to other considerations, such as water availability and scenic conditions.

MAPS

The maps in this book serve as a general guide only. Except for the most elementary day hike, don't hit the trail without a better, more detailed map. For each hike, the book tells you what maps are available and gives you a telephone number to call. The detailed U.S. Geological Survey quads (1:24,000 scale) listed for each hike can be ordered through sports stores or directly from the USGS at:

USGS Map Sales
Box 25286, Federal Center, Building 810
Denver, CO 80225
(888) ASK–USGS
www.usgs.gov

ELEVATION PROFILES

For hikes that involve substantial altitude changes, the hike descriptions include elevation profiles. Use these charts to get a general picture of how much elevation gain and loss a hike entails. The charts are not meant to be a detailed foot-by-foot account of the route, but serve as a quick glimpse of the overall elevation change.

PERMITS AND FEES

When applicable, the hike descriptions alert you to any permit that must be secured or fee paid before using a trail. In Kentucky requirements of this nature are the exception.

SPECIAL CONSIDERATIONS

This heading is included if there is an unusual trail hazard or hiking condition that might affect your use or enjoyment of an area.

Seaton Ridge Loop Trail follows an old country road in Jesse Stuart State Nature Preserve.

Trail Safety and Ethics

MAKE IT A SAFE TRIP

The Boy Scouts of America have been guided for decades by what is the single best piece of safety advice: Be prepared! For starters, this means carrying survival and first-aid gear, proper clothing, compass, and topographic map—and knowing how to use them.

The second-best piece of safety advice is to tell somebody where you're going and when you plan to return. Pilots must file flight plans before every trip, and anybody venturing into a blank spot on the map should do the same. File your "flight plan" with a friend or relative before taking off.

Third in importance is physical conditioning. Being fit makes wilderness travel not only more fun, but also safer. Here are a few more tips:

- Check the weather forecast. Be careful not to get caught at high altitude by a bad storm or along a stream in a flash flood. Watch cloud formations closely so you don't get stranded on a ridgeline during a lightning storm. Avoid traveling during prolonged periods of cold weather.

- Avoid traveling alone in the wilderness; keep your party together and stay on the trail where possible. The latter is particularly important in some parts of eastern Kentucky, where the illegal cultivation of marijuana has become a business. None of the hikes in this book should involve danger of this kind, but remember that hidden fields of marijuana are sometimes protected by dangerous booby traps.

- Don't exhaust yourself or other members of your party by traveling too far or too fast. Let the slowest person set the pace.

- Study basic survival and first aid before leaving home.

- Before you leave for the trailhead, find out as much as you can about the route, especially the potential hazards.

- Don't wait until you're confused to look at your maps. Follow them as you go along so you have a continual fix on your location.

- If you get lost, don't panic. Sit down and relax for a few minutes while you carefully check your topo map and take a compass reading. Confidently plan your next move. It's often smart to retrace your steps until you find familiar ground, even if you think it might lengthen your trip. Lots of people get temporarily lost in the wilderness and survive—usually by calmly and rationally dealing with the situation.

- Stay clear of all wild animals.

- Take a first-aid kit that includes, at a minimum, a sewing needle, aspirin, antibacterial ointment, antiseptic swabs, butterfly bandages, adhesive tape, adhesive strips, gauze pads, two triangular bandages, codeine tablets, two inflatable splints, Moleskin or Second Skin for blisters, 3-inch gauze, CPR shield, rubber gloves, and lightweight first-aid instructions.

- Take a survival kit that includes, at a minimum, a compass, whistle, matches in a waterproof container, cigarette lighter, candle, signal mirror, flashlight, fire starter, aluminum foil, water purification tablets, space blanket, and flare.

HYPOTHERMIA: THE SILENT KILLER

Be aware of hypothermia—a condition in which the body's internal temperature drops below normal. It can lead to mental and physical collapse and death.

Hypothermia is caused by exposure to cold and is aggravated by wetness, wind, and exhaustion. The moment you begin to lose heat faster than your body produces it, you're suffering from exposure. Your body starts involuntary exercise, such as shivering, to stay warm, and it makes involuntary adjustments to preserve normal temperature in vital organs, restricting blood flow in the extremities. Both responses drain your energy reserves. The only way to stop this drain is to reduce the degree of exposure. In full-blown hypothermia, as energy reserves are exhausted, cold blood reaches the brain, depriving you of good judgment and reasoning power. You won't be aware that this is happening. You lose control of your hands. Your internal temperature slides downward. Without treatment, this slide leads to stupor, collapse, and death.

To defend against hypothermia, stay dry. When clothes get wet, they lose about 90 percent of their insulating value. Wool loses relatively less heat; cotton, down, and some synthetics lose more. Choose rain clothes that cover the head, neck, body, and legs and provide good protection against wind-driven rain. Most hypothermia cases develop in air temperatures between 30 and 50 degrees, but hypothermia can develop in warmer temperatures.

If your party is exposed to wind, cold, and wet, watch yourself and others for uncontrollable fits of shivering; vague, slow, slurred speech; memory lapses; incoherence; immobile, fumbling hands; frequent stumbling or a lurching gait; drowsiness; apparent exhaustion; and inability to get up after a rest. When a member of your party has hypothermia, he may deny any problem. Believe the symptoms, not the victim. Even mild symptoms demand the following treatment:

- Get the victim out of the wind and rain.

- Strip off all wet clothes.

- If the victim is only mildly impaired, give her warm drinks. Then get the victim in warm clothes and a warm sleeping bag. Place well-wrapped water bottles filled with heated water close to the victim.

- If the victim is badly impaired, attempt to keep him awake. Put the victim in a sleeping bag with another person—both naked. If you have a double bag, put two warm people in with the victim.

17

ZERO IMPACT

Going into a wild area is like visiting a famous museum. You obviously do not want to leave your mark on an art treasure in the museum. If everybody going through the museum left one little mark, the artwork would be quickly destroyed—and of what value is a big building full of trashed art? The same goes for pristine wildlands. If we all leave just one little mark on the landscape, the backcountry will soon be spoiled.

A wilderness can accommodate human use as long as everybody behaves. But a few thoughtless or uninformed visitors can ruin it for everybody who follows. All backcountry users have a responsibility to follow the rules of zero-impact camping.

Nowadays most wilderness users want to walk softly, but some aren't aware that they have poor manners. Often they're simply following the outdated habits of a past generation of campers—the ones who cut green boughs for evening shelters, built campfires with fire rings, and dug trenches around tents. In the 1950s these practices may have been considered appropriate. But they leave long-lasting scars, and today such behavior is absolutely unacceptable.

These days wild places are becoming rare, and the number of users is mushrooming. To cope with the unending waves of people who want a perfect backcountry experience, then, a new code of ethics is growing. Wilderness visitors today are encouraged to enjoy the wild, but leave no trace of your visit. The basic principles of zero impact are:

1. Leave with everything you brought in.

2. Leave no sign of your visit.

3. Leave the landscape as you found it.

Most of us know better than to litter—in or out of the backcountry. Be sure you leave nothing, no matter how small, along the trail or at your campsite. Pack out everything—including orange peels, flip tops, cigarette butts, and gum wrappers. Also, pick up any trash that others leave behind.

Follow the main trail. Avoid cutting switchbacks and walking on vegetation beside the trail. Don't pick up "souvenirs," such as rocks, antlers, or wildflowers. The next person wants to see them, too, and collecting such souvenirs violates many regulations.

Avoid making loud noises on the trail (unless you are in bear country) or in camp. Be courteous—remember, sound travels easily in the backcountry, especially across water.

Carry a lightweight trowel to bury human waste 6 to 8 inches deep at least 200 feet from any water source. Pack out used toilet paper.

Go without a campfire. Carry a stove for cooking and a flashlight, candle lantern, or headlamp for light. For emergencies, learn how to build a no-trace fire.

Camp in obviously used sites when they are available. Otherwise, camp and cook on durable surfaces such as bedrock, sand, gravel bars, or bare ground.

Put your ear to the ground and listen carefully. Thousands of people coming behind you are thanking you for your courtesy and good sense.

Details on these guidelines and recommendations of zero-impact principles for specific outdoor activities can be found in the guidebook *Leave No Trace*. Visit your local bookstore, log on to www.falcon.com, or call The Globe Pequot Press at (800) 249–7586 for a copy.

BACKCOUNTRY ESSENTIALS

- Where required, get a permit.

- Camp only in appropriate places (see Zero Impact above).

- Stay on trails (where possible), and don't create shortcuts.

- Dispose of human waste in a cat hole at least 200 feet from all water sources and campsites. Dispose of bathing and dishwater well away from water sources.

- Use camp stoves rather than cooking fires whenever possible.

- Carry out all trash. If you can pack it in, you can pack it out.

- Limit your group size to ten or less.

- Suspend food out of reach of animals.

- Do not feed or in any way disturb the wildlife. Do not leave behind food scraps.

- Do not operate any mechanized vehicle in official wilderness areas.

- Do not destroy, deface, disturb, or remove from its natural setting any plant, rock, animal, or archaeological resource.

- Please read Zero Impact (above) for more details on minimizing impact on the wilderness.

Northeastern Kentucky

Mention eastern Kentucky and people tend to think of the Appalachian Mountains, coal mining, and isolated hollows. Those stereotypes may be valid for parts of southeastern Kentucky but not the state's northeastern corner. In northeastern Kentucky the land is more rolling than mountainous; farming is the big activity, and not much is isolated at all. Indeed, lacking a rugged terrain, northeastern Kentucky has traditionally not gotten much attention from hikers. With a number of man-made lakes in the region, boating has been the main source of recreation, not walking. But that may change. In recent years there have been efforts to increase the hiking possibilities, and there are a number of nice walks to be found in the area. Happily, they are located near Interstate 64, the region's main drag running west from the industrial area around Ashland at the West Virginia border.

Just keep in mind that for the most part these hikes run through quiet wooded bottomlands and up and down gentle ridges. In short, the scenery is pleasant but not spectacular, the walking lazy, not particularly challenging. If you're looking for a Mount Everest, northeastern Kentucky probably isn't for you. But if you want to relax as you walk, and think deep thoughts about philosophy, international politics, or maybe just the latest Jerry Seinfeld rerun, you should have a good time.

1 Greenbo Lake

Highlights:	A pleasant walk on wooded ridges, along a small stream and around a fishing lake.
Location:	Greenbo Lake State Resort Park, about 22 miles west of Ashland.
Type of hike:	Day hike or one-night backpack; loop.
Total distance:	7.3 miles.
Difficulty:	Easy.
Best months:	Any month.
Maps:	Greenbo Lake State Resort Park trail guide (park 606–473–7324); USGS Oldtown and Argillite.
Permits and fees:	A permit is required for overnight use of the backcountry shelter on this hike; it's available free of charge at the park lodge.

Special considerations: If you plan to use the overnight shelter, it would be smart to call ahead to make arrangements. The receptionist on duty the evening I arrived knew nothing about permits.

Finding the trailhead: From exit 172 off Interstate 64, take Kentucky Highway 1 north for 14.5 miles and turn left (west) onto KY 1711. In 2.7

Greenbo Lake

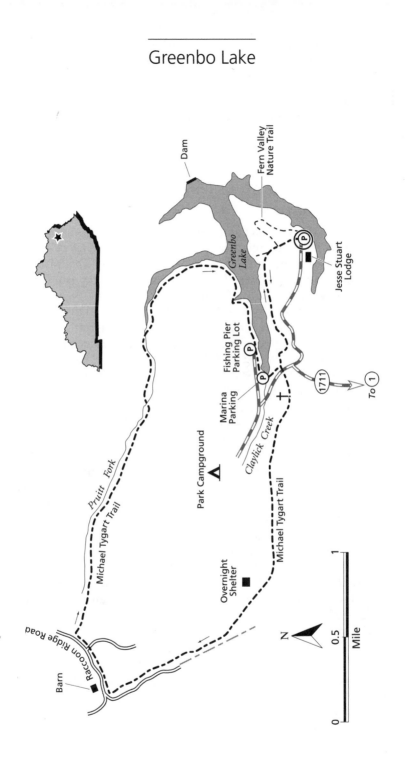

miles, turn right at the sign to the state park lodge, which you reach in another 0.8 mile. Park and walk to the signboard at the eastern end of the parking lot. GPS: 38 28.875 N 82 52.324 W.

Parking and trailhead facilities: Restaurant and overnight accommodations, water, and rest rooms are available in the lodge; a campground is nearby. There are lots of parking spaces.

Key points:
1.8   Overnight shelter.
3.4   Pruitt Fork.
5.8   Shaded lakeside spot.

The hike: The park lodge is named for Jesse Stuart (1906–1984), a prolific author of books on rural life who lived only a few miles away. Another famous native son is country music star Billy Ray Cyrus, who hails from nearby Flatwoods. In contrast, Michael Tygart, an early Kentucky frontiersman, is not so well known. In this part of Kentucky, however, the Tygart name is familiar indeed. It graces a creek, a state forest, and the trail that you will take on this hike. In fact, this is the second Michael Tygart Trail, a point worth noting because lingering references on maps and in guides to the original one can be confusing. The first Tygart Trail was a 24-mile backpacking route partially on private land. In 1998 it and two connected, long-distance trails—Jenny Wiley and Simon Kenton Trails—were closed as a result of landowners' complaints about motorized traffic and rowdiness.

With more than 3,000 acres, Greenbo is one of the largest parks in the state system. The name is a combination of the "Green" in Greenup County and the "Bo" in adjoining Boyd County (Ashland). A half century ago residents of both counties, seeking a recreation facility for their area, initiated the damming of three small streams to create 225-acre Greenbo Lake. The lake's water is clear and inviting, and a favorite of anglers. Unfortunately, swimming is not permitted, and a park official says you can be fined if caught taking a dip—an activity hard to resist on a hot summer day.

From the parking lot by the lodge, Michael Tygart Trail heads north on an old road. At mile 0.2, Fern Valley Nature Trail forks off to your right, and just after that Tygart Trail leaves the road on a path branching off to your left and following the lakeshore westward. The path can be faint, but there are enough yellow blazes painted on trees to keep you on track. The park is loaded with deer, and this is a good place to see them.

After curving south toward the lodge road, the trail winds north and west and, at mile 0.8, hits a park road leading down to the campground and boat dock. You cross the road and proceed west up the hill to the small Buffalo Furnace Cemetery, which has graves dating back to the 1800s. In the early nineteenth century, this part of Kentucky was a major iron producer, and the 36-foot-high Buffalo Furnace was an important part of the industry. At one time, it employed 150 people. The output was transported to the Ohio River for shipment by barge. It was not a long-lived enterprise, however. In 1850 Greenup County had nineteen iron furnaces; the last one ceased operations in 1891. The remains of the Buffalo Furnace are just south of the trail but not visible. West of the cemetery, the trail passes the old pits where the ore was dug.

From the cemetery, the trail climbs to a ridgetop and merges with an old roadbed. At just under 2 miles, you come to Blackberry Shelter, a three-sided wooden structure left over from the old Tygart Trail. It can sleep six comfortably, and when I was there was in good condition. There is also tenting space, but no source of water. Backcountry camping is prohibited everywhere in the park except at this shelter.

From the shelter, the trail heads northwest on the ridgetop and parallels the park boundary. After crossing a power-line clearing, it begins running alongside a gravel road, and at mile 2.8 comes out on gravel Raccoon Ridge Road. You take a right onto the road, passing a horse barn on your left and disregarding a gravel road forking off to your right. At mile 3.2, Tygart Trail leaves the road, splitting right into the woods on a path and descending eastward to a trickle of water named Pruitt Fork, one of the three streams that feed Greenbo Lake. The creek ravine is the most pleasant part of the hike. The remnants of several old homesteads are visible, and the bottomlands retain the openness they once had as farm fields.

After crossing the creek at least a couple of times, you reach a spot where the stream empties into a thin lake arm about as wide as a small river. When I made the trip, beavers had been busy felling trees here. The trail curves south and at mile 5.8, just after the arm meets the main body of the lake, you pass a small cove—a fine spot for a rest. From there to the fishing pier at mile 6.0, there are a number of other delightful places by the water. Don't expect a sandy beach, but you will find rocks to sit on and shade from trees growing along the shore. From the fishing pier, the trail follows a park road

Pruitt Fork empties into an arm of Greenbo Lake.

along the lake to the marina parking lot. You cross first the lot and then Claylick Creek, another of the streams feeding the lake, and take the road going south from the dock and camping area. After a road walk of 0.2 mile, you are once again at the bottom of the cemetery hill. Here you take a left into the woods and retrace your steps on the Tygart Trail east to the lodge parking lot.

2 Lick Falls

Highlights: A wooded walk to a scenic lake overlook where, depending on the time of year and rainfall, you may see a small stream cascading over a high cliff.
Location: Grayson Lake State Park, about 35 miles southwest of Ashland.
Type of hike: Day hike; loop.
Total distance: 2.7 miles.
Difficulty: Easy.
Best months: Any month.
Maps: Grayson Lake State Park map (park 606-474-9727); USGS Bruin.

Finding the trailhead: From exit 172 off Interstate 64, take Kentucky Highway 7 south through the town of Grayson. After 11 miles, turn right onto the road for the Grayson Lake State Park camping area. Bear left at the fork, and in 1.1 miles park in the small lot on the left side of the road across from the campground office. Walk a few steps south on the road to the sign marked TRAILS. Here turn right off the road and walk west across the field 0.1 mile to where the woods begin just behind the amphitheater. GPS: 38 12.025 N 83 01.812 W.

Parking and trailhead facilities: Rest rooms, water, and a campground are available in the park. There's room for about ten cars in the lot and plenty of additional parking space nearby.

Key points:
1.3   Lick Falls Overlook.

The hike: In the 1960s the Corps of Engineers dammed the Little Sandy River and created a long, skinny, 1,500-acre reservoir named Grayson Lake. As with most Corps reservoirs, flood control was the main purpose. Unlike many, this one has some beautiful stretches of shoreline. Instead of mud flats, rock cliffs rise out of the water at a 90-degree angle, some reaching 200 feet in height. This hike follows a relatively new Grayson Lake State Park trail that takes you along one of these palisades areas to an overlook where Lick Branch tumbles over a cliff into the lake. At least, that's what it's supposed to do. The actual condition of the falls depends on whether there has been enough rain to keep the little stream flowing. I visited in a dry spell, and the falls amounted to no more than a trickle. Even so, the

Lick Falls

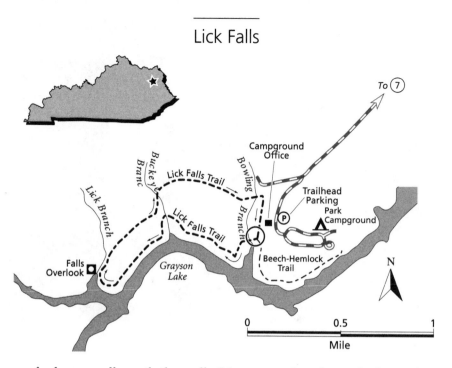

overlook was well worth the walk. It's a great place for a picnic, reading, or just daydreaming.

At the trailhead, there are two paths. Beech-Hemlock Trail goes left, following the lakeshore east for a short (0.8-mile) trip ending near the campground. Lick Falls Trail goes straight, and that's the one you take. It heads west and descends immediately to Bowling Branch just before the stream flows into the lake. After crossing the brook on a bridge, you walk southwest through a hardwood forest and then turn west to parallel the lakeshore. The trail, marked by yellow diamonds, climbs partway up a ridge and winds around an inlet. Here another small creek, Buckeye Branch, empties into the lake. This is a particularly pretty spot, full of ferns and rocks. You then turn south, continuing to follow the lake but staying high above the water. Watch small children; a fall could be deadly.

After descending through a thicket of mountain laurel, you come to the overlook at mile 1.3. The falls are to your right; the cove below is a favorite anchoring spot for boaters, and so you may be looking down on the tops of several watercraft as well as the dark green lake water. At the overlook, the trail curves east and immediately comes to the creek itself just before it plunges over the cliff into the lake. From here the trail goes northeast along the stream bank and comes out on an old road. At this point, the creek goes north; you continue northeast. At mile 1.6, the road forks; take the gravel, right-hand prong, which curves through a pine grove and descends to recross Buckeye Branch. The stream is so small here that it's barely visible. After climbing a short distance, the road flattens out, turns east, and recrosses Bowling Branch. At mile 2.5, the trail turns off the road to your right and enters a

A quiet cove awaits hikers on Grayson Lake.

grassy field. From here you are supposed to walk south through the woods for 0.2 mile back to the trailhead. When I made the trip, however, the grass had overgrown the trail, making it difficult to find. If that's the case, simply walk east through the field to the campground road, and take a right onto the road back to the parking area.

3 Grayson Lake Wildlife Management Area

Highlights:	A walk in secluded woods along Grayson Lake and on the ridgetops above the lake.
Location:	Grayson Lake Wildlife Management Area, about 33 miles southwest of Ashland.
Type of hike:	Day hike; loop.
Total distance:	7.8 miles.
Difficulty:	Moderate.
Best months:	Avoid on hot summer days.
Maps:	Api-Su-Ahts Trail guide, available from the U.S. Army Corps of Engineers office at Grayson Lake (606–474–5107); USGS Willard and Bruin.

Special considerations: This is a relatively new trail, and sections go through grassy areas that could become overgrown if not maintained. Check

Grayson Lake Wildlife Management Area

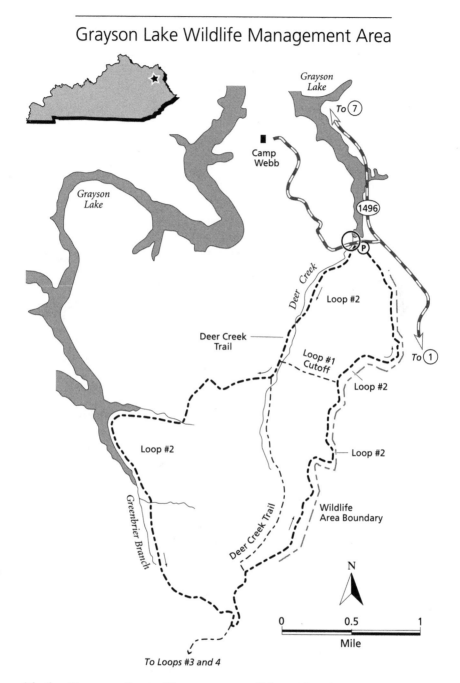

To Loops #3 and 4

with the Corps on the trail's current condition. Also, be aware that while this is a wildlife area, small-game hunting is allowed in some areas.

Finding the trailhead: At exit 172 off Interstate 64, take Kentucky Highway 7 south through the town of Grayson. After 7 miles, turn left onto KY 1496 just west of the Grayson Lake dam. (If you drive over the dam on KY

7, you missed the turn.) In 1.8 miles, turn right off KY 1496 onto a paved road marked with signs for both the Api-Su-Ahts Trail and Camp Robert C. Webb, a conservation camp for young people. In 0.2 mile, stop at the parking area on the left side of the road at the end of the lake's eastern arm. GPS: 38 13.982 N 82 58.199 W.

Parking and trailhead facilities: There's space for six to ten cars but no other facilities.

Key points:
   2.5   Beginning of lakeshore section.
   5.5   First of ridgetop views.

The hike: *Api-Su-Ahts,* which is said to be Pawnee Indian for "morning star" or "early riser," is the name of a collection of hiking trails on the southeast side of Grayson Lake's main trunk. The trails were originally developed in the 1970s by the Boy Scouts, but Mother Nature reclaimed them. In the late 1990s Grayson businessman Tim Wilson, volunteering his time and considerable energies, led an effort to reestablish the paths with cooperation from the Kentucky Department of Fish and Wildlife Resources and the Corps of Engineers. The area, encompassing almost 15,000 acres, is owned by the Corps and leased to the state for wildlife management. It's full of deer, raccoons, and wild turkeys, and while busy KY 7 and a popular lake marina are nearby, you feel you're in the backwoods.

Using old roadbeds and newer gravel roads in addition to trails, the Api-Su-Ahts system consists of four connected walking loops totaling 26 miles. This hike is Loop Number 2, the longest of the four and rated the most difficult. Don't let that stop you. There are a number of ups and downs but for the most part they are gentle, and much of the walk is level—both along Grayson Lake and on the ridgetops. Be aware, however, that some stretches are in the open sun. On a summer day this could be a hot one, although there are spots along the lake to take a swim.

A white blaze above the guardrail at the end of the parking area marks the start of the hike on an old, grass-covered road heading south along Deer Creek. The track is named, appropriately enough, Deer Creek Trail. In several spots along the way, I had trouble finding my way through thick vegetation. These stretches were brief, and I got assurances that the Corps and the state are committed to keeping the trail well maintained in the coming years. However, if high grass makes the trail difficult to see during this early part, just keep the creek close by on your right and you'll be fine.

At mile 0.2, disregard the gravel road crossing the creek and continue straight ahead. In the early morning of a late-spring day, when I made the hike, this was an especially pleasing area, with deer romping in a creekside field and wild turkeys blasting into the air. At mile 0.5, the trail crosses the creek and soon passes a trail splitting off to the east. This is a cutoff that creates Loop Number 1. Continuing south on the old road, you climb slightly, and at 1.2 miles a sign instructs you to make a right-hand turn off the road onto a path going west. You shortly enter a field and continue west, sticking close to the trees lining the left side of the field. This is one of the areas

Sunlight filters through the forest canopy on the Loop 2 Trail.

subject to overgrowth, so watch closely. At a white blaze at mile 1.4, turn right and cross a small streambed, leaving the field and entering a forest of mixed hardwoods and pines.

The trail then climbs west and northwest, making use of old roadbeds, and at mile 1.7 reaches its height before falling to the shore of Grayson Lake at 2.5 miles. You come down close to the lake at an inlet where the water is muddy and altogether uninviting. Keep going; the trail parallels the lakeshore and soon turns into a definite forest road. At this point, the lake is more substantial and better for swimming. The "beach" is mud but it's a hard mud, and there's almost an immediate drop-off, eliminating the need for much wading. The water is about 20 yards below you, and the bank is fairly steep; but the scramble down isn't difficult. The forest road follows the shore west to the spot where Greenbrier Branch empties into the lake and, after crossing a feeder stream, develops into a full-fledged gravel road. Here you begin to climb. After curving to the east, the road dead-ends at mile 4.4 into another gravel road, this one running along the ridge. Take this road—which is a continuation of Deer Creek Trail, which you initially walked from the parking area—to your left (north). (As the sign at the junction explains, if you went right instead of left, you would soon reach the start of Loop Number 3.) The Api-Su-Ahts map and USGS Willard quad both show a lookout tower near the beginning of the third loop. However, this old fire tower—about 0.4 mile southwest of the road junction—is currently in poor condition and off limits to climbers.

The road climbs north, and in just under half a mile an old dirt road splits off to your right. Take this road heading northeast on top of the ridge. A canopy of trees makes this a pleasing walk but also blocks any views. Soon you see WILDLIFE MANAGEMENT AREA signs along the trail; you are now following the wildlife area's eastern boundary line as it meanders north along the ridgeline, gently rising and falling and alternating between old roadbeds and narrow paths. For much of the way, the boundary line is reinforced by a fence. At mile 5.5, a clearing provides the first of several good views to the east. The cliff you see due east in the far distance was left by a surface coal mine that locals say operated in the late 1970s. A federal law regulating strip mining now makes it illegal to leave behind this kind of uncovered "high wall." But what you see is an example of the widespread scarring that mining inflicted on eastern Kentucky over many years.

At mile 6.3, you come to a sign pointing to a right-hand turn and announcing that you're 1.5 miles from the end of the hike. Continuing northeast, you climb and pass a dilapidated one-room cabin covered with metal siding, proving that the siding industry can successfully push its product anywhere. After several more short climbs and descents along the boundary line, the trail descends to the southern end of the parking area.

Options: You can extend the hike 6 miles by adding on Loop Number 3; just go south instead of north at the road junction near Greenbrier Branch. However, be aware that backcountry camping is not permitted in the wildlife management area. You can also shorten this hike by taking the cutoff trail for Loop Number 1, which has a total length of 2.9 miles.

4 The Little Sandy

Highlights:	A short hike along the Little Sandy River and an overlook of the Grayson Lake area.
Location:	The Grayson Lake dam, 31 miles southwest of Ashland.
Type of hike:	Day hike; loop.
Total distance:	3 miles.
Difficulty:	Easy.
Best months:	Autumn or spring, before tree leaves block the overlook view.
Maps:	Map of the below-dam area from the Army Corps of Engineers office at Grayson Lake (606–474–5107); USGS Grayson.

Finding the trailhead: At exit 172 off Interstate 64, drive south on Kentucky Highway 7 for 7.5 miles. Immediately after crossing the earth-filled dam that makes Grayson Lake, turn right onto the road descending to the below-dam recreation area. This turnoff is 0.6 mile south of the KY 1496 turnoff to Hike 3. The Corps of Engineers office, which has information about the lake and surrounding area, is 0.1 mile farther west on the other side of KY 7. Take the below-dam road for 0.5 mile and park in the lot by the rest rooms. The trailhead is across the small field behind the rest room building. GPS: 38 15.258 N 82 59.467 W.

Parking and trailhead facilities: Rest rooms, water, a picnic pavilion, and plenty of parking space are available.

Key points:
    0.0   Banks of the Little Sandy.
    1.2   Overlook.

The hike: On the road below the 120-foot-high dam holding back 20-mile-long Grayson Lake, a sign warns, BLAST OF HORN MEANS FAST RISE OF WATER. Chances are catastrophe will not strike during this brief hike, which starts off following the scenic Little Sandy River as it flows out of the dam on its way to the Ohio River and then climbs easily to an overlook.

Near the dam outflow, wooden steps lead down to a mud-and-gravel path going first west and then north along the river. This is the Corps's Grayson Lake Nature Trail, a highly developed (benches for resting are sprinkled along the way) 1.5-mile loop that you take for the hike's first mile. The robustness of the river and the attractiveness of its muddy banks depend on how much rain has fallen recently and where the Corps is keeping the lake level. But whatever the conditions, the weathered rock outcroppings and ledges that line the far side of the river are interesting. At mile 0.4, a short spur trail leads straight ahead to a large, old sycamore tree while the main trail turns right, ascends steps, and at the top turns north again to continue following the river from a higher elevation. After passing through a grove of pines, the

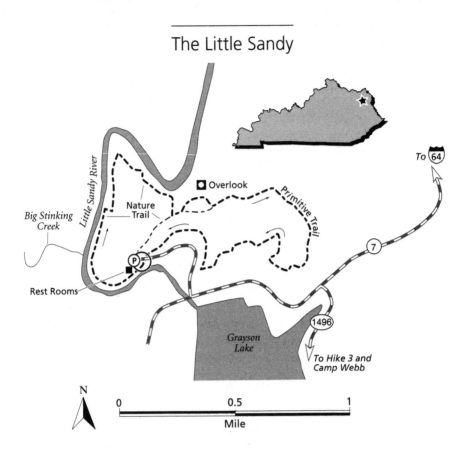

The Little Sandy

Little Sandy River

Big Stinking Creek

Overlook

Nature Trail

Primitive Trail

Rest Rooms

P

To 64

7

1496

Grayson Lake

To Hike 3 and Camp Webb

N

0   0.5   1
Mile

trail curves east and offers a fine view of a pretty farm field across the river. You also pass a short side trail to a "blind" for viewing wildlife, which in this area includes deer, beavers, wild turkeys, blue herons, and Canada geese.

After a brief climb, the nature trail comes to the beginning of the Corps's 2-mile Primitive Trail with a sign warning of long, steep inclines. That's an overstatement; even small children should have no trouble. The nature trail goes south back to the parking area, and you turn left onto Primitive Trail, marked by blue diamonds, and head east. Immediately you take another left, this one on a side trail leading to a scenic overlook of the lake; a sign marks the turn. If the trees are full, you probably won't see anything from the overlook; the side trail reconnects with Primitive Trail, though, so you don't have to backtrack. Back on Primitive Trail, you cross a power-line clearing that is likely to be filled with wildflowers. The trail then heads southeast through a pleasant forest and turns west, staying at a fairly constant elevation near the top of a ridge. After a hairpin turn right (north), you get a westward view of the lake and marina even when the leaves are out. You also get an earful of auto and truck traffic gunning its way across the dam and along KY 7.

From here you descend to a ravine bottom and cross two small streambeds, which may be bone dry, then a creek, and finally the outflow from the dam.

Rock cliffs line the Little Sandy River below the Grayson Lake dam.

A mowed path leads you up a hill to a mulch-covered trail through a field demonstrating various methods of promoting wildlife. The Corps says these are tips that people can use to attract wildlife in their own yards. The trail ends at the road leading down from KY 7; follow it back to your car.

Options: This would be a good hike to combine in a day with another short, easy stroll—Hike 2 to Lick Falls. The turnoff for Hike 2 is about 4 miles south on KY 7.

5 Carter Caves State Resort Park

Highlights:	A backcountry walk up and down ridges to two arches and a fishing lake.
Location:	About 40 miles west of Ashland.
Type of hike:	Day hike or one-night backpack; loop.
Total distance:	6.7 miles.
Difficulty:	Moderate.
Best months:	Spring and autumn.
Maps:	Park map and visitor guide (park 606–286–4411); USGS Tygarts Valley, Wesleyville, Olive Hill, and Grahn.
Permits and fees:	A permit is required for overnight use of the backcountry camping area on this hike. It's available free of charge at the state park welcome center.

Special considerations: If you plan to use the backcountry camping area, calling ahead to make arrangements might save you time. The welcome center personnel on duty when I arrived knew nothing about permits.

Finding the trailhead: At exit 161 off Interstate 64, go east on U.S. Highway 60 for 1.4 miles and turn left (north) onto Kentucky Highway 182. In 2.7 miles, turn left onto the state park road, and after 1 mile park at the welcome center on your right. The trail begins at the stone steps just northeast of the welcome center. GPS: 38 22.642 N 83 07.315 W.

Parking and trailhead facilities: Water, rest rooms, and information are available at the welcome center; there's also plenty of parking both there and in a lot across the road. A lodge with a restaurant and overnight accommodations is nearby in the park, as is a campground.

Key points:
2.5   Shangra La Arch.
4.3   Backcountry campsite.
5.9   Fern Bridge arch.

The hike: The caves beneath Kentucky's Carter County have been drawing visitors for a long, long time. Early settlers extracted raw materials from them, and for decades their exploration has been a source of recreation. Cave

Carter Caves State Resort Park

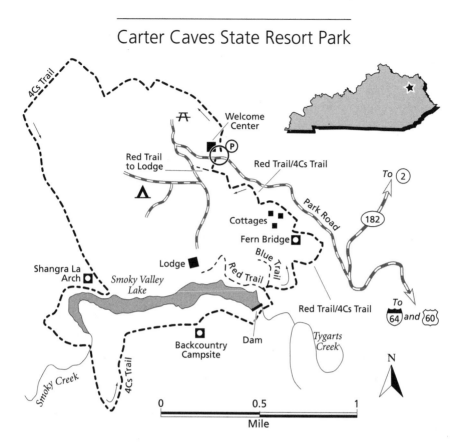

Welcome Center

Red Trail to Lodge

Red Trail/4Cs Trail

4Cs Trail

To 2

182

Park Road

Cottages

Fern Bridge

Blue Trail

Red Trail

Lodge

Shangra La Arch

Smoky Valley Lake

Red Trail/4Cs Trail

To 64 and 60

Backcountry Campsite

Dam

Tygarts Creek

Smoky Creek

4Cs Trail

N

0   0.5   1
Mile

tours were being conducted long before the state park was established in the 1940s. Within the park, there are twenty charted caves, three of them open for guided tours. But although the underground sights are the main attraction, the 1,800-acre park also offers 20 miles of hiking trails. The longest—and the one you follow on this hike—is 4Cs (for Carter Caves Cross Country) Trail through the wooded backcountry of the park and a small section of adjacent Tygarts State Forest.

The 4Cs Trail has one steep stretch—the climb away from Smoky Valley Lake—but otherwise the numerous ups and down are relatively painless as you range from creek bottomlands to ridgetops. The trail makes use of old roadbeds as well as narrow paths, and features interesting limestone and sandstone formations. In all probability you will also see a good number of deer. The mainly hardwood forest includes oak, hickory, and maple. The one thing you won't see, at least not when the foliage is out, is a panoramic view; there are no good lookout points on this hike. Backcountry camping is not allowed in the park except at a designated site located a little more than halfway through the hike. Park officials put the trail's length at 7.2 miles, based on a measurement several years ago. I found the distance to be slightly less.

After climbing the stone steps northeast of the welcome center, turn left at the 4Cs Trail sign; another trail, the shorter Green Trail, goes straight. Walking north, you quickly come to the head of a ravine and turn west onto a narrow, leafy path passing several nice rock outcroppings. The trail is blazed with both orange paint and yellow plastic diamonds. Nevertheless, be especially careful as you wind down to a broad but probably dry streambed at mile 0.6. An old country road following the streambed to your right could fool you into going the wrong way. The trail jogs left, crosses the streambed, and climbs southwest before turning northwest. After crossing over a ridgetop, it then descends into another bottomland, follows a mowed path west through a clearing, and returns to the woods. At mile 1.5, after widening from a path into an old road, the trail reaches another ridgetop; a few paces later it crosses a gravel road coming from the park's riding stables. Immediately afterward, you run into another trail and turn left. As of this writing, a sign at this junction identifies the path to the right as Simon Kenton Trail, an old 9-mile-long route that was partially on private land and is no longer maintained. Park personnel planned to remove the sign. Kenton, by the way, was a Kentucky frontiersman of the Daniel Boone era.

After the junction, you head southeast, make another descent and ascent, and at mile 2.5 pass under the Shangra La Arch—a limestone structure that park personnel say was formed by the erosion of what was once a cave. Steep steps take you down to the arch entrance, and most people are able to walk through it standing up. If you're anywhere near 6 feet tall, though, watch your head! The arch is surrounded by scenic rock cliffs and makes a good rest spot.

Almost immediately beyond the arch, you come to a point just above Smoky Valley Lake, a 40-acre man-made fishing reservoir shaped like a snake. Here you turn right (a left would take you a short distance to the boat ramp) and begin circling the lake's western tail. It's doubtful this water will tempt you, but just in case, swimming is prohibited. After paralleling the base of a tall cliff, you cross over a streambed that may or may not have water in it, then a second with a healthier flow toward the lake; this is Smoky Creek. At mile 3.2, immediately after the crossing, you begin a steep climb southward on a broad, very rocky track. After the trail levels off, you come to a fork; here you turn left and walk north on a dirt road. The road descends and, at mile 3.9, hits another fork; this time you take a path to your right.

After crossing a meadow and another streambed, you come to what a sign identifies as the Johnson Homeplace campsite. A family by the name of Johnson is said to have had a house here once, but nothing is standing now—except a large rock overhang that could provide shelter. There is also plenty of tenting space and supposedly an unmarked spring, although I didn't see it. From here you descend and, at mile 4.7, arrive below the dam. At this point, when I made the trip in late spring, all traces of the trail suddenly evaporated. This bottom area appeared to have been overcome by a torrent of water that left behind trees, brush, old tires, and various other flotsam. The park planned to restore the trail and blazes, but if the same thing happens to you, simply head north toward the dam and climb to the top of the earthen embankment. At the east end of the dam, a wooden suspension bridge

The Shangra La Arch on the 4Cs Trail was once a cave.

carries you over the spillway. At the other end, take the wooden steps up, and then go west following the lake's shoreline. After another set of steps, you meet the Red Trail, which you take to the right. (A left turn would lead to the park lodge.) From here on, the 4Cs and Red Trails are the same, and the trees are marked with red blazes.

Climbing eastward, you soon come to a junction with the Blue Trail, which also leads back to the lodge. Turn right, staying on the Red Trail, and go east, then north, and finally west as you circle the ridge at a constant elevation. An intriguing cliff of pockmarked rock festooned with small trees and mountain laurel lines the left side of the trail, and at mile 5.9 you pass under Fern Bridge. This impressive sandstone arch is 90 feet high and 120 feet long. From there wooden-block steps take you a bit higher; at the top, turn right and continue a level walk west. (There is also a trail to your left at the top of the steps, and no sign marking the correct direction.) The Red Trail, a loop through the main part of the park, eventually circles back to the lodge and lake. But at mile 6.6, you leave it, taking a side trail to your right and dropping quickly down the hillside to the welcome center. You come out on the park road across from the center at Saltpetre Cave, where early-nineteenth-century miners are believed to have extracted the salty, white mineral for use in making gunpowder.

6 Carrington Rock Overlook

Highlights:	A stone arch and ridgetop overlook.
Location:	Daniel Boone National Forest, 18 miles southwest of Morehead.
Type of hike:	Day hike; out-and-back.
Total distance:	7 miles.
Difficulty:	Easy.
Best months:	Any month.
Maps:	Morehead Ranger District trail sheet for Section 10 of the Sheltowee Trace National Recreation Trail; USGS Salt Lick.

Special considerations: There's no water on the trail.

Finding the trailhead: From exit 133 off Interstate 64, take Kentucky Highway 801 south for about 3 miles to U.S. Highway 60 at the town of Farmers. Turn right (west) onto US 60, drive 4 miles to the town of Salt Lick, and turn left (south) onto KY 211. Take this road 3.7 miles and turn left (east) onto Forest Road 129. In 2.5 miles, just after passing a sign for the boat ramp on man-made Clear Creek Lake, turn right into the Iron Furnace picnic area, the starting point for the hike. GPS: 38 02.969 N 83 35.336 W.

Parking and trailhead facilities: Ample parking, rest rooms, a water faucet, and picnic tables are available at the trailhead. A national forest campground is found 0.2 mile south off FR 129.

Key points:
2.2 Natural arch.
3.5 Overlook.

The hike: Two centuries ago this part of Kentucky was a major producer of iron. Like the old Buffalo community near what is now Greenbo Lake (Hike 1), the Clear Creek area played a role in that early industry. The 40-foot-tall furnace built on the banks of Clear Creek in 1839 operated off and on until 1875, turning out tons of pig iron for use in the manufacture of railroad wheels. It also consumed acres and acres of the surrounding forest to make fires hot enough to melt the iron ore. Today the remains of this tall stone tower stand as a reminder of Kentucky's long-ago iron business. The spot also marks the beginning of this leisurely ridgetop walk to a cliff overlooking a large rock formation called Carrington Rock.

After examining the furnace and explanatory plaques north of the parking lot, walk west on the footbridge across Clear Creek and turn left (south) onto the path paralleling the creek. This is Sheltowee Trace National Recreation Trail, which you will take all the way to the Carrington Rock Overlook. The Sheltowee is a north–south route of approximately 260 miles through the Daniel Boone National Forest. *Sheltowee*, which means "big turtle," is said to be the name that the Indians gave to Daniel Boone. Thus, the trail is blazed with white diamonds bearing the outline of a turtle. On maps,

Carrington Rock Overlook

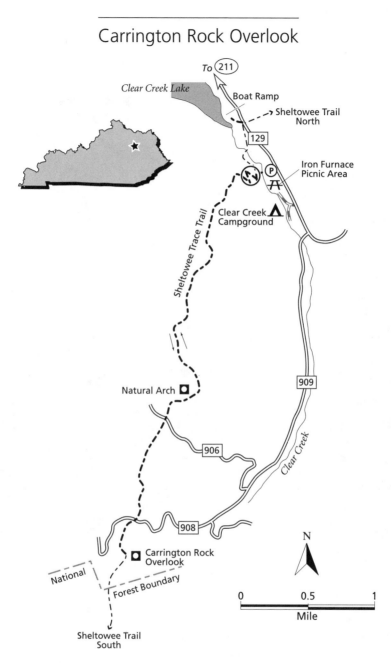

in addition to its name, the trail is identified by the number 100. This section of the Sheltowee—Section 10—begins 0.4 mile to the north on FR 129 at the boat-ramp turnoff; the mileage signs you see on the hike are to that point, not to the picnic area. If you want to enjoy the creek before the hike, there are several nice wading spots on the Sheltowee just north of the footbridge over Clear Creek.

The Clear Creek iron furnace was built in 1839.

Shortly after you turn left on the Sheltowee, the trail begins a series of switchbacks that take you west away from the creek and up the side of the ridge. This is the only serious climb of the hike. At mile 0.5, you reach the top of the ridge and head south on generally level ground. Depending on the season and foliage conditions, there are a few limited views east and west to outlying ridges. Through the trees to the north, you catch glimpses of Clear Creek Lake. After crossing an old roadbed, the trail passes several rock outcroppings and climbs gently. At mile 2.2—just after the trails begins a descent—you come to a medium-sized sandstone arch with ferns and small trees growing out of it. The USDA Forest Service map shows the unnamed arch to the left of the trail, but it's actually on your right and easily missed because it's slightly above the trail. A scramble onto the top of the arch is well worth the effort; the view of the countryside to the north is excellent. But be careful with small children here. It's a dangerous drop-off.

From the arch, the trail descends and, after a quarter mile, comes to unpaved FR 906 in Glady Hollow. (FR 906 goes east to FR 909, which connects with FR 129 just south of the picnic area.) After crossing FR 906, the trail proceeds south along the ridge spine, climbs over a rock formation, and descends gently to FR 908 at 3.25 miles from the trailhead. (FR 908 also connects with FR 909.) The trail crosses the road going southeast, and rises to the head of a shady, fern-filled ravine. It then curves left (east) and uses several switchbacks to make a steep but short climb up the ravine wall. At mile 3.5, after making your way around the face of a rock outcropping—another place to keep your eye on small children—you come out on top of a cliff with a grand view to the west. In the distance is a large rock formation with a cavelike hole that makes a shelter. On the right side of the formation is Carrington Rock, which was supposedly used as a lookout point first by Indians and later by soldiers during the Civil War. The panorama makes this a great lunch spot. It's also where you turn around and begin retracing your steps back to your car. Just beyond this point, the Sheltowee leaves the national forest and enters private land on its way to KY 1274 about 5 miles to the south.

Options: Instead of retracing your steps, you can take FR 908 and FR 909 back to the picnic area parking lot; the distance is about the same. The two gravel roads are used by national forest vehicles but otherwise are closed to motorized traffic.

7 Cave Run Lake

Highlights:	A lakeshore walk and a 360-degree view from atop a fire tower.
Location:	Daniel Boone National Forest, 21 miles southwest of Morehead.
Type of hike:	Day hike or one-night backpack; loop.
Total distance:	10.5 miles.
Difficulty:	Moderate.
Best months:	Any month.
Maps:	Morehead Ranger District trail pamphlet for the Pioneer Weapons Wildlife Management Area; USGS Salt Lick.

Special considerations: This is a hunting area set aside exclusively for "pioneer" weapons, including flintlock and percussion cap rifles, bows, and crossbows. Avoid deer and turkey seasons.

Finding the trailhead: From exit 133 off Interstate 64, take Kentucky Highway 801 south for about 3 miles to U.S. Highway 60 at the town of Farmers. Turn right (west) onto US 60, drive 4 miles to the town of Salt Lick, and turn left (south) onto KY 211. Take this road 3.7 miles and turn left (east) onto Forest Road 129. In 2.5 miles, just after passing a sign for the boat ramp on man-made Clear Creek Lake, pass the Iron Furnace picnic area on your right. Continue for 1.5 miles and turn left (north) onto FR 918, called the Zilpo Scenic Byway. After 0.3 mile, turn right (east) onto gravel FR 918A, and in 1.2 miles pull into the parking area on the north side of the road. The trailhead is across the road at the gated dirt road marked TRAIL 118. GPS: 38 02.833 N 83 33.510 W.

Parking and trailhead facilities: There's space for about ten cars; but no facilities.

Key points:
   1.6   Fire tower.
   4.7   Lakeshore.

The hike: Years ago the farmers in this region tilled the bottomlands of the Licking River while lumbermen harvested trees on the higher ground. Today wood production for furniture and veneers remains a major industry, making the Morehead area Kentucky's biggest hardwood producer. The bottomlands, however, are another story. They are now submerged under 8,300-acre Cave Run Lake, the largest body of water in Kentucky east of I–75. Built by the Corps of Engineers in 1974 by damming the Licking, the reservoir is principally for flood control. But as you'll see if you visit in spring or summer, it's well used by boaters and anglers. While the recreational focus is on the water, the adjoining area south of the lake's main stem offers plenty of walking opportunities. This hike uses a number of these trails to make a long loop through the hills and hollows near the lake and along a section of

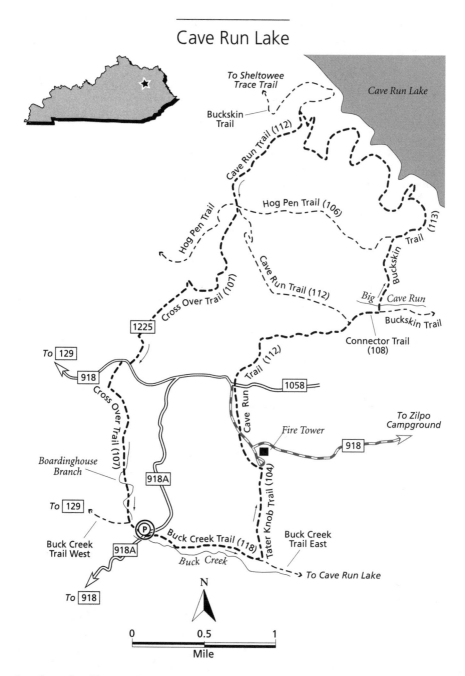

Cave Run Lake

Cave Run Lake

To Sheltowee Trace Trail

Buckskin Trail

Cave Run Trail (112)

Hog Pen Trail

Hog Pen Trail (106)

Cave Run Trail (112)

Buckskin Trail (113)

Cross Over Trail (107)

1225

Big Cave Run

Buckskin Trail

To 129

918

Connector Trail (108)

Cross Over Trail (107)

Cave Run Trail (112)

1058

To Zilpo Campground

Fire Tower

918

Boardinghouse Branch

918A

To 129

Buck Creek Trail West

918A

Buck Creek Trail (118)

Tater Knob Trail (104)

Buck Creek Trail East

Buck Creek

To Cave Run Lake

To 918

N

0   0.5   1
Mile

the shore itself. It's all within the special 7,610-acre pioneer weapons zone set aside by the Forest Service and state Department of Fish and Wildlife Resources for hunters who do not use modern breech-loading firearms. Despite the name, hikers are also welcome—but as in any national forest, make sure to check the local hunting schedule first. It's advisable to avoid the deer and wild turkey seasons.

The hike's first leg is on Buck Creek Trail (118), a tree-lined forest track along a creek of the same name. From FR 918A, follow the trail east for 0.8 mile to Tater Knob Trail (104), which you take to your left (north). Tater Knob Trail climbs 0.8 mile to the parking lot for the Tater Knob fire tower. Just across the lot are steps leading up to the tower, the last one remaining in the Daniel Boone National Forest and well worth the short side trip. The 35-foot-high structure was built in 1934; the lookouts used to live full time in the 14-by-14-foot cabin at the top. Spotter aircraft eventually made towers of this type unnecessary, and this one was removed from service in the mid-1970s. But instead of being torn down, it was preserved and opened to the public. Rebuilt in 1959, it seems solid as a rock, though you will want to carefully shepherd young children up the open stairway. From the top, which has a roof and half walls but is otherwise open to the elements, you have a 360-degree view of the full Cave Run Lake area.

From the tower base, retrace your steps across the parking lot, and just south of it take a right (northwest) onto Cave Run Trail (112), a relatively new path marked initially by white and later blue diamonds. The trail shadows the fire tower access road to FR 918, which it crosses and parallels north to gated FR 1058 at mile 2.3. Go around the gate, cross FR 1058, and continue following Cave Run Trail as it heads north away from the road and along a ridgetop. After providing a good view of the lake off to your right, the trail begins a series of switchbacks downward and, at mile 3.3, reaches a pleasant bottomland with several streams. Here Cave Run Trail heads northwest; you take a short connector trail (108) east for 0.2 mile to Buckskin Trail (113). Take Buckskin Trail, marked by yellow diamonds, to your left (north), first making your way on stones across Big Cave Run Creek

Cave Run Lake remains quiet on a cloudy spring day.

and then climbing. After you pass the eastern terminus of Hog Pen Trail (106) on your left, Buckskin Trail comes out on a small field. Cross the field and begin descending east, then north toward the lake.

At mile 4.7, you arrive just above the lakeshore, which at this spot is likely to be muddy and uninviting. However, after jogging south to get around an inlet, Buckskin Trail comes to a stretch of shore firm enough to make a good stop for resting and swimming, although the rocks may be a bit hard on tender feet. The trail continues northwest along the lake and, after two more jogs to avoid inlets, connects at mile 6.6 with the north end of Cave Run Trail (112). Here you leave Buckskin Trail and take Cave Run Trail left (south) up an easy incline. After reaching the top of a ridge, the trail crosses Hog Pen Trail (106) and immediately afterward, at mile 7.6, comes to an unmarked gravel road. The road, FR 1225, does double duty as Cross Over Trail (107), and you take it to your right (south) for 1.5 miles to paved FR 918. FR 1225 is level but unshaded, and in summer it's certain to be hot. Shortly before reaching FR 918, you can take a path through the woods that cuts off the last bit of road walking. Once you're at FR 918, go right (west) on the pavement for about 100 yards and look for a sign across the road marking the continuation of Cross Over Trail to the south. From here on, Cross Over Trail is an easy, pleasant path descending through the woods, most of it along a lovely little stream named Boardinghouse Branch. After crossing and recrossing the creek numerous times, you come into a field. At the far end is a path, which you take to your left (east). You are now back on Buck Creek Trail (118), and in several minutes arrive at FR 918A and your car.

Options: The hike is easily shortened by taking Cave Run Trail (112) or Hog Pen Trail (106) west instead of continuing to the lakeshore. Also, the fire tower itself makes a good destination for families with young children. The hike can be lengthened by continuing west on Buckskin Trail (113) east to Sheltowee Trace National Recreation Trail. See the Forest Service map covering the pioneer weapons area.

8 Leatherwood Creek

Highlights:	A pleasant, level walk in the woods.
Location:	Daniel Boone National Forest, 21 miles southwest of Morehead.
Type of hike:	Day hike; loop.
Total distance:	4.3 miles.
Difficulty:	Easy.
Best months:	Any month.
Maps:	Morehead Ranger District trail sheet for Leatherwood Loop Trail (116A); USGS Salt Lick.

Finding the trailhead: From exit 133 off Interstate 64, take Kentucky Highway 801 south for about 3 miles to U.S. Highway 60 at the town of Farmers.

Leatherwood Creek

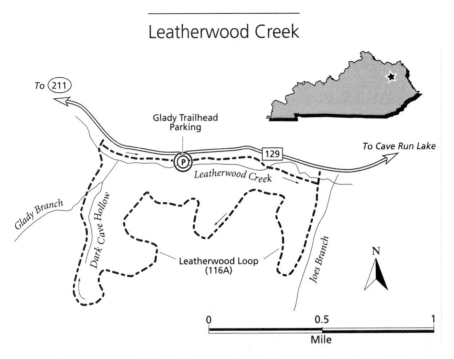

Turn right (west) onto US 60, drive 4 miles to the town of Salt Lick, and turn left (south) onto KY 211. Take this road 3.7 miles and turn left (east) onto Forest Road 129. In 2.5 miles, just after passing a sign for the boat ramp on man-made Clear Creek Lake, pass the Iron Furnace picnic area and continue for 3 more miles to the sign for Glady Trailhead, the starting point of this hike. The sign is on the left side of the road, the gravel parking area on the right. GPS: 38 01.810 N 83 33.232 W.

Parking and trailhead facilities: There's plenty of parking space and authorized no-fee primitive campsites.

Key points:
    0.7   Joes Branch.
    3.4   Dark Cave Hollow.

The hike: Some hikes reward you with a scenic overlook or interesting landmark. This one near Cave Run Lake south of the pioneer weapons area is just a pleasant walk in quiet woods. Instead of dramatic scenery, it offers solitude and an opportunity for reflection. Try it in the late afternoon when the sun's strength and your own energy level are winding down.

The entire hike is on Leatherwood Loop Trail (116A), a 4.3-mile loop that largely follows narrow, old roadbeds left behind by loggers. The trail name comes from Leatherwood Creek, which parallels FR 129 and is just south of the parking area. After leaving your car, walk a few steps north across the gravel parking lot toward FR 129. Just before the road, you come to the trail, which is marked by white plastic diamond shapes on the trees. Take a right and walk east through the camping area. At mile 0.2, using rocks or a log, cross the shallow stream and angle southeast away from the road.

At mile 0.7, the path ends at a dirt-and-grass road running south from FR 129. Turn right onto this track. Just to the east you see little Joes Branch on its way to join Leatherwood Creek. This is pretty bottomland with an open forest of pines and hardwoods. The old road rises gradually, and at mile 1.1 you make a distinct right-hand turn west away from Joes Branch to climb steeply but briefly up the ridgeside to a level area. Here the trail joins another old roadbed and begins a series of northbound and southbound legs as it takes you west along the ridgeside above Leatherwood Creek. There are some ups and downs, but for the most part the trail follows a constant contour. There are ferns and wildflowers to see, but the trail stays below the ridgetop; there are no views.

About a mile from the hike's start, you pass a pond built by the Forest Service for wildlife. As it heads west, the trail makes a number of hairpin turns around rock outcroppings. Where it uses newly cleared ground instead of old roads, the pathway can be faint. But as long as you keep your eye out for the diamond tree marks, you should have no trouble.

At mile 3.3, the trail descends past several large rock formations into Dark Cave Hollow for the final leg north. This is another pleasant bottom area with inviting rest spots. After crossing and recrossing a feeder stream, you cross Glady Branch and take a right onto a dirt road that winds down into a meadow. At mile 4, the road (FR 914) crosses Leatherwood Creek and just beyond dead-ends at FR 129. Cross the creek on pilings, turn right (east), and follow the path back to the parking area.

A small stream trickles along Leatherwood Trail in Dark Cave Hollow.

9 Jesse Stuart State Nature Preserve

Highlights:	A lovely, tree-lined ridgetop with views across the Ohio and Little Sandy River valleys.
Location:	Near the town of Greenup.
Type of hike:	Day hike; loop.
Total distance:	3.3 miles.
Difficulty:	Easy.
Best months:	Any month.
Maps:	USGS Greenup; Kentucky State Nature Preserves Commission trail map of the Jesse Stuart Preserve (office 502–573–2886).

Special considerations: Pets, even leashed, are not allowed.

Finding the trailhead: From Greenup, take Kentucky Highway 1 south for 1.8 miles, turn right onto W-Hollow Road, and after 1.6 miles park in the small gravel lot on your right. The trail starts at the lot. GPS: 38 32.850 N 82 50.515 W.

Parking and trailhead facilities: There's room for seven cars, but no facilities.

Key points:
- 0.0 Trailhead.
- 0.6 Right at fork.
- 0.7 Straight at fork.
- 1.2 Left onto dirt road.
- 1.4 Right onto spur.
- 1.8 Turn around at end of spur.
- 2.6 Straight at junction.

The hike: This 714-acre state nature preserve in W-Hollow was previously the home of Jesse Stuart (1906–1984), a prolific novelist, poet, and short-story writer whose works focused on eastern Kentucky hill life. W-Hollow figured prominently in both his fiction and real life. If you want to get a feel for Stuart's writings, try *Head o' W-Hollow*, a collection of short stories, or *The Thread That Runs So True* about his experience as a teacher in the mountains.

But even if you have never read a word written by the former Kentucky poet laureate, you should enjoy this pleasant loop across ravines and ridges in the preserve's western half. The walk includes a long stretch on a delightful, tree-lined dirt road that winds along the top of a ridge. It offers views of Greenup and the Ohio River to the north and the Little Sandy River valley to the west. This little preserve is a real gem. It has three loops of varying length; this hike takes the longest in a counterclockwise direction. All three start and end at the parking area.

From your car, go through the gate and turn right onto the narrow path. It goes east at first but quickly turns north as it descends a set of wood-and-dirt steps on the way to a small, wet-weather stream. Crossing it, you climb

Jesse Stuart State Nature Preserve

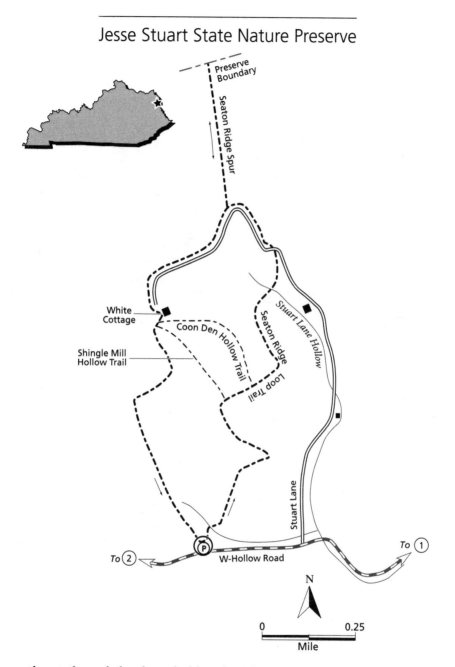

northeast through hardwoods blazed with orange paint, and at mile 0.3 cross a grass clearing above a buried LPG pipeline.

You then drop partway down a ravine, named Shingle Mill Hollow, and walk northwest along its side. At mile 0.6, after turning right and descending, you cross the bottom of the ravine and immediately on the other side come to a fork. Shingle Mill Hollow Trail, the shortest of the three loops, goes left; you bear right (north) onto Seaton Ridge Loop Trail, the longest.

Two old farm buildings dot the landscape near the end of the Seaton Ridge Loop Trail.

Climbing northeast up the ridgeside, you quickly come to another fork where Coon Den Hollow Trail, the third loop, branches off to your left; continue straight. After dipping down briefly into a drainage, you climb steeply up a hill and, at the top, head northwest along the level ridgetop. Through the trees you see cleared pastureland on the next hillside to the northeast.

At mile 1.1, after following a small ravine downhill, you cross the stream at the bottom of Stuart Lane Hollow and, on the other side, climb up to an old dirt road. Turn left and follow the road up through a stand of pine trees. At mile 1.4, just after the road begins a marked curve to the south, you come to a spur trail branching off to your right. Following the spur, you go north on an increasingly narrow ridge spine with views north and west. The path, grass covered and lined with large trees, is especially attractive, making this a nice stretch for lunch or a rest.

The spur ends in 0.4 mile at a fence marking the preserve boundary and blocking further travel. Turn back onto the main Seaton Ridge Loop Trail, which goes south and then southwest on the dirt road. The road hugs the right side of the ridge, allowing you to see a good distance to the west.

After the road curves south, you come into an open grass field, where the trail is marked by stakes in the ground. At mile 2.6, shortly after you pass an old white-clapboard cottage full of personality, the preserve's two shorter loop trails rejoin Seaton Ridge Loop Trail, which goes straight. Heading southeast, the trail briefly follows the same grassy pipeline strip that you crossed earlier. In 0.2 mile, the trail leaves the pipeline clearing, angling right on a roadbed along the edge of the ridge. At mile 3.3, after an easy descent, the old road ends at the parking area.

Southeastern Kentucky

When you think of Appalachia, you are thinking of southeastern Kentucky. This is the Kentucky of mountains, coal mining, Loretta Lynn, the Hatfield-McCoy feud, and, yes, poverty. It is the Kentucky that for decades has been alternately pitied and romanticized by the rest of the nation. When presidents and would-be presidents want to talk about helping the pockets of rural America left behind by progress and prosperity, they come to the hollows of southeastern Kentucky. Photos of ramshackle houses inhabited by gap-toothed adults and poorly clad children are a staple of these whirlwind tours—and of the news media's attention. As with most stereotypes, this one was based on some fact. For generations, residents of this remote corner of the state were dependent on the coal industry's boom-and-bust cycle and the benevolence of government aid programs. With a good rain and only a few hours' warning, Mother Nature regularly sent families fleeing their creekside communities. The steep grades and narrow ravines made modern highway travel only a dream.

But all of this is now changing, as any visitor today quickly realizes. Indeed, in recent years the old Appalachia has become increasingly hard to find. The decline of the state's coal industry is forcing economic diversification. Dams, floodwalls, and modern highways—made possible largely by special federal funding secured by influential members of Congress from Kentucky and other Appalachian states—have mitigated Mother Nature's capriciousness. What has not changed is the area's striking geography. For the hiker, the mountains of southeastern Kentucky offer the most dramatic scenic rewards to be found in any part of the state.

10 Breaks Interstate Park

Highlights:	Breathtaking views into the 1,000-foot-deep gorge known as the Breaks, and a walk down to the fast-moving stream that made the cut.
Location:	Breaks Interstate Park, on the Kentucky-Virginia border about 30 miles southeast of Pikeville.
Type of hike:	Day hike; loop.
Total distance:	4.4 miles.
Difficulty:	Moderate.
Best months:	Any month.
Maps:	USGS Elkhorn City; Breaks Interstate Park trail map (park 800–982–5122 or 540–865–4413).

Finding the trailhead: From Elkhorn City (which is about 23 miles southeast of Pikeville), take Kentucky Highway 80 east for 4 miles to the Virginia line and continue on the same road, now Virginia Highway 80, for another

Breaks Interstate Park

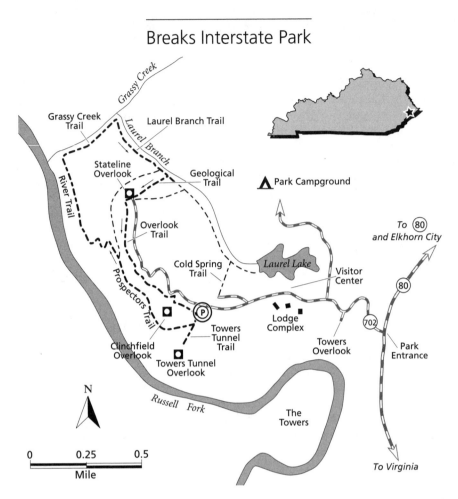

3 miles to the main Breaks Interstate Park entrance on your right. The park is in both states, but the developed portion is in Virginia. Take the main park road (VA 702) past the park restaurant, lodge, and conference buildings and turn left into the Towers Tunnel Overlook parking area 1 mile from VA 80. The trailhead is at the far end of the lot away from the road. (Don't be confused; there is a Towers Overlook 0.3 mile from the park entrance.) GPS: 38 17.189 N 82 18.216 W.

Parking and trailhead facilities: There's space for twenty cars. You'll find picnic tables at the trailhead, along with a restaurant and rest room facilities at the lodge complex 0.4 mile south on the park road. The visitor center, which has trail information and nature displays, is in a separate building across the road from the lodge complex.

Key points:
    0.0   Towers Tunnel Trailhead.
    0.2   Towers Tunnel Overlook.

The hike: Pine Mountain, one of Kentucky's most prominent land features, is a steep ridge running 125 miles along the southeastern corner of the state. For generations, it and the parallel ridge known as Cumberland Mountain formed a barrier that helped iso-

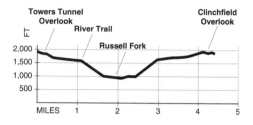

late the region. One of the few passes through Pine Mountain is a 5-mile-long gorge made by the Russell Fork of the Big Sandy River. This 1,000-foot-deep cut across the north end is named the Breaks—because it's a break in the ridge. In the early 1900s the Clinchfield Railroad took advantage of nature's handiwork by constructing a rail line through the Breaks on the western side just above the stream. This engineering marvel, which includes two tunnels within the gorge, is still in use today as part of the CSX system. Indeed, any hike in the Breaks is certain to be accompanied by the plaintive whistle of locomotives pulling long lines of coal-filled cars.

Beyond its interest as a transportation link, the gorge is impressive for its rugged scenery. "The Grand Canyon of the South" is the promotional tag

Swift-moving water frolics through a rocky section of the Russell Fork.

used in the Breaks Interstate Park brochure. Park personnel call it the largest canyon east of the Mississippi. The Kentucky-Virginia border runs along Pine Mountain, and in 1954 the two states created the jointly operated park to showcase this unique area. The 4,600-acre park is well maintained and has paved roads, a swimming pool, a twelve-acre fishing lake, a 122-site campground open April through October, and about 10 miles of relatively short hiking trails.

This hike combines several park trails to make a loop that includes both vistas from the top of the gorge and a visit to Russell Fork at the bottom. The stream has a number of rapids and is popular for rafting. This loop route is entirely in Virginia. Backcountry camping is allowed in the park's undeveloped portion on the Kentucky side but not on the Virginia side.

From the Towers Tunnel Overlook parking area, take yellow-blazed Towers Tunnel Trail south, passing first a path on your left that leads to a picnic shelter and then the beginning of Prospectors Trail on your right. At mile 0.2, you reach the overlook and get a good view south across the Breaks. Just below, you can see the train tracks and, farther to your left, the opening of Towers Tunnel, one of the two railroad tunnels in the gorge. The Towers is a 600-foot-tall hunk of sandstone that juts out from Pine Mountain into Russell Fork. The rock was too hard for the water to cut through and so the railroad, accomplishing what the stream could not, dug a 921-foot-long tunnel to avoid the obstruction.

From the overlook, retrace your steps to Prospectors Trail, which descends gently as it begins to parallel the rim of the gorge above. Be especially careful if it has been raining: This mud path can be slippery. There are a few switchbacks, but much of orange-blazed Prospectors Trail is level. At mile 1.1, Prospectors intersects with River Trail, a narrower path that winds down toward Russell Fork. You turn left onto blue-blazed River Trail and shortly come to a large rock on your right that makes an unofficial overlook and a good rest stop. There is no fence, however, so be careful with children. As you get nearer to the stream, the trail becomes steeper and more difficult. Make sure to follow the blue squares painted on trees; there are several unmarked paths off River Trail.

Just above Russell Fork, River Trail turns right and an unmarked path on your left drops steeply down the bank to the water's edge. This side trail is short (less than 0.1 mile) but difficult; at one point you have to climb over rocks. Nevertheless, several large rocks reaching out into the rapids offer an attractive lunch spot.

Returning to River Trail, you head north on level ground, paralleling Russell Fork through a hardwood forest full of mountain laurel and ferns. At mile 2, after skirting the base of a tall cliff, you pass another side trail to the water, this one an easy 20 feet in length and worth taking. The stream here is churning through another set of rapids, and there are rocks along the shoreline from which to watch the action.

At mile 2.1, River Trail ends just above the spot where Grassy Creek empties into Russell Fork. Here you turn right onto yellow-blazed Grassy Creek Trail and follow the creek upstream. The trail climbs, makes a sharp right turn to the southeast, and levels off before meeting Laurel Branch Trail at mile 2.4. You take red-blazed Laurel Branch Trail right (south) and begin a steady climb back up the gorge wall; this is the most strenuous part of the hike. At mile 3, shortly after passing the other end of Prospectors Trail, turn right onto Geological Trail and take this short, easy path up to the Stateline Overlook parking lot at the top of the gorge; you gain the final bit of elevation on wooden steps. Geological Trail and a companion path named Ridge Trail are self-guided nature trails; a pamphlet explaining plants, rock formations, and other features along these two paths is sold at the visitor center.

From the parking lot at mile 3.4, a paved path leads out to the Stateline Overlook, so named because you are looking northwest into both states. Just below you is the 1,523-foot-long Stateline Tunnel, the second of the two railroad tunnels; the large window you see in the rock marks the tunnel's midway point. From Stateline Overlook, you follow green-blazed Overlook Trail as it heads south along the edge of the gorge rim and past a number of rocky lookout points with excellent views. Watch small children; it's straight down. You are also walking at times along the park road (VA 702). After passing a large outcropping called Pinnacle Rock (fenced off and decorated with NO CLIMB-ING signs), you reach the parking area for Clinchfield Overlook at mile 4.1; the walk out to the overlook itself is 0.1 mile one-way. At 1,920 feet, this overlook is the park's highest observation point, though the view is what you have already seen. Continuing south along the road, you reach your car at mile 4.4.

Options: For a short walk in the park, take Cold Spring Trail to Laurel Branch Trail, a distance of 0.5 mile. You can then either turn right for Laurel Lake or turn left and take Ridge Trail up to the Stateline Overlook.

11 Lilley Cornett Woods

Highlights:	An old-growth forest, said to be the largest remaining in Eastern Kentucky.
Location:	Letcher County, west of Whitesburg.
Type of hike:	Day hike; loop.
Total distance:	2.4 miles.
Difficulty:	Moderate.
Best months:	April through October.
Maps:	USGS Tilford and Roxana.

Special considerations: Access to this state-owned forest is by guided tour only. There are no set tour times; guides are standing by to take visitors into the woods from 9:00 A.M. to 5:00 P.M. daily from May 15 through August 15, and on weekends April 1 through May 14 and August 16 through October 31 (reservations are not necessary during these periods). From November through March, tours are conducted by appointment only. Pets are not allowed, and there are no camping facilities. Telephone: (606) 633–5828.

Lilley Cornett Woods

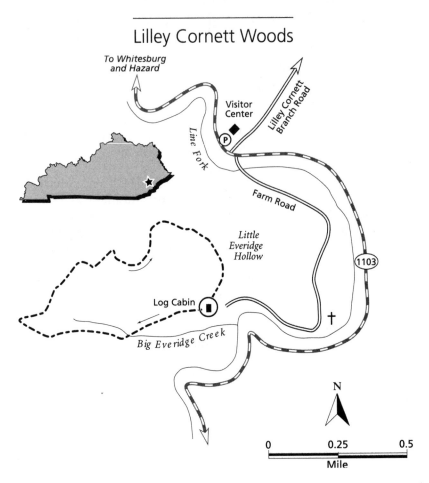

To Whitesburg and Hazard

Visitor Center

Lilley Cornett Branch Road

Line Fork

P

Farm Road

Little Everidge Hollow

1103

Log Cabin

†

Big Everidge Creek

N

| 0 | 0.25 | 0.5 |

Mile

Finding the trailhead: From Whitesburg, the Letcher County seat, take Kentucky Highway 15 northwest for 8 miles and turn left (west) onto KY 7. Take KY 7 for 13 miles and turn left (south) onto KY 1103. In 7.5 miles, turn left at the sign for Lilley Cornett Woods, and park in front of the building, which is the visitor center. A guide will lead you by car from the visitor center to the trailhead. (The distance from Hazard is about the same. From Hazard, take KY 15 south to KY 7. Turn right onto KY 7 and take it to KY 1103.) GPS: 37 05.213 N 82 59.609 W.

Parking and trailhead facilities: There's space for numerous cars; rest rooms, water, and nature displays are found in the visitor center.

Key points:
 0.0 Loop trailhead.
 0.9 Head of Big Everidge Hollow.
 1.7 Head of Little Everidge Hollow.

The hike: As is apparent to anyone who has done much hiking in Kentucky, the state has

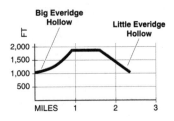

been heavily logged. This hike gives you a chance to step back in time and experience the forest as it was in pioneer days. Lilley Cornett Woods contains the largest parcel of old-growth forest in eastern Kentucky, with trees as old as 400 to 500 years. Put another way, some were probably around at the time of Christopher Columbus. At the visitor center, a display dramatizes this point with a section of an ancient white oak. The tree's annual rings are labeled with important contemporary events—the ring made in 1685, for example, coincided with the birth of composer J. S. Bach.

Lilley Cornett was a local man who began acquiring land along the Line Fork shortly after World War I. Over the years he refused to sell the trees on his property for timber, and after his death his children sought a buyer who would continue to protect them. In 1969, with funding help from The Nature Conservancy and the U.S. Department of Interior, the state bought the 554 acres. Today the land is administered by Eastern Kentucky University and used for forest research. About half of the acreage, including the portion visited in this hike, has never been logged and contains trees of varying ages and types, including hickories, white oaks, and beeches. It also has more then 500 kinds of flowering plants; birds include red-shouldered hawks and barred owls.

The term for what you see is *old-growth forest,* not *virgin forest.* The latter refers to woods that are unaffected by human activities of all kinds, not just logging, explains Dr. William H. Martin, the university's natural areas director. As is true across Appalachia, he says, the bottomlands here were cultivated, and cows and pigs used to graze in the forest—activities that no doubt influenced the woods' growth. But while not technically pristine, Lilley Cornett Woods comes close enough.

After signing in at the visitor center, you are assigned a guide. Often that's a student, but mine was Robert Watts, a native of Appalachia who manages the forest and has been taking visitors into the woods for years. You have a choice between a short hike, estimated at 2 miles, and a long one, said to be about 4 miles. I chose the longer version, though I found it to be considerably less than 4 miles based on GPS readings. The trails are not blazed, and there are no signs or mileage markers.

The longer hike goes up Big Everidge Hollow, parallels the ridgetop, and comes down Little Everidge Hollow. The start is across KY 1103 at an old log cabin near Line Fork—a drive of a little more than a mile from the visitor center on an unpaved farm road. Your guide may go with you in your car. The road is gated to keep out unescorted visitors. The purpose of the security, Robert said, is to prevent fire, vandalism, wildflower digging, and camping. Instruments used in research, such as stream-flow measuring devices, are left in the woods.

From the log cabin, you walk west on a mowed path, cross Big Everidge Creek at mile 0.3, and climb, though not steeply, to reach a rock outcropping just below the ridgetop at mile 0.9. There are a few limited views across KY 1103 but no real vistas. The focus of this hike is trees, and along the way Robert pointed out a number of old ones. "Just guessing," he said, gesturing at a red oak, "I'm going to say at least 400 years old." After spying a white

This white oak in Lilley Cornett Woods is believed to be about four hundred years old.

oak of the same vintage, he explains that this species was prized for use in making barrels for aging bourbon.

We paralleled the ridgetop eastward along the boundary with a privately owned parcel. After starting down Little Everidge Hollow at mile 1.7, we took a series of switchbacks, went through hemlocks, and came back out at the log cabin at mile 2.4.

12 Bad Branch

Highlights:	A 60-foot waterfall, and the bare-rock crest of Pine Mountain with vistas to the north.
Location:	Bad Branch State Nature Preserve in Letcher County south of Whitesburg.
Type of hike:	Day hike; partial loop.
Total distance:	7.2 miles.
Difficulty:	Moderate.
Best months:	Any month.
Maps:	USGS Whitesburg; Bad Branch preserve map from Kentucky State Nature Preserves Commission (502-573-2886).

Special considerations: Dogs are prohibited in the nature preserve.

Finding the trailhead: From Whitesburg at the intersection of U.S. Highway 119 and Kentucky Highway 15, take US 119 south over Pine Mountain. In 7.2 miles, turn left (east) onto KY 932 (Flatgap Road). After 1.7 miles, turn into the gravel parking area on the left side of the road. The trailhead is at the edge of the parking area. GPS: 37 04.058 N 82 46.309 W.

Parking and trailhead facilities: There's space for about fifteen cars, but no facilities.

Key points:
  0.0 Bad Branch Trailhead.
  0.7 Side trail to falls.
  0.9 Falls.
  2.6 Beginning of loop.
  4.2 Top of Pine Mountain.

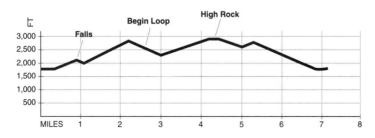

Bad Branch

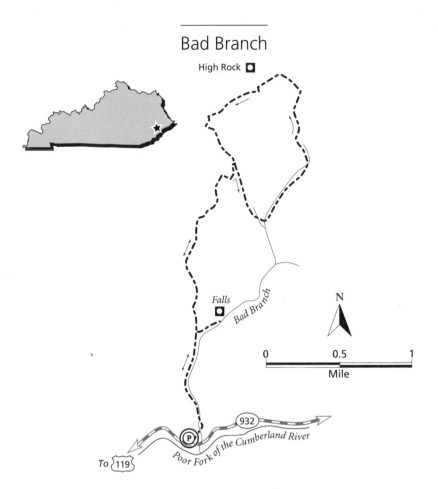

High Rock

Falls

Bad Branch

N

0   0.5   1
Mile

932

P

Poor Fork of the Cumberland River

To 119

The hike: The 2,343-acre Bad Branch State Nature Preserve is one of the prettiest hiking spots in eastern Kentucky and not well known outside the Whitesburg area. Bad Branch, designated a Kentucky Wild River, is a clear stream flowing down the south side of Pine Mountain. It empties into the Poor Fork of the Cumberland River just below the parking area. On this hike you follow Bad Branch upstream part of the way as you climb Pine Mountain to a sandstone cliff known as High Rock. From this big slab of rock on the top of the mountain, you have excellent views north of Whitesburg and the valley cut by the North Fork of the Kentucky River. On the way up you pass a short side path to a lovely spot where Bad Branch takes a 60-foot plunge over a cliff. The surrounding forest, last logged in the 1940s, is full of wildflowers, ferns, and rhododendrons. The one-word comment written by a previous visitor in the sign-in log at the trailhead expressed my sentiment exactly: "Wow."

This is a lollipop-shaped route—a loop on top of a straight out-and-back trail. From the trailhead, walk northeast on an old road and immediately come to a roofed bulletin board with a map and history of the preserve. Continuing north, you cross Bad Branch, cut through a grove of old-growth

Bad Branch River drops 60 feet down the side of a cliff.

hemlocks that escaped the loggers, and immediately recross the stream, putting it once again on your right. Paralleling the stream, you begin to climb and, at mile 0.7, come to a path on your right leading to the base of the falls. This side trail, which is marked by a sign, goes down to a ravine and then climbs steeply through rocks before dropping to the base of the falls at mile 0.9. The falls area is full of old paths. If you get confused, just turn right at the steep embankment in front of the cliff face and parallel the cliff to the falls. The cascading water makes a refreshing shower, and there are large rocks for lounging. The trail does not go up to the top of the falls, and you should be extra careful to stay on the trail—for your own safety and to protect the rare plants growing near the falls.

After retracing your steps to the main trail, continue climbing to the north. The trail, which is now blazed with orange squares, becomes narrower as you proceed up the hollow through an increasingly thick forest of hardwoods and young hemlocks. At several points, you take what is literally a tunnel through thick rhododendrons. At mile 2.2, you reach a high point and begin descending to the start of the loop portion, at mile 2.6. A word of caution: The trail between the high point and the beginning of the loop was faint and poorly blazed when I was there; both I and other hikers I met had trouble finding our way, in part because it was early fall and leaves covered the path. The potential trouble comes at a spot where the trail turns abruptly from west to north and enters a patch of rhododendrons. This easy-to-miss turn is GPS 37 05.508 N 82 46.250 W. If you come to a tree with three red stripes—apparently an old boundary mark—you have gone too far west. Go back 10 feet and turn north.

On the way down to the beginning of the loop, you go over a small rock outcropping and then curve around a large boulder. Just below the boulder, the trail dead-ends into an old logging road; this is the start of the loop, and from here the trail is easily followed. The shortest route to the top of Pine Mountain is left on the old road; that way it's only 0.6 mile to the cliff overlook. But I suggest going right so you take the longer portion when you are fresher. After turning right (southeast), you follow the road for only a short distance before the trail veers off to your right into the woods. At mile 3, after crossing two arms of Bad Branch in rapid succession, you turn left onto a pleasant old roadbed and go northeast, with the stream on your left. At mile 3.5, the road forks to your right and the trail turns left to cross the stream. It shortly joins with another old road heading north up the hollow. After narrowing again, the trail traverses open woods and climbs steeply to reach the cliff atop Pine Mountain at mile 4.2. From here you have a panorama to the north that includes Whitesburg and the palisades made by the North Fork of the Kentucky River. For a picture of southeastern Kentucky's rough geography, this one can't be beat. Needless to say, it's a dangerous spot. Watch small children carefully.

From here the trail ducks briefly into the woods and comes out again on the cliff. Walking over flat slabs of stone, you follow the cliff edge southwest 0.2 mile before turning farther south and descending steeply to an old roadbed. Turn left onto the roadbed and continue descending to the south, but more gently. At mile 5, you are back at the beginning of the loop, where you turn right and begin retracing your steps down the hollow to your car.

13 Raven Rock

Highlights: An easy walk to several lookout points on Pine Mountain.
Location: Kingdom Come State Park, just outside the town of Cumberland midway between Whitesburg and Harlan.
Type of hike: Day hike; loop.
Total distance: 2.3 miles.
Difficulty: Easy.
Best months: Any month.
Maps: USGS Benham; Kingdom Come State Park trail guide (park 606–589–2479).

Finding the trailhead: Coming from Whitesburg on U.S. Highway 119, take the first Cumberland exit and drive toward Cumberland a short distance to Park Road on your right. Take Park Road up Pine Mountain for 1.3 miles and turn left at the sign for the lake and hiking trails. The trailhead is next to the lake at the end of the parking lot. Coming from Harlan on US 119, take Kentucky Highway 160 into the center of Cumberland and from there Kingdom Come Drive 0.5 mile to Park Road on your left. GPS: 36 59.364 N 82 59.104 W.

Parking and trailhead facilities: There's a large parking area adjacent to a visitor center, rest rooms, a telephone, and a miniature golf course. The park picnic area, where camping is allowed, is nearby.

Key points:

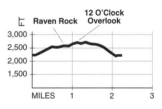

0.0   Lake Trailhead.
0.1   Laurel Trailhead.
0.8   Raven Rock.
1.1   Side path to 12 O'Clock Overlook.
1.2   Halcomb Overlook.
1.5   Nature Haven Trailhead.
2.1   Lake outflow.

The hike: Raven Rock is a 290-foot-tall hunk of sandstone that sticks up out of Kingdom Come State Park near the top of Pine Mountain. From the rock's sloping top, there is an excellent view across the ridges to the southwest. This hike then takes you up to the crest of Pine Mountain and several good overlooks to the north. The 1,238-acre park, which bills itself as Kentucky's highest, is undeveloped as state parks go; there is no lodge, marina, or even a campground (primitive camping is allowed in the picnic area). But it is a park, and this is no walk in the wilderness. It is, rather, a relaxing stroll over

Raven Rock

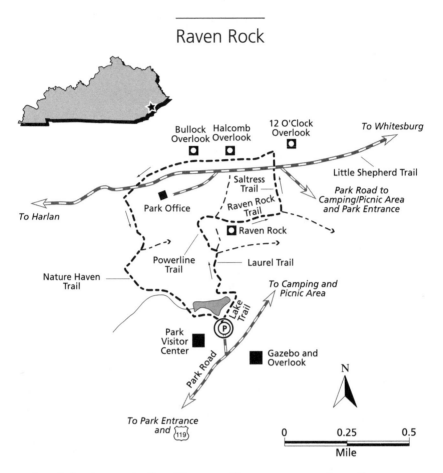

a series of short, easy trails with rewarding panoramas along the way—perfect for families with small children or an evening outing. The park's name comes from the title of a novel popular in the early 1900s—*The Little Shepherd of Kingdom Come.* The author, John Fox Jr. (1863–1919), was a Kentuckian, and the book deals with Kentucky mountain life and the Civil War.

The park has more than a dozen short trails weaving in and around Raven Rock. This hike cobbles together several to make a loop that hits most of the (figuratively and literally) high spots. From the edge of the parking lot next to the small lake, take gravel Lake Trail to the east end of the lake, turn left onto the gravel road, and go west a short distance along the lake's north edge. At mile 0.1, turn right onto a stone path going uphill to a sign for Laurel Trail. Taking Laurel Trail, you climb gently north to a fork at mile 0.3. Here Pine Trail goes right to a playground, but you go left on Powerline Trail. After wiggling northward in an easy ascent through thin woods, you come out at mile 0.5 on a rock slab next to a utility pole and under a power line—hence the trail name. This is a section of Raven Rock but not the top. Nonetheless, you get a great view into the valley south of Pine Mountain. In the early morning that I visited, a low white cloud blanketed the valley bottom, making a beautiful sight.

Morning clouds blanket the valley as seen from Raven Rock.

From here you follow Raven Rock Trail east across the slab and duck into a wooded area of pines and mountain laurel. After descending slightly, you pass Possum Trail on your left, cross two small bridges, and come to a wall of rock. This is Raven Rock just below its highest point, and when I was there the stone was marred with painted graffiti—a constant problem, according to park personnel. You go east along the rock, climb a set of wooden steps, and follow a sign directing you right to a scenic viewpoint, which you reach at mile 0.8. This is the top of Raven Rock. Be careful and keep a close eye on young children. The rock tilts at a 45-degree angle toward the south, and the north side is a straight drop-off. On a far ridge to the southwest, you can see a "high wall" of exposed rock left by a strip mine, a method of extracting coal that has left lasting scars across Appalachia. Federal law now requires mine operators to cover all high walls, but many sites mined before the law's 1977 passage remain unreclaimed. To the southeast is 4,145-foot Black Mountain, the state's tallest.

Back at the sign, you continue east 0.1 mile to a fork, unmarked when I was there. Take the left prong, which is Saltress Trail, and climb gently over a rise and then down to a paved road. This is Little Shepherd Trail (KY 1679), a rough, scenic, lightly traveled route along the crest of Pine Mountain from Whitesburg to Harlan. On your right a road forks right off Little Shepherd Trail and goes downhill through the picnic area, past the lake, and to the park entrance. You turn left (west) onto Little Shepherd Trail and ascend a rise to a short side path at mile 1.1. The side path leads to the 12 O'Clock Overlook and an unlimited view north across the Cumberland Plateau. Immediately below the overlook, you see KY 160 paralleling the mountain.

Continuing west on Little Shepherd Trail, you quickly come to the Halcomb Overlook, where the view is spoiled by a utility wire, and then at mile 1.3 to the Bullock Overlook, the last observation point of the hike. Just before the Bullock Overlook, you pass a road forking left to the park office; disregard it. At mile 1.5, turn left off Little Shepherd Trail onto Nature Haven Trail, a path that curves southward as it descends through the forest to meet the lake's outflow at mile 2.1.

Follow this drainage up to the west end of the lake and parallel the southern shore to reach your car at mile 2.3.

14 Martins Fork Lake

Highlights:	An up-and-down walk around a man-made lake on dirt roads, most of them wooded and pleasant.
Location:	Southern Harlan County, just north of Cumberland Mountain and the Kentucky-Virginia line.
Type of hike:	Day hike or one-night backpack; out-and-back.
Total distance:	4.6 miles.
Difficulty:	Moderate.
Best months:	Spring or fall.
Maps:	USGS Harlan and Rose Hill (Va./Ky.); *Martins Fork Lake Facilities Guide* from the U.S. Army Corps of Engineers (local Corps office 606–573–7655).

Special considerations: This is a popular hunting area; be especially mindful of the deer and turkey seasons. (This U.S. Army Corps of Engineers property observes state dates.) There is no potable water on the trail.

Finding the trailhead: From the junction of U.S. Highways 119 and 421 at Harlan, take US 421 south for 10.5 miles and turn right onto Kentucky Highway 987 in the town of Cawood. Drive 4.6 miles southwest on KY 987 and turn into the parking area on the right side of the highway just below the Martins Fork dam. The trailhead is at the end of the parking area nearest the dam. GPS: 36 45.069 N 83 15.356 W.

Parking and trailhead facilities: There's space for a dozen cars; there are no facilities immediately at the trailhead, but you will find rest rooms, a playground, a beach, picnic tables, and the local Corps of Engineers office 1.4 miles south on KY 987.

Key points:
```
0.0   Cumberland Shadow Trailhead.
1.6   Crane Creek.
2.6   Broad Branch.
4.0   Harris Creek.
```

The hike: Eastern Kentucky towns on the Cumberland River long had to endure the constant threat of devastating floods, and Harlan faced a triple

Martins Fork Lake

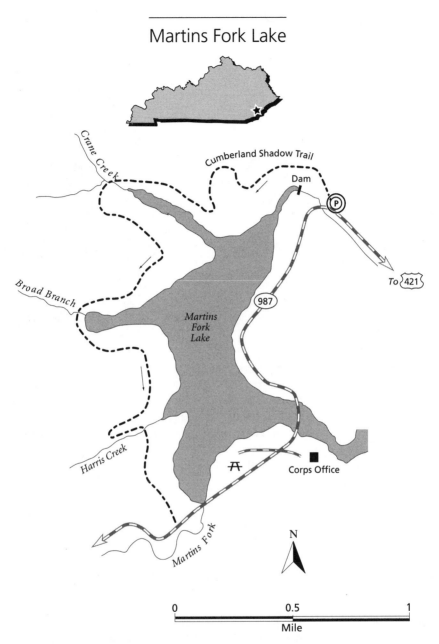

danger: Martins Fork and Clover Fork come together in the middle of the city and immediately flow into Poor Fork to form the Cumberland. As part of a series of flood-control measures along the river, the U.S. Army Corps of Engineers dammed Martins Fork in the 1970s to create a reservoir at the base of Cumberland Mountain. The lake ranges in size from 274 to 578 acres, depending on the season and rainfall, and with the surrounding land the Corps project totals 1,360 acres.

Martins Fork Lake features pristine inlets.

Using a series of dirt roads, this hike takes you around the lake's western shore, crossing three major tributaries along the way: Crane Creek, Broad Branch, and Harris Creek. As a result, the hike is a series of climbs from the bottomland up the ridgeside and back down again. The climbs for the most part are modest in length and grade, and seldom reach the ridgetop itself. Consequently, there are no scenic vistas of the countryside; much of the time you don't even see the lake itself. This is a simple walk in the woods, most of it quiet and pleasing. However, over the years the Martins Fork area has been host to lots of coal mining, and a small section of this hike takes you across an old strip mine, its scars very much visible, including seeping red water.

Because the bottomlands along the creeks are especially hot and buggy in summer, you'd be wise to avoid that time of year. There are four designated primitive campsites along the trail, but none has water. Indeed, they have no facilities of any kind—and precious little flat space for tents. Backcountry camping is not restricted to the designated sites, however. The local Corps office likes to know in advance of visitors' camping plans, but a permit is not required. At the end of the trail, instead of retracing your steps, it's quicker to walk back to your car on KY 987—a distance of 2 miles. But be careful on the bridges, which have no shoulders.

The entire hike is on Cumberland Shadow Trail, marked CST on signposts. From the parking lot, walk toward the dam and turn right (east) at the end of the lot just before crossing the concrete drainage culvert. At the turn, which is easily missed, there's a rubber-covered cable to help you pull yourself up the sharp incline. There's a second such contraption just beyond the spot where the trail turns north and climbs toward an old dirt road. You go left on this road and continue going up for a brief period. Above the dam but below the ridgetop, the road levels off and follows a stable contour through young trees. Disregard the side road off to your left at mile 0.5; it dead-ends into a power-line crossing. Climb briefly again before descending southward to a small cemetery with graves dating to the early 1900s.

Past the cemetery, the trail follows the Crane Creek inlet upstream (northwest). After descending to the creek bottomland, which was hard mud when I was there, the trail forks. You go left around a metal gate and turn right onto a gravel road; a signpost marks the turn. This road is unattractive, but you leave it in less than 0.1 mile, turning left to cross Crane Creek at mile 1.6. Again, a signpost marks the turn. From the creek, take a path up the ridge to another dirt road, which you take to your left. After ducking under another gate—which the Corps uses to try to discourage off-road vehicles—you climb as you follow the inlet back toward the lake's main stem. Reaching a level shoulder at mile 1.9, you come to a sign pointing left to the first primitive campsite. The roadbed here is winding, leaf covered, and especially pleasant. It turns southwest and then south as it descends to Broad Branch, which you cross on a bridge at mile 2.6.

There is supposed to be another primitive campsite here, but I couldn't find it. On the other side of the bridge, the trail follows a mowed area south through the brush, turns right onto another old road, and then left to begin the ridge climb. You initially go south but then make a hairpin turn to the northeast. After reaching its height, the track passes another campsite, this one on your right, and descends toward Harris Creek.

Nearing the creek, you go through a cleared area marked as a wildlife food plot. You are now on the old strip-mine site. At a signpost, the road makes a hairpin turn to the left (east) and descends past a basin collecting unsightly red water, some of it draining into Harris Creek. At mile 4, the road forks and you go right across the creek. From the creek you climb steeply, going first south and then east, and pass a turnoff to a cleared area above the lake. This is the last and most pleasant of the designated campsites; in addition to a good lake view, it has an old picnic table. From here you descend south along a drainage, and at mile 4.6 come to a gate and KY 987. The Corps office is 0.6 mile to the left on the highway, your car 2 miles.

15 Gibson Gap

Highlights: Pleasant stream crossings and impressive ridgetop overlooks.

Location: Cumberland Gap National Historical Park, just south of Middlesboro along the Kentucky-Virginia border.

Type of hike: Day hike or one-night backpack; loop.

Total distance: 9.7 miles.

Difficulty: Moderate.

Best months: April through June and September through October.

Maps: Cumberland Gap National Historical Park visitor map; USGS Middlesboro South, Wheeler (Tenn./Va.), and Varilla (Ky./Va.).

Special considerations: Bring a flashlight if you want to explore the opening into a large rock known as Skylight Cave. Also bring plenty of water; there are no safe sources of drinking water on this hike. Backcountry camping is allowed at designated spots along the ridgetop but you need a free permit from the park visitor center on U.S. Highway 25E just south of Middlesboro.

Finding the trailhead: From Middlesboro, take US 25E south through the Cumberland Gap Tunnel, and at the far end exit onto US 58. Follow US 58 east into Virginia, and turn left onto the road into the national park's Wilderness Road Campground. Pass the turnoff to the picnic area, and park near the campground office just before the road forks to make a loop through the campsites. The sign for the start of Gibson Gap Trail is a short walk south on the road that forms the left-hand fork. GPS: 36 36.192 N 83 37.799 W.

Parking and trailhead facilities: There are several designated parking spaces by the office; the campground has water, rest rooms, and 160 overnight sites, some with electricity.

Key points:

4.8   Gibson Gap.

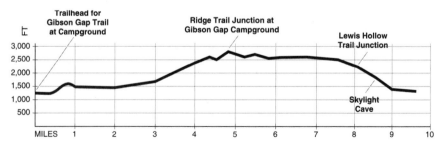

The hike: Cumberland Gap is nature's gate through the Appalachians. It was first used by Indians and later, thanks largely to Daniel Boone, by white

Gibson Gap

settlers. In 1775 Boone and a crew of thirty axmen blazed a trail through the gap that became known as the Wilderness Road. For years it was a thoroughfare not only for pioneers headed west but also for western farmers and hunters transporting their produce east. This hike gives you a good feel for the terrain that confronted Boone and all who have followed him to this isolated region. It's a climb but not a difficult one, and the idyllic streamside spots and the ridgetop views of the surrounding mountains in Kentucky, Virginia, and Tennessee are well worth the effort.

Cumberland Gap itself, which is about 5 miles west of Gibson Gap, was paved over long ago, and for years was part of U.S. Highway 25E, a major north–south highway. Prodded by the region's lawmakers, Congress eventually put up millions of dollars to replace the road with twin 4,600-foot-long highway tunnels through Cumberland Mountain. The tunnels opened in 1996, and in the late 1990s the National Park Service had ambitious plans to remove the pavement from the gap and restore the area to its Wilderness Road appearance.

From the Gibson Gap Trailhead at the campground, head southeast. At mile 0.1, turn left and walk north on a forest road coming from US 58. Disregard the side path, which leads to an old corral. Soon the trail jogs right and makes the first of what are several crossings of Station Creek. Especially in spring, this is a delightful stream that provides a number of fine lunch spots on the way up the ridge. At mile 0.7, you come to a sign marking the entrance to the park's backcountry. Here the trail leaves the creek temporarily and makes a steep but short climb before beginning a series of gentle ups and downs through rhododendron shrubs and hardwoods.

The trail has mileage markers, and just after mile 2, if the season is right, you will see jonquils blooming, a hint that there must have been a gardener around at some point. Sure enough, if you look closely, not far from the trail you find the crumbled remains of a building. After mile 3, the grade steepens and you get your first glimpses of the green Virginia valley to the south, although summer views are restricted by foliage. The trail switchbacks northward and then makes a long sweep west. After passing a large rock outcropping, you descend through a canopy of rhododendrons to a streambed, turn north, and begin the final climb to the ridgetop. At mile 4.8, you pass an outdoor privy, announcing your arrival at Gibson Gap. The park has designated the gap a backcountry campsite; there is a fire pit and a nearby but unreliable water source. This is also where Gibson Gap Trail intersects with 19-mile-long Ridge Trail.

Ridge Trail, the longest in the park and almost wide enough to serve as a road, starts 14 miles to the east at Civic Park and ends 5 miles to the west

Table Rock is an interesting sight on the Ridge Trail.

at the Pinnacle Overlook near Cumberland Gap. At Gibson Gap, you take a left onto Ridge Trail and begin a generally level walk west. The ridgetop is the boundary between Kentucky and Virginia, and the trail repeatedly weaves across it, permitting good views into both states as well as a third, Tennessee, which meets the other two just west of Cumberland Gap. There is a particularly spectacular overlook to the southwest just before Ridge Trail descends to a junction with Lewis Hollow Trail at mile 8.1.

Turn left onto Lewis Hollow Trail and descend southeast along a branch of Station Creek. At mile 8.6, the trail crosses the stream, and just to your left is a large overhanging rock christened Skylight Cave because ceiling openings allow in some daylight. It's not really a cave, but you can go back into the opening several hundred feet. For children, it's a big adventure. Park rangers say the rock formations you see on the Virginia side of the ridge are generally limestone, and on the Kentucky side sandstone. For most of the hike's final 1.1 miles, you are coasting downhill. After passing a side trail to a picnic area and soon crossing a road to the same picnic area, the trail ends at the campground road near the office and just north of the Gibson Gap Trailhead.

Options: To lengthen your hike, continue east on Ridge Trail to the Pinnacle Overlook. The round trip from the Lewis Hollow Trail junction to the overlook will add 3.4 miles to the Gibson Gap loop. See Hike 17.

16 Hensley Settlement

Highlights:	The rough, wooden buildings of an abandoned Appalachian settlement, and a striking panorama from the ridgetop.
Location:	Cumberland Gap National Historical Park, just south of Middlesboro along the Kentucky-Virginia border.
Type of hike:	Day hike or one-night backpack; out-and-back.
Total distance:	7.7 miles.
Difficulty:	Moderate.
Best months:	April through June and September through October.
Maps:	Cumberland Gap National Historical Park visitor map; USGS Varilla (Ky./Va.).

Special considerations: Take plenty of water; depending on the time of year, there may be some at Hensley Settlement, but otherwise it's likely to be a dry trip. Overnight camping at the park's designated backcountry sites requires a permit, which you can get free at the park visitor center on U.S. Highway 25E just south of Middlesboro.

Finding the trailhead: From Middlesboro, take US 25E south through the Cumberland Gap Tunnel, and at the far end exit onto US 58. Follow US 58 east into Virginia for 9.6 miles, turning left onto Virginia Highway 690. This narrow paved road winds northeast for more than 2 miles to a stop sign at

Hensley Settlement

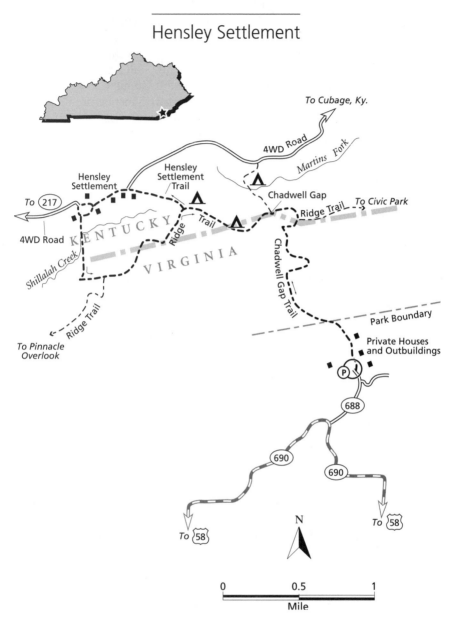

unpaved VA 688. Turn left onto VA 688, and soon you see a sign pointing left to Chadwell Gap. Make the turn and drive up the incline to the trail-head. The total distance from Middlesboro is 14.5 miles. GPS: 36 39.244 N 83 30.119 W.

Parking and trailhead facilities: The parking area, which is marked by a hand-lettered sign, has space for about ten cars. Note the donation box. This is private land whose owners allow hikers to leave their cars.

Key points:

3.2   Hensley Settlement.

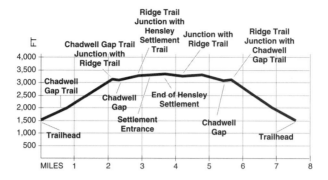

The hike: Cumberland Gap is associated with Daniel Boone, but a latter-day, lesser-known pioneer named Sherman Hensley also left his mark on the long, steep mountain ridge that separates the southwestern tip of Virginia from eastern Kentucky. In 1903 Hensley moved his family to the top of Cumberland Mountain and started a self-sufficient farming community that lasted until the early 1950s. Today the buildings and fences that remain provide a glimpse into the hard, isolated life of Appalachia before the arrival of electricity and paved roads. The pamphlet *Hensley Settlement* written by William E. Cox and sold at the park visitor center provides good background on this little village and its lifestyle.

Hensley Settlement is on the Kentucky side of the ridge, but the best way to get there is from the Virginia side using Chadwell Gap Trail. This was a

The old Hensley Settlement schoolhouse still stands.

75

route the Hensley clan took when venturing down into the modern world for goods they could not grow or make themselves. From the trailhead parking area, walk north on the unpaved road past the several houses and through the metal farm gate, making sure to relatch it. Disregard the road to your right, and continue north to a national park boundary sign and a second gate at mile 0.3. Open the gate or, if your pack isn't too big, slip through at the right end. The trail, still an old road, continues to climb northwest though the woods at a gradually increasing grade. The concrete foundation you pass is what's left of a large scale where coal trucks were weighed before leaving the mountain. The mine itself, which has not been in operation for about fifty years, is located farther up the ridge to your left and out of sight. The coal was brought down to the trucks by conveyor belt, now long gone. Behind the old foundation, however, you can still find old furnaces where coal was burned to make coke.

Past the foundation, the trail narrows and steepens as a series of switchbacks takes you steadily up the mountain. Park rangers say this is the steepest trail in the park, but the grade is doable, and there are no cliffs to endanger straying children. In spring, before the leaves come out, you can get a view every now and then of the Virginia valley to the south. At about mile 1.5, an unmarked path goes off to your left; disregard it and continue climbing. You soon come to a set of concrete steps that lead past a huge overhanging rock, and at mile 2.1 Chadwell Gap Trail dead-ends into Ridge Trail.

Ridge Trail meanders for 19 miles across the spine of Cumberland Mountain, which marks the Kentucky–Virginia border. To reach Hensley Settlement, you turn left onto Ridge Trail and walk west. But first, take the narrow path that leads south to the rock outcropping on the ridge edge. Hold on to any small kids, and enjoy a wonderful panorama of the lush valley farmland below on the Virginia side. This is a great lunch spot.

Chadwell Gap Trail was rerouted some years ago, so despite its name, its intersection with Ridge Trail is not at the gap itself. The gap is 0.2 mile to the west, where a side path branches north off Ridge Trail 0.2 mile to a backcountry campsite on Martins Fork. Just west of the gap, there is another designated campground, and you pass a third before turning right off Ridge Trail at a sign pointing to Hensley Settlement. This side trail, which is canopied by trees like a shady country lane, reaches the settlement entrance at mile 3.2. The old buildings, which were refurbished starting in the 1960s, are identified on a sign at the entrance. From May through October, volunteers may live in one or two of the houses. Also, in season, park vehicles drive visitors up using one of the two four-wheel-drive roads that connect the settlement to Kentucky. As you walk through the settlement, admire the hand-hewn-log construction of the buildings and the beauty of the flat farm fields. But for a reminder of how tough life here could be, make sure to stop at the cemetery. Sherman Hensley lived to the age of ninety-seven (he died after he left the mountain) but a number of headstones mark the resting places of young children. A LITTLE TIME ON EARTH HE SPENT / TILL GOD FOR HIM THE ANGELS SENT reads the inscription above the remains of a fourteen-month-old.

You reach the far end of the settlement at mile 3.7. You can either return the way you came or take a loop route back to Ridge Trail. For the loop, follow the path heading south from the end of the settlement. It crosses Shillalah Creek, where you may get your feet wet, and passes a large outcropping called Indian Rock. Just below the rock, 0.5 mile from the end of the settlement, you hit Ridge Trail, which you take east for 0.6 mile to the turnoff for Hensley Settlement. From there retrace your steps on Ridge Trail to Chadwell Gap Trail and back down the mountain.

Options: For a longer hike, you can continue west on Ridge Trail to the park's drive-in campground off US 58, or go all the way to the Pinnacle Overlook. From Chadwell Gap, the additional one-way distances would be 12.1 and 12.4 miles, respectively. You can also go east for 6.6 miles to the trailhead at Civic Park. In each case you will need to arrange a shuttle back to the Chadwell Gap Trail parking area.

---

17 Pinnacle Overlook

Highlights:	A walk along a beautiful mountain stream to an overlook above Cumberland Gap.
Location:	Cumberland Gap National Historical Park, just south of Middlesboro along the Kentucky-Virginia border.
Type of hike:	Day hike; out-and-back.
Total distance:	7.8 miles.
Difficulty:	Moderate.
Best months:	April through June and September through October.
Maps:	Cumberland Gap National Historical Park visitor map; USGS Middlesboro North and Middlesboro South (Ky./Va./Tenn.).

Finding the trailhead: From Middlesboro, go south on U.S. Highway 25E and take the exit for the Cumberland Gap National Historical Park Visitor Center, which comes before you get to the Cumberland Gap Tunnel. Instead of entering the visitor center parking lot, drive east (away from Middlesboro) on the road that runs in front of the visitor center, parallel to US 25E. This is Pinnacle Road, which winds its way up to the Pinnacle Overlook. You don't go that far, however; 1.2 miles from the visitor center, turn right onto Kentucky Highway 988, and in another 2.8 miles turn right at the sign for the park's Sugar Run Area. The trailhead is just beyond the southwest end of the parking lot near the rest room building. GPS: 36 38.189 N 83 40.138 W.

Parking and trailhead facilities: You'll find spaces for about fifty cars, along with rest rooms, water, and picnic tables.

Key points:
0.0   Sugar Run Trailhead.
0.5   Junction with other leg of trail.

Pinnacle Overlook

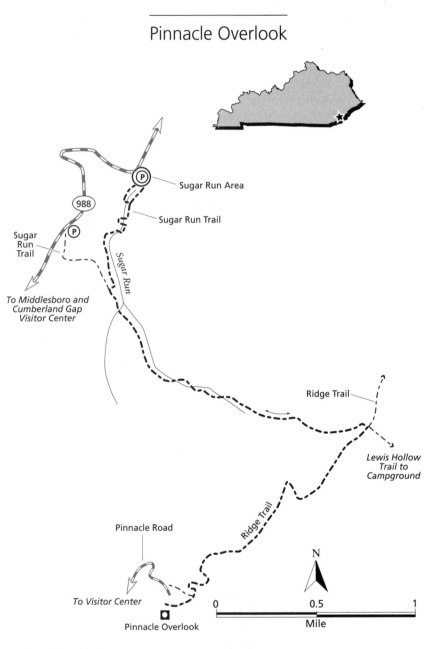

Sugar Run Area

Sugar Run Trail

988

Sugar
Run
Trail

To Middlesboro and
Cumberland Gap
Visitor Center

Sugar Run

Ridge Trail

Lewis Hollow
Trail to
Campground

Pinnacle Road

Ridge Trail

To Visitor Center

Pinnacle Overlook

N

0   0.5   1
Mile

2.2   Ridge Trail.
3.9   Pinnacle Overlook.

The hike: Sugar Run is a small, picturesque stream running down the Kentucky side of Cumberland Mountain. In spring the hollow is full of wildflowers. This hike follows Sugar Run upstream and then takes Ridge Trail southeast along the mountain's crest to the Pinnacle. From this 2,440-foot observation point, you look down on Cumberland Gap and across the mountains of three states: Kentucky, Virginia, and Tennessee. On clear days you can see all the way to North Carolina. The Pinnacle is the park's single most dramatic feature.

Sugar Run Trail provides an easier, more gradual ascent of Cumberland Mountain than you get on the Virginia side. It's also one of the prettiest walks you will find anywhere in Kentucky. The trail isn't hard to follow, but when I took the hike there was no trailhead sign—and few markings along the way. From the southwest end of the parking lot, take the paved walkway a short distance to a fork. You can go either way, because the two prongs soon meet. But on busy spring days, the left path is likely to be less crowded. Turning left, you follow a dirt path and rise slightly, the creek on your right. At mile 0.1, you come to a bridge, which you disregard; the bridge carries the right-hand prong, which you didn't take.

Continuing with the creek on your right, you go a short distance to a second bridge; this one you do cross, and almost immediately come to a third bridge, which you also cross, putting the creek again on your right. Moss-covered rocks, pine trees, and rich stands of rhododendrons make this a lovely stretch. At mile 0.3, the trail crosses the stream again. Now, with Sugar Run on your left, you begin to move away from the creek and to climb. At mile 0.5, you come to a junction with another leg of Sugar Run Trail, this one starting at a pull-off on KY 988 nearer the visitor center. The road

Pinnacle Overlook looks down into Cumberland Gap, Tennessee.

79

itself is a short distance to your right; turn left to continue your trek southeast up the mountain.

The trail is now an old roadbed, broad and easy to follow. After crossing a feeder stream on a bridge, you begin to climb steadily. The creek is below you out of sight, though you can hear it gurgle. After a series of level sections, the trail again meets the stream, and cuts along a rock outcropping. At mile 1.5, you cross Sugar Run twice in rapid succession; afterward the stream dwindles into a trickle before disappearing altogether. At mile 2 you emerge from the hollow into more open, level terrain with hardwoods. This signals your approach to the ridgetop. At mile 2.2, Sugar Run Trail ends and you turn right onto Ridge Trail. When I was there, the junction was marked by a sign for the Pinnacle but not one identifying Ridge Trail. If you miss the turn—as I managed to do—you will go only a few yards before running into the turnoff for Lewis Hollow Trail, which leads to the park campground. (See Hike 15.)

From the junction, Ridge Trail climbs gently and then more steeply to the southwest as you weave along the Kentucky-Virginia line. This is another old roadbed and easily followed. After a steep climb to the north, you reach a level spot on the Kentucky side with limited views. You then curve back to the Virginia side and, at mile 3.1, come to an outcropping with excellent views southeast into Virginia and Tennessee. From this unnamed lookout, descend to a Ridge Trail registration box for hikers going the other way, and then climb again. Disregard the old road on your right and continue south. At mile 3.7, immediately after the dirt path turns into a paved walkway, you come to a fork. The right prong descends to the parking lot at the end of Pinnacle Road; you turn left for the Pinnacle. Just beyond the fork are the earthworks of one of the old forts built around Cumberland Gap during the Civil War. Control of this key transportation route was an objective of both the North and South. But while virtually impregnable—the American Gibraltar, a Union general called the Gap—the forts were also difficult to resupply. As the sign explains, IT WAS EASIER FOR THE WAR TO JUST GO AROUND THEM. First the Confederates held and abandoned the Gap, then the Federals did the same. Each side held the Gap twice.

The paved path reaches the walled Pinnacle lookout at mile 3.9. Directly below is the little Tennessee town of Cumberland Gap. Farther southwest you see the twin highway approaches to the Cumberland Gap Tunnel disappear into the mountain. The tunnel opened in 1996, eliminating the need for a difficult and dangerous stretch of US 25E up the mountain and through the Gap. You can see the Gap itself; just beyond is Tri-State Peak, where Kentucky, Virginia, and Tennessee meet. (See Hike 18.) The body of water farther in the distance is Fern Lake, and north of that is the city of Middlesboro. The Pinnacle is also a good spot for seeing hawks. This is where local birders station themselves for the annual hawk census. From the Pinnacle, retrace your steps to the Sugar Run parking lot.

18 Tri-State Peak

Highlights: A short walk to the ridgetop spot where Kentucky, Tennessee, and Virginia meet plus stops at Cumberland Gap and two Civil War fort sites.
Location: Cumberland Gap National Historical Park, just south of Middlesboro.
Type of hike: Day hike; out-and-back.
Total distance: 2.8 miles.
Difficulty: Easy.
Best months: Any month.
Maps: Cumberland Gap National Historical Park visitor map; USGS Middlesboro South (Ky./Va./Tenn.).

Finding the trailhead: The trailhead is in the Tennessee town of Cumberland Gap. From Middlesboro, take U.S. Highway 25E through the Cumberland Gap Tunnel and exit onto US 58. In 0.9 mile, turn left at the sign for the Iron Furnace and descend into the town of Cumberland Gap. In 0.6 mile, turn right onto Pennlyn Avenue, go several blocks, turn right onto Llewellyn Street, and park in the lot for Iron Furnace visitors. The trailhead is between the parking area and the furnace. GPS: 36 36.062 N 83 40.125 W.

Parking and trailhead facilities: There's room for about ten cars. There are no facilities immediately at the trailhead, but restaurants and stores are available nearby in Cumberland Gap.

Key points:
0.0 Wilderness Road Trailhead.
0.5 Cumberland Gap.
0.9 Fort Foote.
1.3 Tri-State Pavilion.
1.5 Fort Farragut.

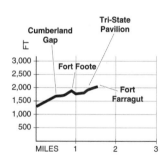

The hike: The states of Kentucky, Virginia, and Tennessee meet just south of Cumberland Gap at a point on the Cumberland Mountain ridge named Tri-State Peak. The spot is marked by a small pavilion with a plaque for each of the states. This short outing takes you from the pleasantly funky town of Cumberland Gap through the Gap itself and up to Tri-State Peak, with additional stops at the earthen remains of two Civil War forts. This short hike is a chance to follow literally in history's footsteps. Afterward you can get refreshments and a dose of local lore from Harvey Fuson, proprietor of the Old Drug Store on Cumberland Gap's main drag. The town, he will be glad to explain, used to be a bustling transportation center, and locals saw a bright future ahead. Alas, it's a future whose arrival has been slowed considerably by the rerouting of US 25E through the tunnel. The highway now bypasses the town as well as the Gap. "I've been here since I was born, and people kept saying, 'It's

Tri-State Peak

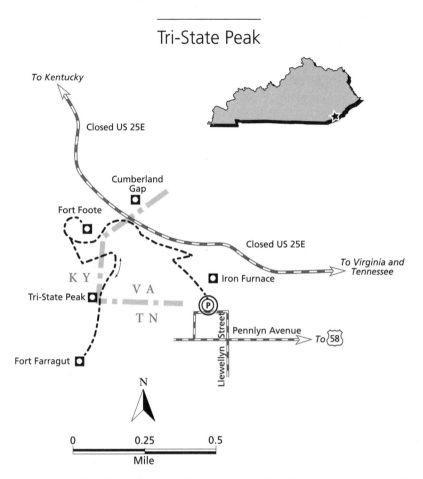

To Kentucky

Closed US 25E

Cumberland
Gap

Fort Foote

Closed US 25E

To Virginia and
Tennessee

K Y

V A

Iron Furnace

Tri-State Peak

T N

P

Pennlyn Avenue

To 58

Llewellyn Street

Fort Farragut

N

0   0.25   0.5
Mile

going to be another Gatlinburg,'" Harvey says of his hometown. "But all I've ever seen it do is get smaller."

Named for the route west that Daniel Boone blazed through the Gap in 1775, Wilderness Road Trail starts just west of the stone walls remaining from a furnace that produced iron in the nineteenth century. While the town is in Tennessee, the Virginia line cuts just in front of the furnace, and so the hike actually begins in that state. The gravel path heads northwest into a forest that is young and a bit scruffy. At mile 0.1, you make a sharp right turn and climb gently to the east. You then turn left and head northwest, still climbing. At mile 0.5, turn right and ascend a short side trail to Cumberland Gap.

The National Park Service has big plans to tear up the pavement of the now-closed US 25E segment running through the Gap and restore the area to its pioneer-day appearance. Work was scheduled to begin in 2001. That, however, had definitely not happened when I was there. Instead, what I saw was a four-lane highway complete with lane markings and utility lines—but no vehicles. What a weird scene! A perfect set for a science fiction movie about the end of the world. Still standing was a large sign telling nonexistent motorists that they were passing through Cumberland Gap. It was a good lesson in history's transitory nature: a walking path yesterday, a paved highway today, and, perhaps, a path once again tomorrow.

For about 20 feet you follow the right-of-way through the Gap on the west side of the old highway, and then turn left and climb gently to the west. You immediately come to a partial pyramid made of stones commemorating Daniel Boone's 1769 route from North Carolina to Kentucky. Following a sign for Tri-State Peak, take a dirt road up the ridgeside, going first west and then southwest past a sign marking the site of a Union commissary. Here the woods are more substantial than below the Gap, the walking far more pleasant. At mile 0.8, you come to a side trail leading right to the site of Fort Foote. The 0.1-mile climb takes you to a bluff with a good view of the Pinnacle (see Hike 17) to the northeast. There is little remaining from the Civil War fortification, but you get a good idea how the combatants tried to defend both sides of the Gap.

After backtracking to the main trail, you climb southward. After the leaves have fallen, the town of Cumberland Gap is visible below you on your left. At mile 1.3, you reach the top of Tri-State Peak. The three states meet at the intersection of the three concrete lines in the pavilion floor, not at the government survey marker several inches away. If your foot is big enough, you can stand literally in the three states at once. The only view—west down into Middlesboro—is obstructed by trees and a power line.

From the pavilion, continue south along the ridge for another 0.2 mile to the earthen remains of Fort Farragut straddling the Kentucky–Tennessee border. From a mowed area next to the pavilion, a narrow path runs just below the ridge's knife-edge crest. In several spots you can scamper up to the top

The boundaries of Kentucky, Tennessee, and Virginia meet inside the Tri-State Peak Pavilion.

for a view that's better than the one from the pavilion. The ridgetop also makes a good spot for lunch. Once you reach the sign designating the Fort Farragut site, you can take a short circular walk around the earth works. The path continues to the southwest as part of a long-distance Tennessee backpacking trail named Cumberland Trail. From Fort Farragut, retrace your steps to the Iron Furnace parking area.

19 Chained Rock

Highlights: A lovely wooded trail past a natural arch to an unusual lookout near the top of Pine Mountain.
Location: Pine Mountain State Resort Park outside Pineville, 15 miles north of Cumberland Gap National Historical Park.
Type of hike: Day hike; out-and-back.
Total distance: 2.8 miles.
Difficulty: Moderate.
Best months: Any month.
Maps: USGS Pineville and Middlesboro North; *Pine Mountain State Resort Park Visitor's Guide* (park 800-325-1712 or 606-337-3066).

Finding the trailhead: From the intersection of U.S. Highways 25E and 119 south of Pineville, take US 25E south for 0.3 mile and turn right onto the park road to Laurel Cove Amphitheater and Chained Rock Overlook. Continue for 0.7 mile; at the top of a hairpin curve, turn right onto the road marked LAUREL COVE LOWER SHELTER. This road dead-ends into a parking lot in 0.1 mile. Laurel Cove Trail starts just beyond the parking lot near the large pavilion. GPS: 36 44.622 N 83 42.331 W.

Parking and trailhead facilities: You'll find space for about fifty cars, as well as portable toilets, water, and a picnic pavilion. The park lodge, with overnight and restaurant facilities, is about 6 miles away; the park campground is near the lodge.

Key points:
0.0   Laurel Cove Trailhead.
0.6   Arch.
1.3   Chained Rock Trail.
1.4   Chained Rock.

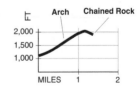

The hike: At the edge of a rock cliff face on Pine Mountain above the town of Pineville, a huge rock appears to perch precariously. For years local lore had it that only a chain tethering the rock to the mountainside kept the little town below from being flattened. There was, of course, nothing to the story. There was no chain, and the rock wasn't about to go anywhere. Park naturalist Dean Henson explains that the rock

Chained Rock

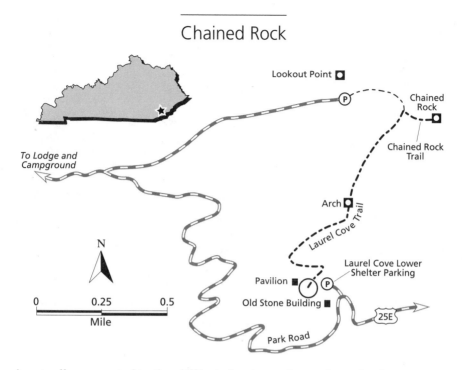

is actually connected to the cliff but, due to erosion and weathering, appears to be separated. In 1933, however, apparently inspired when an out-of-state couple passing through Pineville was completely taken in by the story, the local Kiwanis Club formed a committee to turn fiction into fact. In an act of truly superhuman proportions, citizens with help from the federal Civilian Conservation Corps hauled a big chain up the mountain by mule and anchored the chain to the rock on one end, the rock cliff face on the other. It was a master stroke of community promotion, gaining Pineville attention in hundreds of newspapers across the country.

Today this 101-foot-long, 1.5-ton chain is still in place, and Chained Rock makes an amusing destination for a hike up Pine Mountain. Kids will love it. The outcropping makes a great lookout, too, with views south to Cumberland Mountain, east along Pine Mountain Ridge, and north down into Pineville.

Pine Mountain was Kentucky's first state park and is certainly one of its prettiest. This hike follows delightful Laurel Cove Trail most of the way to Chained Rock. Blazed with both green and blue plastic diamonds and with white paint, it's billed as the park's longest and hardest trail. Still, while the hike's inbound leg is mostly uphill, the grades are not severe.

From the Laurel Cove Trailhead near the pavilion, you ascend initially northeast and then northwest, and after a short level stretch reach a small unnamed sandstone arch at mile 0.6. This graceful structure is a toy version of those found so plentifully in Kentucky's Red River Gorge. After the arch, you drop down briefly to a streambed—dry when I was there—and then climb some more as you cross and recross the streambed. At mile 0.8, a short side

Laurel Cove Trail passes underneath a small sandstone arch on its way to Chained Rock.

trail leads to a rock slab with limited views south; the rock makes a nice resting spot.

After continuing up through beautiful stands of rhododendrons, you descend on stairs beside a rock outcropping and then climb again, curving northeast as you leave the hollow and emerge into more open woods. Immediately after reaching the top of a ridge shoulder, the trail descends north, passes a large rock overhang, and dead-ends into Chained Rock Trail. To your left, Chained Rock Trail leads to 2,200-foot-high Lookout Point at the end of the park's scenic ridgetop road. You turn right and descend on stone steps and rocks to Chained Rock at mile 1.4.

The good views are from the top of the huge outcropping to which the rock is "attached." There is no set route up the outcropping, and you should watch children carefully. As for the chain, it's made of 1⅜-inch steel, and each link weighs 4.5 pounds, according to park information. When you've had enough of the vistas, retrace your steps down to the parking lot.

Options: The park has a number of other trails, all of them short. A favorite is Hemlock Garden Trail, a loop that starts and ends at the lodge. Including a spur to Inspiration Point, a small bluff at the head of a hollow, this trail is about a mile in length. It winds through old-growth hemlocks as well as interesting rock formations that should intrigue children. Despite its brevity, the scenery makes this hike worthwhile. To reach the lodge, return to US 25E, go south for 0.4 mile, and turn right onto KY 190. In 1.6 miles, KY 190 goes left and you bear right, following the signs for the lodge.

Red River Gorge

The Red River Gorge is Kentucky's most popular hiking area. The 27,000 acres in the federally designated Red River Gorge Geological Area and adjacent Clifty Wilderness offer 60 miles of trails ranging from short hops of less than a mile to backpacking possibilities of several days. Carved out of the Cumberland Plateau eons ago, the gorge serves up a mix of massive cliffs with panoramic views, narrow ravines with peaceful streamside picnic spots, and intriguing rock arches in all sizes. Christmas ferns, rhododendrons, mountain laurel, and a wide variety of wildflowers cover the area. From families with small children to experienced trekkers, there's something here for every kind of hiker. The tall cliffs also attract lots of rock climbers.

That, of course, means trail traffic can be heavy, especially on summer weekends, a good time to avoid. But otherwise, each season has advantages—even winter, when water falling over the cliffs freezes into columns of ice. The gorge is in Eastern Kentucky about an hour's drive from Lexington, and easily reached on the Bert T. Combs Mountain Parkway, named for a former governor. For a preview of the rugged terrain, you can drive a scenic 35-mile loop through the area using Kentucky Highways 15, 77, and 715. Part of the drive is along the Red River, which supposedly once had a red tint, hence the name. The loop also takes you through the Nada Tunnel, a one-lane, 900-foot-long cut made in the early 1900s to accommodate a logging railroad.

On KY 715 east of its junction with KY 77, a reconstructed log cabin dating to the 1800s gives a glimpse of how settlers here lived. The cabin and a nearby barn with old farming tools are open to the public seven days a week, April through October. Behind the barn, a USDA Forest Service trailer has information, maps, and personnel to answer questions. The book *Kentucky's Land of the Arches* by Robert H. Ruchhoft (Pucelle Press, Cincinnati, 1986) gives the geological and human history of the gorge, including a detailed explanation of how the area's sandstone arches and shallow caves, known as rock houses or rock shelters, were formed. Essentially, they are the result of uneven erosion. The hard sandstone that tops the area was able to withstand the weathering process, while the soft underlying layers were eaten away.

The gorge is part of the Daniel Boone National Forest, and the Forest Service has a fifty-four-site fee campground at Koomer Ridge off KY 15. Backcountry camping is allowed except within 300 feet of a road or developed trail or within 100 feet of the base of any cliff or the back of any rock shelter. This last restriction is to protect the gorge's archaeological sites; as long as 10,000 years ago Native Americans were living in the rock shelters and cliffs. In April 2000 the Forest Service initiated a fee system for overnight users. Vehicles parked in the gorge area between 10:00 P.M. and 6:00 A.M. must have a pass hanging on the rearview mirror. Passes are sold at Forest Service district offices as well as stores in the gorge area and Lexington. For a list of outlets, go to the Web site www.southernregion.fs.fed.us/boone/ recpass.htm. You can buy passes covering one night ($3.00), three nights ($5.00), seven nights ($10.00), or a year ($30.00). The Stanton Ranger District (606–663–2852) has jurisdiction over the gorge and is a source of information.

Two notes of caution. The gorge cliffs claim lives all too frequently. Hikers, especially those with small children, should be alert to the danger of falling. Also, while this is a popular recreation area, it is open to hunting according to regular state seasons. Be extra careful and wear bright orange during the modern-gun season for deer, usually in November.

20 Koomer Ridge

Highlights: A forest walk, much of it on or near ridgetops, to a small rock arch and a scenic stream.
Location: The Red River Gorge area of the Daniel Boone National Forest, 16 miles east of Stanton.
Type of hike: Day hike or one-night backpack; loop.
Total distance: 7.7 miles.
Difficulty: Moderate.
Best months: Any month.
Maps: USDA Forest Service map of the Red River Gorge; USGS Slade.
Permits and fees: Overnight users must obtain a pass to display on cars parked in the Red River Gorge area.

Finding the trailhead: From exit 33 off the Bert T. Combs Mountain Parkway, go north for 0.1 mile on Kentucky Highway 11 and turn right onto KY 15, which leapfrogs the parkway several times as both head east toward Campton. After 5 miles, turn left into Koomer Ridge Campground. Bear left at the first fork, and immediately take another left onto a road that dead-ends in a few yards at a parking lot for trail users. Walk back out to the campground road. Officially the trail starts just across the road but the first 0.2 mile simply parallels the road north to the tenting area, which is the true trailhead. After taking either the road or trail to the tenting area, go past the rest rooms to the trail signs at the edge of the forest. GPS: 33 47.063 N 83 38.169 W.

Parking and trailhead facilities: There are rest rooms and water at the campground, and lots of parking space.

Key points:
0.8 Hidden Arch.
3.3 Chimney Top Creek.
5.8 Right Fork of Chimney Top Creek.

The hike: Logging, aided by the construction of rail lines, came to this remote gorge with a vengeance in the late 1800s, and by the 1920s much of

Koomer Ridge

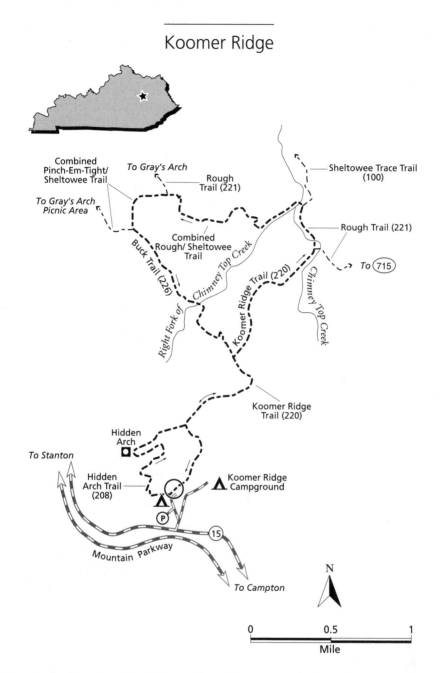

Combined Pinch-Em-Tight/ Sheltowee Trail

To Gray's Arch

Rough Trail (221)

Sheltowee Trace Trail (100)

To Gray's Arch Picnic Area

Combined Rough/ Sheltowee Trail

Rough Trail (221)

Chimney Top Creek

Buck Trail (226)

Koomer Ridge Trail (220)

Chimney Top Creek

To (715)

Right Fork of Chimney Top Creek

Koomer Ridge Trail (220)

Hidden Arch

To Stanton

Hidden Arch Trail (208)

Koomer Ridge Campground

(P)

(15)

Mountain Parkway

To Campton

N

0   0.5   1
Mile

the area had been stripped bare. The effects are apparent today in the relatively small size of the trees, especially up on the accessible ridges. Indeed, in some sections lumbering continued into the 1960s—before the gorge got special protection as a geological area. But humanity's past excesses are not able to dull the beauty of the stark cliffs, intriguing rock arches, and lush ravines—or coves, as they are called here—that cover the area. This hike along ridgetops and a creek bank using several different trails is a good sampler of what the Red River Gorge has to offer. For me, the highlight is the stretch along Chimney Top Creek, a lively stream lined with delightful wading pools. Like most trails in the gorge, these are blazed with a white diamond. Because of trail changes over the years and a tradition of rounding up fractional mileage, distances on trail signs in the gorge are often inaccurate. Those you see on this hike are no exception.

Two trails leave the tenting area: Koomer Ridge Trail (220), heading north, and Hidden Arch Trail (208). You take the latter, which goes west and north before swinging east to join Koomer Ridge Trail about half a mile north of the campground. The reason to take Hidden Arch Trail is that it's beautiful. The trail follows a narrow, pretty ridgetop through hardwood trees, mountain laurel, and rhododendrons to an overlook with views to the north—the best you get on this hike when the foliage is out. Watch small kids; the drop-off is steep. The trail then descends on wooden steps to a large outcropping of pockmarked rocks and little Hidden Arch, which would be just that if not for the people who built this trail. More stairs take you under the cliff wall before the trail climbs through rhododendrons to meet Koomer Ridge Trail 1 mile into the hike.

Take Koomer Ridge Trail to your left (north) for a quick, flat walk to meet the southeastern end of Buck Trail (226) at mile 1.8. Later in the hike you will take Buck Trail, but for now continue on Koomer Ridge Trail as it winds northeast and descends, gently at first and then more steeply, to the western bank of Chimney Top Creek. This creek flows north to the Red River, and Koomer Ridge Trail follows it briefly before dead-ending into Rough Trail (221) at mile 3. Rough Trail, the longest in the gorge, runs generally east–west

Chimney Top Creek is lined with delightful wading pools.

from KY 715 to KY 77. You take it to your left and continue following the creek north for 0.2 mile before crossing to the eastern bank. The crossing point is marked by a white diamond on a tree but is easily missed; you can't go too far past it, however, because the path on the western bank soon ends. There is no bridge, and, depending on the creek's level, wading may be necessary. Look downstream about 15 yards for a line of rocks to get you across dry footed.

Rough Trail continues to parallel the creek and, in another 0.1 mile, joins with Sheltowee Trace National Recreation Trail (100), a north–south walking route of approximately 260 miles through the Daniel Boone National Forest. You take a left onto the combined Rough/Sheltowee and immediately cross back over the creek, again wading or finding a makeshift bridge of stones and logs. The combined trail climbs northwest above the creek and then west up the ridgeside and through an area of about one hundred acres that burned in 1999. Rangers believe a campfire got out of control. After following a constant contour around the head of a ridge, you come to a large, bald rock that makes a nice resting spot. Go directly across the rock and pick up the trail again, heading north and then west before Rough and Sheltowee Trails split at mile 4.5.

Rough Trail goes northwest while the Sheltowee joins with Pinch-Em-Tight Trail (223) and heads west along the ridge toward the Gray's Arch picnic area on Tunnel Ridge Road 1.6 miles away. You take the combined Sheltowee/Pinch-Em-Tight, but go only 0.4 mile to the start of Buck Trail (226). Turn left onto Buck Trail, going southeast and descending to reach the Right Fork of Chimney Top Creek at mile 5.8. Bear right along the creek before making several easy crossings and climbing through rhododendrons away from the stream and up the ridge. At mile 6.4, Buck Trail dead-ends into Koomer Ridge Trail, and you are now back near where you were early in the hike. Turn right onto Koomer Ridge Trail and walk 1.3 miles south to the tenting area.

Options: To enlarge the loop to include Gray's Arch, one of the gorge's most popular attractions, continue northwest on Rough Trail (221) to the arch and then south to near the Gray's Arch picnic area. There you can take Pinch-Em-Tight Trail (223) east to Buck Trail (226). This will add about 4 miles to your trip. See Hike 21.

21 Gray's Arch

Highlights:	A 50-foot-high natural arch, and a small, shady creek with inviting wading pools.
Location:	The Red River Gorge area of the Daniel Boone National Forest, 15 miles east of Stanton.
Type of hike:	Day hike; loop.
Total distance:	3.3 miles.
Difficulty:	Moderate.
Best months:	Any month.
Maps:	USDA Forest Service map of the Red River Gorge; USGS Slade
Permits and fees:	Overnight users must obtain a pass to display on cars parked in the Red River Gorge area.

Finding the trailhead: From exit 33 off the Bert T. Combs Mountain Parkway, go north for 0.1 mile on Kentucky Highway 11 and turn right onto KY 15, heading east toward Campton. After 3.5 miles, turn left onto gravel Tunnel Ridge Road (Forest Road 39) and drive north 1 mile to the Gray's Arch picnic area on your right. GPS: 37 48.481 N 83 39.456 W.

Parking and trailhead facilities: You'll find picnic tables, rest rooms, and parking for at least a dozen cars, but no water.

Key points:
- 1.0   Gray's Arch.
- 1.4   King Branch.

The hike: Natural arches are formed over thousands of years as water and wind eat away soft rock and leave harder strata behind. The Red River Gorge offers one of the largest collections of sandstone arches in the country. Altogether there are reportedly more than a hundred in the area. Without a doubt Gray's Arch is among the most spectacular. It rises 50 feet, spans 80 feet, and appears even bigger because you approach it from the bottom of a ravine, the formation towering over you. The rest of the scene is equally impressive. Surrounding cliffs drip with water except on the driest of summer days, and thick ferns and rhododendrons carpet the forest floor. This is a perfect spot for a leisurely lunch—or just daydreaming—provided you avoid a busy summer weekend. Gray's Arch is one of the most popular destinations in the gorge. Past the arch, however, the number of hikers is certain to thin out. A delightful little stream named King Branch offers beautiful, quiet spots.

From the picnic area parking lot, take Gray's Arch Trail (205) to the north. Notice the memorial plaque to Jim Graf, a young man killed in a fall from the top of Gray's Arch in 1986. The gorge is full of signs warning hikers of the danger of falling. This hike, however, is safe even for small children—as long as you stay off the top of the arch. Rappelling, a popular activity in the gorge, is prohibited from the arch.

Gray's Arch

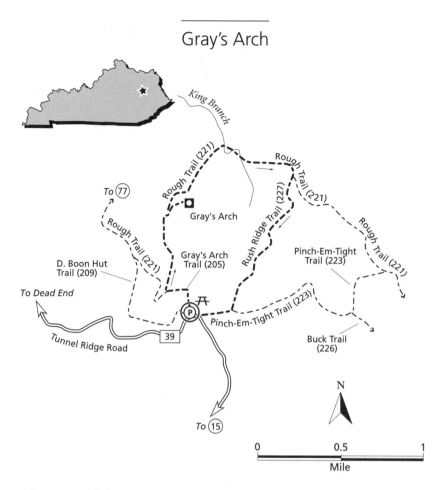

0   0.5   1
Mile

The name of this trail is a misnomer because it doesn't go to the arch. After jogging west, Gray's Arch Trail dead-ends in 0.2 mile into Rough Trail (221), which is what actually gets you to the arch. Blazed with white diamonds, Rough Trail is the main hiking route across the gorge area. You take it to your right, walking north. Notice the magnolia trees with huge elephant-ear-like leaves. At mile 0.6, the trail makes an easy-to-miss curve to your right; if you continue going straight, you end up in a cleared area well used as a campsite. Immediately after the curve, the trail comes to a fence and turns left. The fence blocks a path leading to the top of Gray's Arch. Continue north on Rough Trail as it slopes gently downhill. Just after you see Gray's Arch off to your right, the trail descends on a series of steep wooden stairs into a ravine. Here, at mile 1, Rough Trail turns left, but you follow a sign pointing straight ahead to the arch. This short side trail takes you up to the base of the arch, which is covered with soft orange-brown sand—proof that the erosion process continues.

While backcountry camping is generally allowed in the Daniel Boone National Forest, it is not permitted near the arch. When it's time to move on, return to Rough Trail and continue downhill to the north. In 0.4 mile, after

Gray's Arch is one of the most popular destinations in Red River Gorge.

passing a large rock outcropping, you come to King Branch on its way to the Red River. Walking upstream and eastward, you cross the creek three times. There are no bridges, but a modest jump should get you over with dry feet unless it has been raining and the water level is up. If you want to get wet, the shaded creek bank offers a number of good wading spots. The gorge was logged into the 1960s, and the trees along the ridges near the roads are young, their trunks no thicker than your waist. Down in this little valley, however, the growth is older, taller, and more pleasing.

At mile 1.5, the trail leaves the creekside and veers up the side of the ridge. This is the only strenuous leg of the hike. Part of the climb is almost straight up; a series of wooden-block steps helps considerably. At mile 2, just after reaching the ridgetop, Rough Trail connects with Rush Ridge Trail (227), which you take to the south. The signs at this intersection can be confusing. When I was last there, Rush Ridge Trail was not identified at all. Just be sure to bear right after you reach the ridgetop.

After 1 mile of level walking, Rush Ridge Trail ends at Pinch-Em-Tight Trail (223) combined with Sheltowee Trace National Recreation Trail (100). Take a right onto the combined Pinch-Em-Tight/Sheltowee and walk west 0.2 mile to Tunnel Ridge Road (FR 39). Turn right onto the road; in 0.1 mile, you are back at your car.

Options: If you want a longer loop, instead of taking Rush Ridge Trail, continue southeast on Rough Trail until it hits Pinch-Em-Tight Trail and take it back to Tunnel Ridge Road. This increases the hike's total distance to just over 4 miles. Also, at the Gray's Arch picnic area, D. Boon Hut Trail

(209) leads for 0.7 mile to the remains of an old saltpeter mine and shelter where a board with the carved letters D BOON was discovered. That prompted speculation, never substantiated, that Daniel Boone himself once may have been in residence.

22 Courthouse Rock and Double Arch

Highlights: A commanding ridgetop view of the Red River Gorge, and an unusual rock arch.
Location: The Red River Gorge area of the Daniel Boone National Forest, 18 miles east of Stanton.
Type of hike: Day hike or one-night backpack; loop.
Total distance: 6.1 miles.
Difficulty: Moderate.
Best months: Any month.
Maps: USDA Forest Service map of the Red River Gorge; USGS Slade.
Permits and fees: Overnight users must obtain a pass to display on cars parked in the Red River Gorge area.

Special considerations: To make this a loop, the last 1.4-mile leg is on Tunnel Ridge Road (Forest Road 39). The road is gravel and not heavily used, but it is a road, and small children will have to be watched. Along the trails, several steep stairways and a high, narrow ridgetop also present a potential danger for unattended children.

Finding the trailhead: From exit 33 off the Bert T. Combs Mountain Parkway, go north for 0.1 mile on Kentucky Highway 11 and turn right onto KY 15, heading east toward Campton. After 3.5 miles, turn left onto gravel Tunnel Ridge Road (FR39). Continue for 3 miles past the Gray's Arch picnic area then turn right at the road marked AUXIER RIDGE. This road dead-ends in 0.1 mile at a parking lot. The trail starts on the west side of the lot. GPS: 37 49.169 N 83 40.877 W.

Parking and trailhead facilities: There's space for numerous cars, but no facilities.

Key points:
2.1   Courthouse Rock.
3.8   Double Arch.

The hike: Courthouse Rock, a boulder the size of an office building, is one of the landmarks of the gorge area. Another is Double Arch, which has a large opening topped by a small one and is positioned prominently on a ridgetop. This hike connects these two works of nature, and also includes

Courthouse Rock and Double Arch

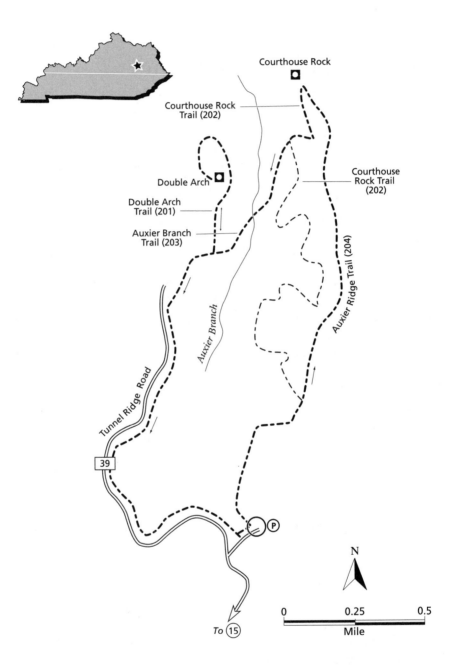

Courthouse Rock

Courthouse Rock
Trail (202)

Double Arch

Courthouse
Rock Trail
(202)

Double Arch
Trail (201)

Auxier Branch
Trail (203)

Auxier Ridge Trail (204)

Auxier Branch

Tunnel Ridge Road

39

P

To 15

N

0   0.25   0.5
Mile

unobstructed views of the gorge area from a narrow ridge that you cross on the way to Courthouse Rock.

At the trailhead, take Auxier Ridge Trail (204) north. The path soon turns left and descends gently through a tunnel of rhododendrons to a ridge that you follow with little elevation change to a junction with Courthouse Rock Trail (202) at mile 0.9. Despite the name of this second trail, continue north on Auxier Ridge Trail. You can get to Courthouse Rock both ways, but this is by far the more scenic. After the junction, keep your eye out for a bend in the trail to your right (east); it's easy to miss and to continue, instead, straight on a well-worn path that ends at a spot used by overnight campers. At about mile 1.5, you reach the first of what are progressively better panoramas. The tall, white cliff you see to the east is flat-topped Ravens Rock, where two hang gliders were killed in the 1970s in a gliding tournament. Farther along, several short paths lead left to the edge of a cliff and fine views westward. The trail then tightens into a narrow bridge of rock from which you have unsurpassed views of the Red River valley. Be careful; on both sides it's a straight drop-off.

The trail then climbs over a small rock outcropping, sidesteps another, and comes to a long stairway of metal steps followed by a second made of wood, both very steep and long. At the bottom on the left, at mile 2.1, is the other end of Courthouse Rock Trail (202), and directly in front of you is Courthouse Rock itself. With a little difficulty, you can climb partway up the rock on both its east and west sides. But beware of trying to get all the way up. Veteran ranger Don Fig says that the Forest Service on more than one occasion has had to rescue people who were able to scramble to the top but then couldn't get down. Unless you have climbing experience and equipment, don't try it, he advises.

After exploring the rock, take Courthouse Rock Trail and head south below the cliffs you just walked across. In 0.3 mile, you come to a fork: Courthouse Rock Trail goes left, but you go right onto Auxier Branch Trail (203). It takes you down to Auxier Branch, a beautiful creek in a small hollow. This is an excellent place for a rest. After briefly following the creek upstream, you cross it on rocks and climb first southwest and then west. At mile 3.1, the trail dead-ends into Double Arch Trail (201); a left would take you to the end of Tunnel Ridge Road, but you go right, walking north and level along the base of the cliff that holds Double Arch. After curving west around the end of the cliff, the trail stops at the bottom of steps up to the arch. At the top of the step is another great view, this one of the ridge that you crossed to get to Courthouse Rock. It's also another long drop-off, so be careful. Double Arch is so named because a thin line of rock separates the bottom opening from a small eye-shaped slit on top. In *Kentucky's Land of the Arches,* author Robert H. Ruchhoft says the lower arch measures 30 feet across and 11 feet in height, the upper 25 feet and 1.5 feet, respectively. It's the only sizable arch in the area with two openings, according to Ruchhoft.

From the arch, retrace your steps to the Auxier Branch Trail junction, and then continue on Double Arch Trail for 0.2 mile to the parking area at the end of Tunnel Ridge Road. The climb to the road uses steps and switchbacks.

Double Arch features a large opening at the bottom and a smaller one above it.

The road, which you take back to the parking area, offers a few limited views and a good deal of shade. At mile 6.1, you reach your car.

Options: You can avoid the road walk by retracing your steps to Courthouse Rock Trail (202) and taking it to the right to Auxier Ridge Trail (204), then Auxier Ridge Trail to your car. This increases the hike's total length to about 8 miles.

23 Tower Rock

Highlights:	A short walk to a tall rock, perfect for families with small children.
Location:	Clifty Wilderness in the Red River Gorge area of the Daniel Boone National Forest, 21 miles east of Stanton.
Type of hike:	Day hike; out-and-back.
Total distance:	0.8 mile.
Difficulty:	Easy.
Best months:	Any month.
Maps:	USDA Forest Service map of the Red River Gorge; USGS Pomeroyton.
Permits and fees:	Overnight users must obtain a pass to display on cars parked in the Red River Gorge area.

Finding the trailhead: From exit 33 off the Bert T. Combs Mountain Parkway, go north for 0.1 mile on Kentucky Highway 11 and turn left onto combined KY 11/15, heading west toward Stanton. After 1.5 miles, turn right onto KY 77. In 4.3 miles, afer passing through the one-lane Nada Tunnel and crossing the Red River, turn right onto KY 715. In 3.2 miles, cross a stone bridge over Gladie Creek; continue east on KY 715 for 1 mile beyond. The Tower Rock Trailhead sign is on the left side of the road, and across from it on the right is a narrow shoulder for parking. Be careful parking; the shoulder is indeed narrow, and below lies the Red River. GPS: 37 49.643 N 83 35.937 W.

Parking and trailhead facilities: There's space for two to three cars. No facilities are available at the trailhead, but the Gladie Historic Site—with rest rooms, information, and exhibits on turn-of-the-twentieth-century life in the gorge—is less than a mile west on KY 715.

Key points:
0.3   Tower Rock.

The hike: The Red River Gorge includes a number of short trails to popular landmarks: Sky Bridge Trail (214), Princess Arch Trail (233), and Angel Windows Trail (218) are all less than a mile. Tower Rock Trail is another of these short hops, but it's one easily overlooked. Because of this and also

Tower Rock soars up about 90 feet from the trail.

Tower Rock

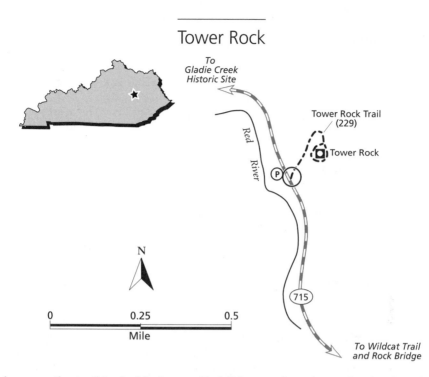

To
Gladie Creek
Historic Site

Tower Rock Trail
(229)

Tower Rock

Red River

P

715

To Wildcat Trail
and Rock Bridge

N

0   0.25   0.5
Mile

because the trail is doable by small children and yet has a destination that rewards hikers of all ages, I have included it.

Tower Rock is just that: a huge hunk of rock towering straight up. The Forest Service doesn't have an official height measurement, but one employee estimates 90 feet, and that looks right. Certainly the rock is tall enough to be popular with the climbing community. You are likely to see some climbers in action during your visit.

From the trailhead sign on KY 715, Tower Rock Trail (229) climbs north through a pleasant forest of pines and rhododendrons before turning south to a large split rock, which you walk through at mile 0.3. Just beyond is Tower Rock, as impressive in size as a European cathedral. In his book *Kentucky's Land of the Arches,* historian Robert H. Ruchhoft explains that the rock is sandstone that has resisted the weathering process while the ridge it was once part of has eroded away. A loop trail, marked by white diamonds, circles the rock. At the south end, there is a low ledge, and it's possible to scramble up a few feet. But otherwise—unless you are an experienced climber—Tower Rock is impregnable. The loop ends in 0.2 mile back where it started, and you retrace your steps down to the road.

24 Swift Camp Creek

Highlights: A peaceful walk in the woods to a sizable creek perfect for cooling off on a hot day.

Location: Clifty Wilderness in the Red River Gorge area of the Daniel Boone National Forest, 7 miles northwest of Campton.

Type of hike: Day hike or one-night backpack; loop.

Total distance: 5.3 miles.

Difficulty: Easy.

Best months: The hot summer.

Maps: USDA Forest Service map of the Red River Gorge; USGS Pomeroyton.

Permits and fees: Overnight users must obtain a pass to display on cars parked in the Red River Gorge area.

Special considerations: To make a loop, the hike's last 1.1-mile leg is on a paved but lightly used road.

Finding the trailhead: From exit 40 off the Bert T. Combs Mountain Parkway, take combined Kentucky Highways 15 and 715 northeast for 1 mile, where the two routes split. Follow KY 715 to your right, and drive 3 miles north to the Wildcat Trail parking lot on your left. GPS: 37 47.443 N 83 35.794 W.

Parking and trailhead facilities: There's off-road parking space for numerous cars, but no facilities.

Key points:
3.0 Swift Camp Creek.

The hike: The 12,600-acre Clifty Wilderness, one of two designated wildernesses in Kentucky, was heavily logged before it received protected status in 1985. The old roads and paths used by loggers and homesteaders are still visible, so you won't experience the remoteness found in the large wilderness tracts in the western United States. Nevertheless, for a quiet walk in the woods, the Clifty area can't be beat. The cliffs and rock outcroppings are intriguing, and Swift Camp Creek, once used by lumbermen to float logs down to the Red River, makes an excellent picnic spot, especially on a hot summer day.

Wildcat Trail (228), which you take east to the creek, starts just across KY 715 from the parking area. The road marks the western boundary of the wilderness area. Although it initially heads south, at mile 0.1 the trail makes a sharp but poorly marked turn to your left (east). Numerous old paths in this area can be confusing; look for the Wildcat Trail blaze, a white diamond. The trail essentially parallels KY 715 until mile 0.5, where it turns right onto an old dirt road. (A left here would take you to the original Wildcat Trailhead on KY 715. The trailhead was moved several years ago because of insufficient

Swift Camp Creek

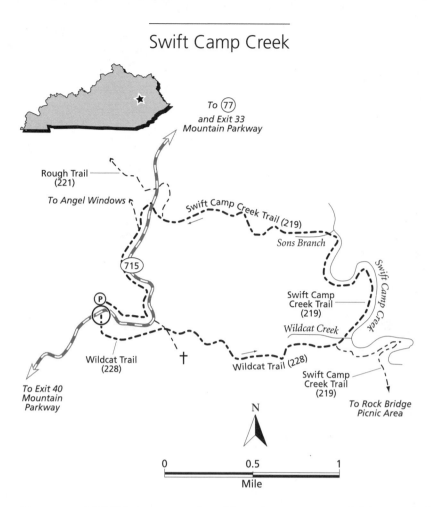

To (77)
and Exit 33
Mountain Parkway

Rough Trail
(221)

To Angel Windows

Swift Camp Creek Trail (219)

Sons Branch

Swift Camp Creek

715

P

Swift Camp
Creek Trail
(219)

Wildcat Creek

Wildcat Trail
(228)

Wildcat Trail (228)

Swift Camp
Creek Trail
(219)

To Exit 40
Mountain
Parkway

To Rock Bridge
Picnic Area

N

0   0.5   1
Mile

parking space.) Walking east on the old road, you come quickly to a fork and bear left; the right prong goes up a hill to a private cemetery. The road narrows to a path, and after a level stretch begins descending, gently at first and then more steeply. The rhododendrons and ferns are thick, and moss-covered rocks along the trail gradually grow into cliffs pocked with cavelike shelters. When I took this walk, a couple of deer bounded through the trees about 25 yards away, their tails flapping madly.

At mile 1.7, Wildcat Trail dead-ends into Swift Camp Creek Trail (219), which you take to your left. Old Forest Service maps show an arch—Timmons Arch—across the creek from the trail junction, but the arch is not visible from this side of the stream. Swift Camp Creek Trail runs a total of about 7 miles—from Rock Bridge at the southeast corner of the Clifty Wilderness north and then west to KY 715. Combined with Rough Trail (221), it permits a backpacking trip across much of the gorge area. (See Options.)

Heading north along Swift Camp Creek as it makes its way toward the Red River, you cross Wildcat Creek and several smaller streams that are likely

Swift Camp Creek makes an excellent spot for picnics and wading.

to be nothing more than a trickle in summer. Swift Camp Creek remains below you at an unreachable distance—and often out of sight—as you slab around the ridges above the stream. At mile 3, the trail descends to just above the creek, and at last you can easily reach the water. Swift Camp Creek will never be an Olympic diving venue, but it should have pools deep enough for a good dunking.

Don't wait too long to take a dip, because soon —at mile 3.2—the trail leaves the creek and begins climbing toward KY 715. Be alert for the turn; it's easy to miss. A white arrow painted on a large rock points left to a narrow set of steps heading away from the stream. Take the steps, cross a small feeder stream named Sons Branch, and begin climbing westward along a ravine. The first part of the climb is steep but brief. Soon the trail levels off, and it remains that way as you walk through young pines. Just before reaching KY 715, the trail forks. You take the left prong and come out on the road across from a short (0.3-mile) trail to two small arches called Angel Windows. The right prong hits the road 0.2 mile north at a trailhead parking lot for Swift Camp Creek and Rough Trails. Your car is an easy walk of 1.1 miles south on KY 715.

Options: For a longer trip, take Rough Trail (221) west from KY 715; it goes for about 7 miles, ending at KY 77. If you take Swift Camp Creek Trail from its beginning at Rock Bridge and continue on Rough Trail to KY 77, the total distance is about 14 miles; you would, of course, have to arrange a shuttle back to Rock Bridge. For directions to Rock Bridge, see Hike 25.

25 Rock Bridge and Turtle Back Arch

Highlights:	The area's only arch with water flowing beneath it, and an arch hidden off the trail.
Location:	The Red River Gorge area of the Daniel Boone National Forest, 8 miles north of Campton.
Type of hike:	Day hike or one-night backpack; loop.
Total distance:	4 miles.
Difficulty:	Moderate.
Best months:	Any month.
Maps:	USDA Forest Service map of the Red River Gorge; USGS Pomeroyton.
Permits and fees:	Overnight users must obtain a pass to display on cars parked in the Red River Gorge area.

Special considerations: Part of this hike is on unofficial, unmarked trails; bring a compass.

Finding the trailhead: From exit 40 off the Bert T. Combs Mountain Parkway, take combined Kentucky Highways 15 and 715 northeast for 1 mile, where the two routes split. Follow KY 715 to your right, driving 1 mile north and turning right onto gravel Rock Bridge Road (Forest Road 24), which dead-ends in 3 miles at a picnic area. Rock Bridge Trail (207) begins at the edge of the road on the south side of the picnic area. GPS: 37 46.209 N 83 33.941 W.

Parking and trailhead facilities: There's plenty of parking space, as well as rest rooms and picnic tables.

Key points:
- 0.6 Rock Bridge.
- 2.0 Turtle Back Arch.

The hike: This is a hike of extremes—from a paved nature trail to a bit of off-trail exploration. The route takes you to two Red River Gorge landmarks. First is Rock Bridge, the area's only true natural bridge because it has a stream—Swift Camp Creek—flowing beneath it. Second is Turtle Back Arch, a medium-sized arch on a ridgetop above Swift Camp Creek. Trying to find it is a challenge.

Rock Bridge Trail (207) is a 1.3-mile loop designed as a self-guided nature trail and, most of the way, covered with asphalt. Despite this unattractive surface, it is one of the most scenic walks in the gorge. Taking the southern leg of this loop path, you descend quickly on steps into a lush ravine of ferns and rhododendrons. Soon you are following a picturesque little stream—Rockbridge Fork—to a small waterfall with a sandy beach. It's a beautiful spot worth a visit in itself. After the falls, the stream meets Swift Camp Creek; just beyond is Rock Bridge, both graceful and craggy at the same time. Lumbermen used to float logs beneath it on the way downstream to the Red River. The arch was formed when a waterfall eroded soft interior rock but not the hard limestone layer on top.

Rock Bridge and Turtle Back Arch

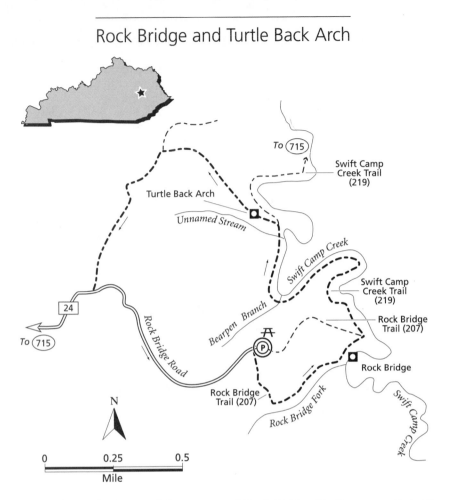

After the arch, the creek jogs east and Rock Bridge Trail goes north to the start of Swift Camp Creek Trail (219). At this junction, which you reach at mile 0.8, Rock Bridge Trail turns west and climbs back to the picnic area; this northern leg of the loop is 0.5 mile. You, however, take Swift Camp Creek Trail north and immediately pass into the Clifty Wilderness. Cliffs line the left side of the trail, and the creek parallels it on the right. Soon after entering the wilderness, you pass a side path down to the creek at the site of what was once a dam built by loggers to raise the water level so they could float trees downstream. The dam washed away long ago.

The walking is fairly level, although the trail rises high above the stream. At mile 1.6, after a pronounced loop eastward, you come to a bridge over Bearpen Branch. At the far end of the bridge, instead of a dirt path, you walk upstream on Bearpen Branch's rock bottom to get past rock outcroppings along both sides of the stream. Once past the outcroppings, the trail scampers up the far bank and immediately passes between two large boulders.

Swift Camp Creek flows under Rock Bridge.

Next to the one on your left, a side trail leads left to a cliff face where a local moonshiner once kept his still.

Continuing north on the trail, you soon hear the trickle of falling water, and at mile 1.8 cross a small, unnamed stream. You are now close to Turtle Back Arch, but without directions it's doubtful you would find it. It's a sneaky little devil. Frustrated and thoroughly defeated by my inability to locate it, I once camped on the ridgetop—only to learn later that I had slept almost literally on top of the arch. About 150 feet past the stream, you see an unmarked path off to the left of the trail. Take it for a brief distance west to a flat, open area that has obviously been used as a campsite. There turn north and wind your way up the hillside to the flat, thin top of the ridge. So far you have come a total of about 300 feet from Swift Camp Creek Trail.

On the ridgetop, turn left (west); in a few feet, step over a low rock outcropping and come to a second, much taller one—about 15 feet in height. When I was there, a climbing rope had been thoughtfully provided; secured at one end to a tree on top of the rock, the rope made it easy to pull myself up. The Forest Service did not install the rope and advises against using it for fear use and the elements could cause it to deteriorate. If there's no rope, fingers and feet will have to suffice. Continuing west on the ridge, you easily climb over two relatively small rocks and then come to another big outcropping. Instead of climbing this one, take the little path running along the rock's left side. It's a snug fit between the rock wall on your right and the bushes on your left. But shortly—at mile 2—you reach an opening in the cliffside, meaning you have found the elusive Turtle Back Arch (GPS: 37 46.649 N 83 34.052 W). The arch opening is big enough for an adult of average size to walk through bent over. The walls of the arch, so eaten away that they look like Swiss cheese, provide a close-up look at the effects of the erosion process that produces these structures.

You can, of course, simply retrace your steps to your car. But by using two unofficial trails across the ridge and a stretch of gravel Rock Bridge Road, you can take a loop back to the picnic area. This way you get the bonus of a good ridgetop view. For the loop return, squeeze your way back to the front of the large rock outcropping, and climb to the top. It's easy if you boost yourself up using the tree growing next to the rock at the beginning of the path. Once you're on top, go west along the ridgetop, passing over the arch. You quickly skirt a rock outcropping and come to a large one that you have to climb. A couple of tree branches I found leaning against the rock wall made the job easier. On top is an unmarked path, which you take to your left. But first, go right, and in a few feet you come to an open spot that provides an excellent overlook to the north.

A left on the unmarked path takes you northwest. It climbs gently at first but then levels off, and at mile 2.5 dead-ends into another trail, which you take to your left (south). This is a wide, ridgetop trail pleasantly covered with pine needles. But, like the previous one, it has no identifying or directional signs. At mile 3.1, the trail dead-ends into lightly used Rock Bridge Road; turn left and you are back at your car in another 0.9 mile.

Options: You can easily turn this day hike into an overnighter. Near Turtle Back Arch, there are a number of nice camping spots that meet Forest Service rules for the backcountry (no camping within 300 feet of a road or developed trail). Swift Camp Creek Trail north of the arch is worth exploring. It goes through a beautiful gorge that gives the trail a more remote feel than the stretch featured in Hike 24.

26 Natural Bridge and Hood Branch

Highlights:	A visit to Kentucky's best-known rock arch followed by a walk in the backcountry of Natural Bridge State Resort Park.
Location:	Natural Bridge State Resort Park, 13 miles east of Stanton.
Type of hike:	Day hike; loop.
Total distance:	5.4 miles.
Difficulty:	Moderate.
Best months:	Any month.
Maps:	Natural Bridge State Resort Park trail pamphlet (office 606–663–2214); USDA Forest Service map of the Red River Gorge; USGS Slade.

Natural Bridge and Hood Branch

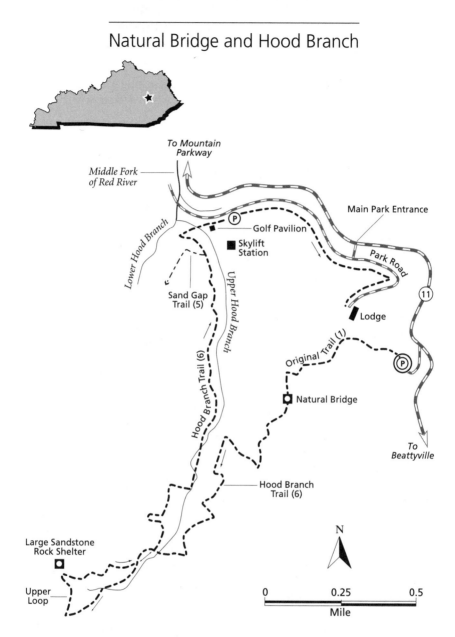

Special considerations: The mileage total includes 1.1 miles on paved park roads from the end of the trail back to the lodge and parking area. Back-country camping is not allowed in the park. Dogs, even on a leash, are prohibited on park trails.

Finding the trailhead: From exit 33 off the Bert T. Combs Mountain Parkway, take Kentucky Highway 11 south. In 2 miles, you come to a right-hand turn to the park's Hemlock Lodge. This is the main park entrance—but continue past it. In 0.5 mile, turn right onto a road marked for various park features, including trails and the swimming pool. Park in the large lot 0.2 mile beyond. A paved path at the lot's north end leads to all trails. GPS: 37 46.537 N 83 40.720 W.

Parking and trailhead facilities: There's plenty of parking space, and nearby are a snack bar, a swimming pool, two campgrounds, and a lodge with a restaurant and overnight rooms.

Key points:
 0.6   Natural Bridge; Hood Branch Trailhead.
 2.0   Upper Loop side trail to large rock shelter.
 2.4   Large rock shelter.
 4.3   End of Hood Branch Trail; beginning of road walk.

The hike: Natural Bridge State Resort Park joins the southern end of the Forest Service's Red River Gorge Geological Area. The park has been a popular tourist attraction for decades and is highly developed. There's even a chairlift to whisk you to Natural Bridge so you don't have to hoof it up the steep hill. Likewise, most of the trails in the park are short and close to the busy lodge area. This hike and Hike 27 are exceptions; both range into the park's little-used backcountry for longer, pleasant walks across deserted ridges and hollows. The park's interior scenery is, for the most part, not spectacular. But it offers plenty of streams, wildflowers, rock outcroppings—and quiet.

This hike combines a stop at the park's main attraction—Natural Bridge—with a walk along Upper Hood Branch, a major drainage of the park's 1,900 acres. Taking the paved path at the north end of the parking lot, you quickly come to a fork. Go right and you are at the start of Original Trail (1), a wide, heavily used, steep path of sand and gravel that gets you to the base of Natural Bridge at mile 0.6. This sandstone arch measures 78 feet in length and 65 feet in height. It's not the area's biggest; Gray's Arch is 2 feet longer and almost as tall, and Whittleton Arch just north of the park spans 100 feet. But Natural Bridge is definitely impressive, not just for its size but for its graceful lines as well. And the view from its top at 1,280 feet is stunning. To get there, ease yourself through the narrow passageway (known as Fat Man's Misery) on the left side of the arch, and climb the steps. The top seems as long and wide as an airport runway. But it has no railings, so watch children. The best view is north across the valley of the Middle Fork of the Red River, the stream that runs along KY 11.

There are a number of other short trails to nearby park landmarks, like Lover's Leap, Devil's Gulch, and Balanced Rock. (See the park trail pamphlet.) But on this hike, you leave all of that behind and head south on Hood Branch Trail (6), a 3.7-mile-long dirt path that starts at the base of Natural Bridge and ends on the park's north side near the lower terminus of the chairlift.

From the southeastern end of Natural Bridge, Hood Branch Trail descends through rhododendrons, then winds along the base of a cliff well above Upper Hood Branch. At mile 1 (measuring from the parking lot), you cross a small feeder stream on a bridge—the first of a number that you will encounter—and walk west before making a sharp turn south. The trail continues snaking east and west as it follows a level contour to the south. At

110

Natural Bridge forms a 78-foot arch.

mile 2, descend to the stream, cross it, and immediately come to a fork. Here the main Hood Branch Trail turns right (north) but you turn left on a side trail that makes a westward loop to a large rock shelter. This side trail—called the Upper Loop—is just less than a mile in length and is included in the total 5.4 miles listed for this hike.

Turning left on the side trial, you go a short distance before bearing left again, this time at the beginning of the loop itself. After climbing up a ravine and turning north, the side trail passes beneath a huge sandstone rock shelter, which makes an interesting rest spot. This cavelike structure was formed when soft interior rock eroded away, leaving a top layer of hard sandstone standing. From the rock shelter, the side trail crosses a footbridge and passes along a cliff face to a smaller rock shelter. Then descending, you return to the start of the loop and in short order reconnect with the main Hood Branch Trail at the streamside fork.

Heading north, the main trial generally follows the level creek bottomland. At mile 3.4 you cross the stream on a bridge and immediately recross it. The trail then passes a shelter built in the 1930s by the old Civilian Conservation Corps and begins following an old roadbed. You pass a turnoff for Sand Gap Trail (5) shortly before descending to the end of Hood Branch Trail at mile 4.3. The chairlift parking lot and a miniature golf course are to your right. The golf pavilion has a snack bar.

From the end of the trail, it's a 1.1-mile walk on park roads back to the lodge area. Take the road going east and, at the intersection in 0.7 mile, go straight for 0.4 mile to the lodge. The parking lot is just below the lodge.

Options: One alternative to the road walk is to take the eleven-minute chairlift ride up to Natural Bridge and walk down to the lodge area. As of this writing, the chairlift runs from 10:00 A.M. to 6:30 P.M. (7:30 P.M. on Saturday), Easter weekend through October; the charge is $3.00 for a one-way ticket. Another alternative, though probably less appealing because of the distance, is to walk back to Natural Bridge on Sand Gap Trail. (See Hike 27.) There are no other trails from this part of the park.

27 Natural Bridge Park Perimeter

Highlights: A ridgetop walk—with several good views—along the boundary of 1,900-acre Natural Bridge State Resort Park.

Location: Natural Bridge State Resort Park, 13 miles east of Stanton.

Type of hike: Day hike; loop.

Total distance: 8.6 miles.

Difficulty: Moderate.

Best months: Any month.

Maps: Natural Bridge State Resort Park trail pamphlet (state park office 606–663–2214); USDA Forest Service map of the Red River Gorge; USGS Slade.

Special considerations: No backcountry camping is allowed in the park, so this has to be a day hike—and it may be too long for some people. However, the mileage total includes 1.1 miles on park roads, which can be eliminated—along with a steep walk of 0.8 mile down from Natural Bridge—by riding the park's chairlift. (See Options.)

Finding the trailhead: From exit 33 off the Bert T. Combs Mountain Parkway, take Kentucky Highway 11 south for 2 miles and turn right at the state park's main entrance. The lodge is straight ahead, but you make an immediate right and, in 0.7 mile, park in the lot near the chairlift and miniature golf course. Walk west across the field to the trailhead sign for Sand Gap and Hood's Branch Trails at the edge of the woods just beyond the golf course. GPS: 37 46.908 N 83 41.482 W.

Parking and trailhead facilities: There are plenty of parking spaces; rest rooms and a snack bar are available at the golf pavilion.

Key points:
3.9 Ridgetop.

The hike: This is a hike for people who enjoy walking a long distance through pleasant woods and don't require lots of dramatic sights along the way to keep them going. The ridgetop section of this trek is thoroughly enjoyable and has several good vistas. But much of the scenery is pretty tame. Even if their young legs are up to it, children are likely to be bored on this one.

The guts of the hike are found along the park's Sand Gap Trail (5). The name is misleading because the trail doesn't go across a Sand Gap—and while there is a Sand Gap Arch just outside the park, you don't see it. What the trail does do, for much of its length, is follow the park boundary through an area that very few visitors ever see. Indeed, while the trail is easy to follow, it is used little enough that low-lying sections near Lower Hood Branch are likely to be overgrown. When I took the hike, the offending vegetation included painful nettles. Consider wearing long pants.

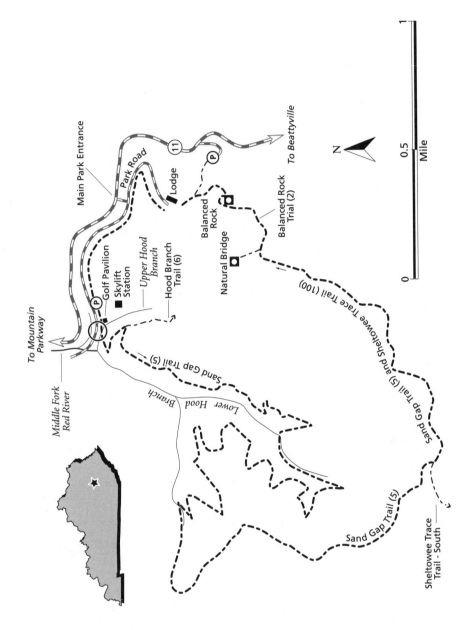

The park trail guide assumes you will walk the trail starting near Natural Bridge and going clockwise, to end up at the miniature golf course on the north side of the park. I recommend the reverse. The Lower Hood Branch section near the golf course is more difficult and less rewarding than the ridgetop boundary portion, and better tackled when you're fresh. I found the length of Sand Gap Trail to be less than 7 mile; officially, it's 8.5. As this was written, park personnel were planning to remeasure the trail.

Sand Gap Trail and Hood Branch Trail (6) leave together from the edge of the miniature golf course and climb briefly but steeply. Sand Gap Trail, which you take, soon splits off to your right, heading initially west and then south to shadow the upstream path of Lower Hood Branch. The trail stays on the ridgeside in a forest of pines and hardwoods until it descends to cross the creek at mile 1.3. Nettles spilling onto the path were particularly bothersome on the far side of the stream when I took the hike. The trail climbs along the creek bed and then settles into a lengthy level period as it winds north and then west. At mile 3.5, you cross a stream—dry when I was there—that feeds into Lower Hood Branch, then climb west out of the valley on an old road.

At mile 3.9, you are on top of the ridge along the state park boundary, and here the character of the trail changes noticeably. Instead of thick vegetation, the woods are open and the trail is wide, flat, and attractively covered with pine needles. Going southeast, you get views of distant ridges to the south and west. Soon you see Forest Service signs marking a Daniel Boone National Forest tract on your right. The views peter out, but the walking is delightful—the kind that lets you put your feet on autopilot and sink deep into thoughts. The trail is frequently on an old roadbed and veers back and forth across the park's legal boundary line.

At mile 5.4, the trail dead-ends into another wide forest track, and you make a sharp left. In addition to Sand Gap Trail, you are now also on Sheltowee Trace National Recreation Trail (100), a long-distance hiking route through the Daniel Boone National Forest blazed with the likeness of a turtle. *Sheltowee,* the Indian name for Daniel Boone, means "turtle." If you were to head right at this junction instead of left, in less than a mile you'd walk across a narrow ridge and the top of a rock arch named Whites Branch Arch.

After joining the Sheltowee, the trail narrows into a path. It heads east and then north with little change in elevation before coming to an overlook with a fine panorama that includes Natural Bridge. At mile 6.7, just past the overlook, Sand Gap Trail ends at the park's Balanced Rock Trail (2), which you take for 0.8 mile down to the lodge area. At this junction, Natural Bridge is just a short walk to your left (north); if you haven't yet seen this arch, the side trip is definitely worthwhile. (See Hike 26.)

To complete this hike, turn right onto Balanced Rock Trail and go down the first of a series of stairways that are long and steep enough to make you thankful you are not coming up. The path goes north along a massive cliff of pockmarked rock and soon descends to Balanced Rock—a rounded boulder that, thanks to uneven erosion, is perched atop a small pedestal of rock in apparent defiance of gravity. The trail passes a rock shelter and ends near

Erosion seems to have given this pockmarked rock a face.

the lodge at mile 7.5. From here follow the sidewalk to the lodge and take the road going downhill. At the intersection in 0.4 mile, continue straight (west) for another 0.7 mile to the chairlift parking lot.

Options: If you want to shorten this hike by about 2 miles, you can avoid the Balanced Rock Trail section down to the lodge and the road walk by riding the chairlift back to your car. Instead of turning right onto Balanced Rock Trail, take it left to Natural Bridge and walk across the arch to the lift's upper station. The chairlift operates from 10:00 A.M. to 6:30 P.M. (7:30 P.M. Saturday) Easter weekend through October; a one-way ticket costs $3.00 as of this writing.

28 Pilot Knob

Highlights:	An overlook west and north into the Kentucky Bluegrass region.
Location:	Pilot Knob State Nature Preserve, 10 miles northwest of Stanton.
Type of hike:	Day hike; out-and-back.
Total distance:	2 miles.
Difficulty:	Easy.
Best months:	Any month.
Maps:	Pilot Knob map from the Kentucky State Nature Preserve Commission (office 502–573–2886); USGS Levee.

Special considerations: Dogs are not permitted in the nature preserve; neither is camping.

Finding the trailhead: From exit 16 off the Bert T. Combs Mountain Parkway, take Kentucky Highway 15 north, and in 3 miles turn right onto Brush Creek Road. This road is not identified, but it's the only paved road to the right in the community of Westbend. Also, at the intersection on KY 15 there is a historical marker noting Daniel Boone's supposed visit to Pilot Knob. Brush Creek Road immediately crosses over the parkway; in 1.5 miles, the pavement ends. Park in the gravel area on your right. GPS: 37 54.720 N 83 56.715 W.

Parking and trailhead facilities: There's space for about six cars, but no facilities.

Key points:
  1.0   Overlook.

The hike: Pilot Knob is not in the Red River Gorge, but it's just 20 easy miles away. This big hill or little mountain—depending on your point of view—rewards the hiker with a wonderful vista. As the story goes, it was from the top of Pilot Knob that Daniel Boone in 1769 got his first view of the gently

Pilot Knob

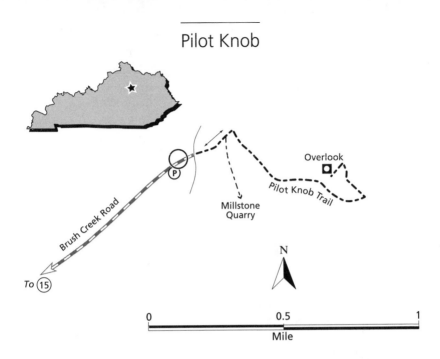

rolling, fertile region now known as the Bluegrass. Pilot Knob is one of a number of knobs lining the western front of eastern Kentucky, and there is no iron-tight evidence that the famous explorer made his observation from this particular one; however Dr. William Martin of Eastern Kentucky University says Boone is known to have camped in the area, and Pilot Knob would have been the most obvious promontory. What is certain is that this 1,440-foot lookout provides a good lesson in Kentucky geography. Behind you, to the east and south, are the forested ridges and high country of the Cumberland Plateau. In front of you, to the west and north, begins the relatively flat farmland of central Kentucky.

The state nature preserve commission calls this hike strenuous. Given the short distance—just 1 mile to the top—and what I found to be a relatively gentle grade, I rate it as easy. You be the judge. From the parking area at the entrance to the 648-acre nature preserve, take the old gravel road going northeast. In a short distance you cross a creekbed, climb wooden steps on the far side, and pass through a metal gate. From here you follow a footpath north to a boxed sign-in sheet at mile 0.1. "Well-kept secret," one previous visitor had written, a sentiment I shared at the end of my hike. Immediately afterward, you come to a junction. Pilot Knob Trail, the path you are following, goes left; to your right is an area where millstones were quarried in the late 1700s and 1800s. (See Options.)

The trail heads southeast and climbs first gently, then more steeply, at one point making use of a series of steps. The way becomes level as you circle the knob, first south and then east. You then climb to the north, passing a rock outcropping on your left and crossing an open area, which was full

Central Kentucky's gently rolling farmland is visible from Pilot Knob.

of wildflowers when I was there in late spring. The trail turns south just before reaching the overlook at mile 1. Continue past the OVERLOOK sign to the rock ledge or you will miss the best view. But be sure to watch small children, because this is an unprotected drop-off. The views are to the west, north, and south. In the southwest you see the water tower for the city of Richmond as well as the buildings of Eastern Kentucky University. This is a spot to enjoy. Afterward, retrace your steps to your car.

Options: At the junction near the trailhead, you can take a short side trip to a site where pioneers once quarried and shaped millstones. Several in various phases of development are positioned along the trail. Free pamphlets explaining the process are available in a box. The easily followed trail, which includes a small loop, is about half a mile long.

Lower Rockcastle

The Lower Rockcastle River—the stretch from just west of London to its entry into the Cumberland—flows through a beautiful, secluded section of the state that tends to get little attention from hikers. Perhaps that's because the recreational focus here is on the water. The Rockcastle and Cumberland, both swollen by backup from Lake Cumberland's Wolf Creek Dam, are large streams, and Laurel River Lake is nearby. In few parts of Kentucky do boaters and anglers have as many opportunities as they do here. But the Lower Rockcastle region is ideal for hikers as well. The river's last 16 miles have been designated a Kentucky Wild River, and the ridges and ravines along the largely untouched shore offer a number of good hikes. The area is within the Daniel Boone National Forest, and the USDA Forest Service maintains numerous trails and campsites. On the east side of the river, the London Ranger District (606–864–4163) has jurisdiction and can provide information; on the west side, the Somerset District (606–679–2010) is in charge.

29 Laurel River Lake

Highlights:	A relaxing walk along the wooded shoreline of a man-made but attractive lake.
Location:	The Flatwoods recreation area on Laurel River Lake in the Daniel Boone National Forest, 16 miles southwest of London in eastern Kentucky.
Type of hike:	Day hike; loop.
Total distance:	3.4 miles.
Difficulty:	Easy.
Best months:	Any month.
Maps:	Map 7 from the London District of the Daniel Boone National Forest; USGS Vox.

Finding the trailhead: From exit 38 off Interstate 75 at London, take Kentucky Highway 192 west for 8.4 miles and turn left (south) onto KY 312. In 3.5 miles, at a stop sign in the town of Keavy, turn right onto KY 3430, and 1.7 miles later turn right onto Flatwoods Road. In 2.6 miles, just after you pass a right-hand turn for the Flatwoods picnic area, bear right to the Flatwoods boat ramp and park in the lot. Flatwoods Trail (470) starts on the lake bank by the ramp. GPS: 36 57.147 N 84 12.433 W.

Parking and trailhead facilities: You'll find parking for several dozen cars, as well as rest rooms.

Key points:
   1.5   Good lakeside spot.

Laurel River Lake

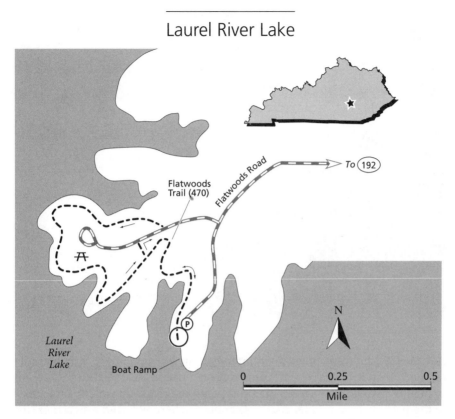

Flatwoods Trail (470)

Flatwoods Road

To (192)

Laurel River Lake

Boat Ramp

P

N

0   0.25   0.5
Mile

The hike: The Laurel River was dammed in the early 1970s by the Corps of Engineers to create a 5,600-acre lake for hydroelectric power and other purposes. Thanks at least in part to a prohibition on private homes and businesses within 300 feet of the waterline, the re- sulting Laurel River Lake is tree lined and free of vis-

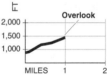

ible commercialization. It is also relatively deep for a man-made lake—about 260 feet. In short, it's a quiet (except for the motorboats) and appealing body of water. This hike takes you along several small inlets on the multifingered lake's eastern shore. The dirt path is shaded by pines and hardwoods, and ranges from running directly along the water to rising a good distance above it. This isn't the Caribbean, and you won't find sandy beaches. But the mix- ture of dirt and stones at the water's edge is not uninviting, and the hike leads you by a number of spots good for a swim on a hot day. Of course, you are on your own; there are no lifeguards. The Laurel River is a tributary of the Cumberland River, not the Rockcastle. But the Laurel is just east of the Rockcastle and part of the Lower Rockcastle area.

Flatwoods Trail (470), which you take, begins next to the water at the south- west end of the ramp parking lot, and follows a long inlet north. The trail gradually rises above the shore and continues north around the streambed that feeds this finger before turning south down the other side of the ravine.

121

Trees line man-made Laurel River Lake.

At mile 0.8, the trail comes to an intersection; turn right onto a path climbing north. After 0.1 mile, you come out on a paved road next to rest rooms in the Flatwoods picnic area. Turn right onto the road and walk 0.1 mile east to the parking area on the road's other side, where you find a sign marking the continuation of Flatwoods Trail. Here the path ducks back into the woods, initially going north and then curving west to follow another finger of the lake. Ferns make this a particularly attractive section.

At mile 1.4, you pass a side trail coming in on your left from the end of the picnic area road. You bear right, continuing to follow the shoreline, and shortly come to a spot just above the rocky shore that makes a pleasant, convenient place to stop for a swim. At mile 1.9, after the trail curves around several small inlets, you cross an old roadbed at the water's edge and then climb above the water. At mile 2.6, you come to a fork and bear right. While you may not recognize it from this direction, the left prong of the fork is the path you took up to the picnic area road early in your hike. This means that in another 0.8 mile, after retracing your steps, you are back at the boat ramp and your car.

30 Cane Creek

Highlights: A secluded creek with beaver activity.
Location: Daniel Boone National Forest, 11 miles southwest of London in eastern Kentucky.
Type of hike: Day hike; out-and-back.
Total distance: 5 miles.
Difficulty: Moderate.
Best months: Any month.
Maps: Map 7 from the London District of the Daniel Boone National Forest; USGS London SW.

Special considerations: The trail along the creek is subject to overgrowth. Check with the London District office of the Daniel Boone National Forest on current conditions.

Finding the trailhead: From exit 38 off Interstate 75 at London, take Kentucky Highway 192 west for 10.5 miles and turn right into the Bald Rock picnic area. The trail starts just beyond the rest rooms at the edge of the woods. GPS: 37 01.949 N 84 13.338 W.

Parking and trailhead facilities: There's space for fifteen to twenty cars, along with rest rooms, drinking water, and picnic tables.

Key points:
1.2   Creek bank.

The hike: Except for a steep climb at the end, this hike is all level or downhill. The only reason it's rated moderate is that in some sections you may have trouble finding the trail. This is the Daniel Boone National Forest, and I felt a little like Daniel Boone as I whacked away weeds and brambles at several spots near the creek. A ranger was surprised when I told him later about the trail's condition, and he promised to have it cleared immediately. Obviously, this stretch isn't used much by hikers, and that's too bad. Here Cane Creek, a tributary of the Rockcastle River, is a lazy little stream lined with rocky banks and small cliffs that make a walk along it thoroughly enjoyable, rough patches and all. When I was there, a beaver had been busy, a gnawed tree standing as evidence of the animal's industry.

The Bald Rock picnic area was once the site of a fire lookout tower. Its use was discontinued in 1970, and the structure torn down. You won't find a bald rock there, either; that's the name of a nearby community. From the picnic grounds, you follow Sugar Tree Hollow Trail (407) north into the Cane Creek valley. It's a loop trail, and you can take it in either direction. The longer eastern leg, which I recommend for the trip down, starts just behind the rest rooms. It's a pleasant, narrow path that descends north along a ravine. At mile 0.7, the trail comes to a fork. You go right onto Cane Creek Trail (410), which winds its way to the creek and then follows its flow northwest. (The left prong of the fork leads 0.5 mile back up to the picnic area.) I found

Cane Creek

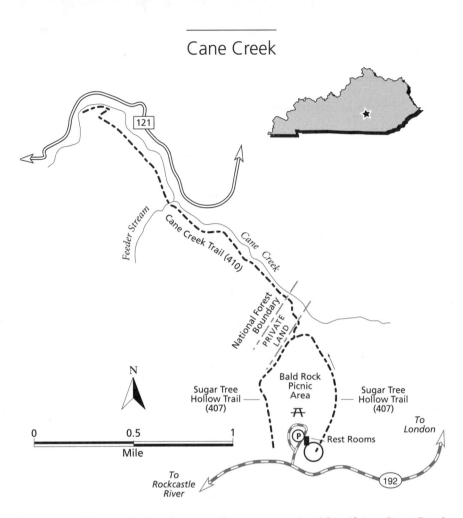

this intersection confusing, because there was no sign identifying Cane Creek Trail. If that's still the case when you take the hike, just remember that Cane Creek Trail is the only path that runs off the Sugar Tree Hollow loop.

After the junction, Cane Creek Trail crosses the national forest boundary for a brief stretch across private property. And you see farm buildings below on the right. You go north, cross a small feeder stream, and follow it briefly on what appears to be an old road. When you come to a fork, go left; a right would take you to a barn. At mile 1.2, after skirting a farm field, you see Cane Creek about 20 feet below on your right. Some parts of the trail between Sugar Tree Hollow Trail and Cane Creek are hard to find, and the area is confused by old farm roads. Just be sure to go north and keep the field on your right.

Soon after reaching the creekside, the trail crosses a red-painted boundary line that shows you are back on national forest land. It was here that I found the beaver-attacked tree, chips still on the ground, and what looked like a beaver dam nearby. At mile 1.6, a large rock in the water makes a good

Cane Creek is a lazy little stream lined with rocky banks.

resting place, and there's another pretty spot at mile 1.9 where you cross a bridge over a feeder stream just as it empties into the creek. After the bridge, the trail widens from a path into an old roadbed. At mile 2.4, after moving away from the creek and above it, the trail makes a sharp right and descends, bringing you once again to the water. At mile 2.6, the creek turns to the west and the trail dead-ends into it.

Directly across the creek is Forest Road 121, which connects with KY 192. If there hasn't been a lot of rain, you could easily wade across and pick up a shuttle car. Otherwise, you must turn around and retrace your steps along the creek to the intersection with Sugar Tree Hollow Trail. At the trail junction, take a right onto the loop's western leg, which climbs steeply and comes out on the western side of the picnic grounds at mile 5.

31 Rockcastle Narrows

Highlights:	A beautiful path through a lush drainage area with waterfalls, and a walk along the Narrows of the Rockcastle River.
Location:	Daniel Boone National Forest, 16 miles southwest of London in eastern Kentucky.
Type of hike:	Day hike or one- to two-night backpack; loop.
Total distance:	10.9 miles.
Difficulty:	Moderate.
Best months:	Any month.
Maps:	Map 3 from the London District of the Daniel Boone National Forest; USGS Ano.

Special considerations: The trails in some spots are not well marked; the Forest Service says it has trouble keeping signs in place. Make sure you bring a compass.

Finding the trailhead: From exit 38 off Interstate 75 at London, take Kentucky Highway 192 west for 15.5 miles to a spot where the road turns sharply right and KY 1193 forks to your left. Park in the off-road clearing left of this junction near the signboard. The trail starts immediately across KY 192 from the parking area. GPS: 36 59.872 N 84 16.992 W.

Parking and trailhead facilities: There's space for fifteen cars, but no facilities at the trailhead; water and rest rooms are available at Bee Rock Campgrounds 4 miles west on KY 192.

Key points:
- 1.3   First waterfall.
- 2.3   Cane Creek.
- 4.6   Rockcastle River.

The hike: Just before it flows into what was once the Cumberland River and is now officially Lake Cumberland, the Rockcastle River makes a tight loop to the east. On a map, it looks like a big ear. Here tall cliffs on both sides force the stream into a thin chute called the Rockcastle Narrows that is popular with kayakers. This hike takes you down to and along the Narrows before catapulting you up the steep banks at the northern tip of the ear.

Along with the river segment, the hike includes one of the prettiest paths you will find in Kentucky—the stretch from the parking area down into the Cane Creek valley. You descend through an area full of little streams and lovely waterfalls; it's worth a hike just by itself. This 2.6-mile section is part of Sheltowee Trace National Recreation Trail (100), the long north–south hiking route through the Daniel Boone National Forest. You also take this segment of the Sheltowee to return to your car at the end of the hike; it's the only backtracking on what is otherwise a loop route.

From KY 192, the Sheltowee descends gently along a ravine that soon develops into a stream. After several crossings and a walk through a stand of

Rockcastle Narrows

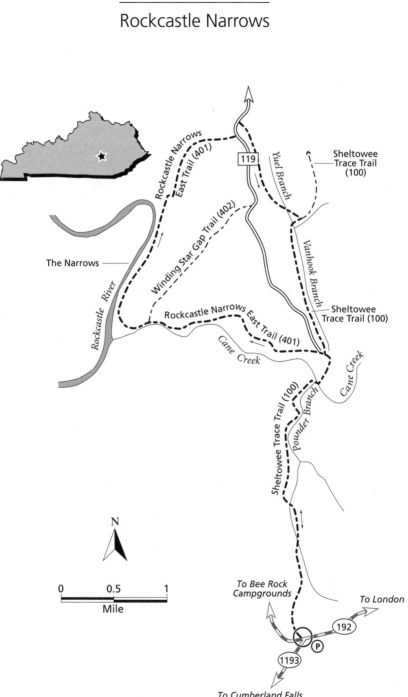

Rockcastle Narrows East Trail (401)

119

Yuel Branch

Sheltowee Trace Trail (100)

Winding Star Gap Trail (402)

Vanhook Branch

The Narrows

Rockcastle River

Sheltowee Trace Trail (100)

Rockcastle Narrows East Trail (401)

Cane Creek

Cane Creek

Sheltowee Trace Trail (100)

Pounder Branch

N

0   0.5   1
Mile

To Bee Rock Campgrounds

To London

192

P

1193

To Cumberland Falls

pines, you come into an area extensively damaged in 1991 by a powerful windstorm. The stream you are following flows into Pounder Branch, which you then follow north until it flows into Cane Creek. The first waterfall along the way, and my favorite, is a small one just to the right of the trail at mile 1.3. The water flows off a large rock into a pool and makes a fine spot for a refreshing dip in summer.

At mile 2.2, the trail crosses a large rock and turns sharply right to descend into a gorge where Pounder Branch and Cane Creek meet. You first take a bridge over Pounder and then immediately another, longer one across Cane, which by this point has grown from the lazy little flow featured in Hike 30 into an adult-sized stream. From here the Sheltowee continues north along a wall of rock and, after climbing to the northeast, comes to a good view of Vanhook Falls. The trail doesn't lead directly to the waterfall, but it's possible to scramble over to it; the Forest Service puts it's height at 40 feet. Immediately afterward, you cross Vanhook Branch and, at mile 2.6, come to a trail junction. Here the Sheltowee goes right (north), while you go straight (west) on Rockcastle Narrows East Trail (401).

When I took the hike, there was no sign identifying Rockcastle Narrows East Trail. Nor were there any directions just beyond at a three-way fork. In fact, at several key points throughout the hike, there was no indication which way to go. A ranger said signs had been placed along the trails and apparently had been removed. This is not Alaska wilderness, and with a compass you can find your way. But you do have to be on your toes. At the three-way fork, take a left and begin winding your way west at a level grade along the ridgeside above Cane Creek. At mile 3.4, the trail makes a sharp left and drops to near the creek. A mile later, shortly after passing a nice streamside spot with a good-sized pool and sandy shore, you come to Winding Stair Gap Trail (402) on your right. Again, the junction was not marked on my hike. Winding Stair Gap Trail runs 1.2 miles northeast to Forest Road 119, which connects back to the Sheltowee.

Continuing on Rockcastle Narrows East Trail, you soon turn right and begin following the Rockcastle River through the Narrows. This unmarked turn can be momentarily confusing because there is also a path to your left, which ends in a short distance at a makeshift campsite. Cane Creek flows into the Rockcastle just beyond the trail but, at least when the foliage is out, their confluence is not visible.

The Rockcastle River stays below the trail, but there are numerous side paths to the boulder-strewn banks. The large rocks make a good place for sunning yourself. The yellow rings you see on trees along the river mark the boundary of a state wildlife management area, with more restrictive hunting regulations. At the upper end of the river's loop, keep your eye out for the spot where the trail turns right, away from the water (GPS: 37 02.463 N 84 18.217 W). The turn is marked by a white diamond painted on a tree, but it's easily missed because a more distinct path continues along the river. The turn comes about 1.5 miles after the Winding Stair Gap Trail junction and less than 0.1 mile after you cross a small stream. Just remember that if you find yourself following the riverbank west, you've missed the turn.

A small waterfall forms a refreshing pool along the Sheltowee Trace Trail.

From the turn, you climb steeply northeast to a cliff face, turn left, and climb some more. It's a tough haul to the top. Once there, the trail soon turns right onto an old roadbed, and at mile 6.5 dead-ends into gravel FR 119. Go left (north) on the road and in about 300 feet, at the trail marker, turn right. The path descends gently to the south, crosses Yuel Branch, and comes to Sheltowee Trace Trail at mile 7.1. From here you take the Sheltowee south to your car. The first 1.2-mile segment, which is new to you, follows Vanhook Branch back to the Rockcastle Narrows East Trail junction. From there you retrace your steps 2.6 miles to KY 192.

32 Bee Rock Overlook

Highlights:	A walk along the western side of the Rockcastle River to an overlook over the valley.
Location:	Bee Rock Campground in the Daniel Boone National Forest, 20 miles southwest of London in eastern Kentucky.
Type of hike:	Day hike; loop.
Total distance:	4.5 miles.
Difficulty:	Moderate.
Best months:	Any month.
Maps:	Map 3 from the London District of the Daniel Boone National Forest (office 606–864–4163); Rockcastle Narrows map from the Somerset District; USGS Ano.

Finding the trailhead: From exit 38 off Interstate 75 at London, take Kentucky Highway 192 west for 15.5 miles to a spot where the road turns sharply right and KY 1193 forks to your left. Continue on KY 192 4 miles to the bridge over the Rockcastle River. At the far end of the bridge, turn right into Bee Rock West Campground. (You don't want Bee Rock East Campground on the near side of the bridge.) Drive 0.9 mile to the end of the campground road and park. The trail starts at the south end of the parking area. GPS: 37 01.512 N 84 18.984 W.

Parking and trailhead facilities: You'll find parking for a dozen or so cars, along with rest rooms, water, and campsites.

Key points:
    1.0   Rockcastle Narrows.
    3.6   Overlook.

The hike: This hike follows the Rockcastle Narrows on the west bank, just across from the hike featured in Hike 31. But the two treks are different in character. On this one, the trail and woods have a more open, less remote feeling, and the hike is capped by an excellent view of the valley below. This vista is from the top of a cliff known as Bee Rock, so named because years ago it was supposedly the home of a large throng of honeybees.

From the parking lot, head south on Rockcastle Narrows Trail (503), following the river upstream. You immediately notice that there are a number of other paths going the same direction. Don't worry; they all merge sooner or later. Rockcastle Narrows Trail is blazed with a white diamond, but throughout the hike the markings are few and far between.

Early in the hike the river you see beside you is wide. That's because once it leaves the Narrows, the Rockcastle is technically part of Lake Cumberland. The Rockcastle runs into the Cumberland River just south of here, and the water level of both is affected by the Wolf Creek dam even though the dam that creates Lake Cumberland is miles away.

Bee Rock Overlook

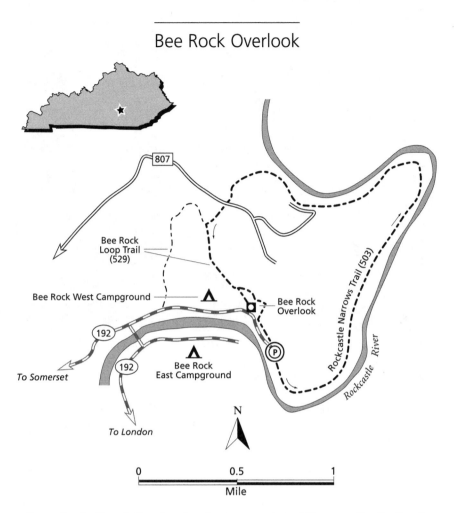

Soon the trail and the riverbank curve east and then north. By the time you've walked about a mile from the trailhead, the river has become the thin, fast stretch of water known as the Narrows. The tall cliffs that have squeezed it into this shape rise above you on both sides of the stream. The trail stays above the river the entire way, but there are side paths down to it. About mile 1.5, you and the riverbank curve west. Here the trail broadens from a path into a pleasant old roadbed, which rises gently before dead-ending into a gravel road at mile 2. A lack of signs made this junction confusing when I took the hike.

Turn left onto the gravel road, which climbs to Forest Road 807 on top of the ridge. You will eventually get to FR 807 too, but now you turn right and take the gravel road as it descends closer to the river and ends in less than 0.2 mile. Here you take an unmarked path to your left, climbing the riverbank until you reach another path to your left, this one marked with a sign that says 503, the number for Rockcastle Narrows Trail. Take the left trail and begin climbing west on switchbacks. After leveling off, the trail slabs

131

Bee Rock looks down on a stretch of the Rockcastle River.

along the ridgeside a short distance and then climbs steeply to a cliff face. Go right, circle the cliff, and continue west. The trail then jogs south, traveling briefly through heavy vegetation that can make the way hard to find; just keep going up and you should have no problem. After winding its way through boulders and climbing wooden steps, the trail levels off just before reaching FR 807 at mile 3.

The trail continues across this gravel road and shortly dead-ends into a track of grass and dirt. This is Bee Rock Loop Trail (529), which runs from the campground up the ridge and back down to the campground. The junction was not marked when I was there. Take Bee Rock Loop Trail to your left, walking south and then southeast. At mile 3.6, almost immediately after passing a side trail to your left, you come to the Bee Rock Overlook and a fine view of the river below and ridges to the south and east.

The hike's final leg is all downhill, some of it steeply so. Return to the side path you passed just before the lookout—it's now on your right—and take it a short distance to a railing. Here you begin winding your way down the cliffside, at one point passing through a cavelike opening. You come to the campground road at mile 4.2. Your car is 0.3 mile to your left.

33 Rockcastle-Cumberland Confluence

Highlights:	An overlook view of the spot where the Rockcastle River flows into the Cumberland, and a level 4-mile walk along the Cumberland's upstream shoreline.
Location:	Daniel Boone National Forest, 19 miles southwest of London in eastern Kentucky.
Type of hike:	Day hike or one-night backpack; loop.
Total distance:	9.1 miles.
Difficulty:	Easy.
Best months:	Any month.
Maps:	Map 5 from the London District of the Daniel Boone National Forest; USGS Sawyer.

Finding the trailhead: From exit 38 off Interstate 75 at London, take Kentucky Highway 192 west for 15.5 miles to a spot where the road turns sharply right and KY 1193 forks to your left. Turn left onto KY 1193, and in 0.7 mile curve right onto Kentucky 3497. After 3.8 miles, turn right into the small, unpaved parking area for Ned Branch Trail (405). The trail starts at the edge of the woods. GPS: 36 57.544 N 84 19.538 W.

Parking and trailhead facilities: There's space for four cars, but no facilities.

Key points:
2.6 Overlook.
3.8 Cumberland River.

The hike: In terms of water volume, Lake Cumberland is the largest manmade lake east of the Mississippi River. One reason is that it's deep—90 feet on average. Another is that it's long—101 miles. In all, Lake Cumberland has 1,255 miles of shoreline. The widest part—the part that on a map looks like a lake—is the 50-mile stretch from the dam east to Burnside. But the dam affects the river's water level all the way to Cumberland Falls, and so the remaining 50-mile section that you explore on this hike is also officially a lake, even if it's shaped like a snake. After a climb to an overlook above the Rockcastle's confluence with the Cumberland, you follow the Cumberland upstream for 4 miles. Whether you're walking along the Cumberland River or Lake Cumberland is your call.

From the parking area, Ned Branch Trail (405) descends north to the Rockcastle River though a lush area of pines, ferns, and rhododendrons. On the way down you skirt rock outcroppings and make several easy stream crossings. Just before reaching the river, the trail divides. Lakeside North Trail (411) goes straight, following the Rockcastle north for 0.7 mile. Ned Branch Trail, which you continue to follow, turns left and crosses Ned Branch. Just beyond the crossing, the little stream makes an elbow-shaped turn that backs up the water, creating a pool and a scenic rest spot. From here the

Rockcastle-Cumberland Confluence

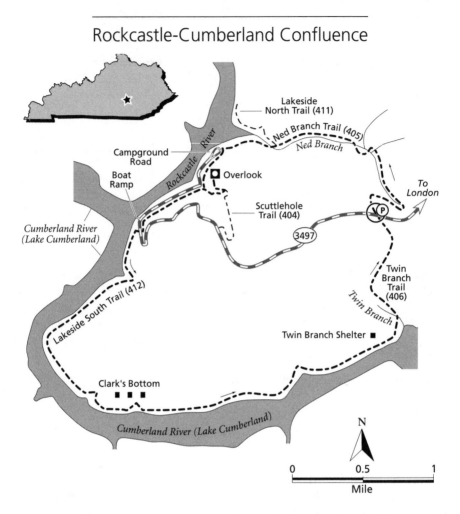

trail parallels the river southwest and, at mile 1.9, dead-ends into a paved road running through Rockcastle Campground. This Forest Service fee facility has rest rooms, drinking water, and twenty-four campsites.

You follow the road along the river for 0.4 mile, then turn left (south) onto Scuttlehole Trail (404), which is marked by a sign. In 0.1 mile, the Scuttle-hold Trail turns left and climbs steeply eastward to the base of a cliff. There you bear right and go up a steep wooden stairway with about a hundred steps. Be careful; these are slippery even in dry weather. At the top, turn left (a right would take you to KY 3497) and curve west. At 0.3 mile from the road, you reach an overlook with a stone fence in front of the drop-off. If you continue along the cliff, you come to two more overlooks in quick succession. All three have a good view southwest to the point where the Rockcastle flows into the Cumberland. But the third vista is the best, because it also allows a look north up the Rockcastle. This view is well worth the climb.

Return to the campground road and continue southwest along the Rock-castle. Just before reaching the confluence of the two rivers, you pass the

Boats moor along the Rockcastle River where it flows into the Cumberland.

London Dock Marina. In addition to taking care of boaters' needs, this private, Forest-Service-sanctioned facility sells food and drinks. After leaving the waterfront, the campground road becomes KY 3497. Continue on it 0.4 mile past the marina to a sign on your right marking the beginning of Lakeside South Trail (412). For the next 4.2 miles, this trail takes you along the Cumberland River/Lake Cumberland shore, almost all of it level. If you expect to find a swimming spot, you will probably be disappointed. When I made the trip on a hot June day, I looked in vain for a place to take a dip. I was anxious to cool off but not anxious enough to brave the muddy riverbank with all the trees, plastic bottles, and other flotsam washed up on it. Still, the walk is pleasant. The trail stays in the woods, a short distance away from the water. In about 2 miles, you pass through a collection of cottages; this is Clark's Bottom, a private summer community. At mile 7.9, you come to Twin Branch Shelter, a well-maintained, three-sided overnight facility for backpackers. It sits about 50 feet above the water, and can sleep six comfortably. There are a number of suitable tent sites nearby.

Just beyond the shelter, Lakeside South Trail curves away from the river and becomes Twin Branch Trail (406). When I was there, the change in names was not marked by a sign. The trail climbs steeply and then descends to small, clear Twin Branch. After crossing the stream, you make a steady ascent almost all the way back to KY 3947. It's the only time on the hike that you have to work. At mile 9.1, you reach the road across from the parking area.

Cumberland Falls Area

On February 12, 1780, Zachariah Green and three fellow hunters boating down the Cumberland River had quite a surprise. It turned out that rumbling they heard wasn't their stomachs. Green, his brother, and two companions are believed to have been the first non–Native Americans to discover the existence of Cumberland Falls. It was a tough lesson indeed, but they were lucky enough to make it ashore before being swept over the huge cascade. Plunging 68 feet and spanning 125 feet, the waterfall is a powerful, beautiful, and, yes, noisy force of nature that has been impressing visitors ever since Zachariah and his hapless hunting party first reached it. But while "the Niagara of the South," as the waterfall has long been promoted, is the main attraction, the area has lots of other intriguing scenery and terrain. In addition to the 1,657-acre Cumberland Falls State Resort Park (606–528–4121), the hikes in this section explore two nearby attractions in the Daniel Boone National Forest—the Natural Arch Scenic Area and the Beaver Creek Wilderness. For information about either, calling the Somerset Ranger District (606–679–2010) is your best bet. The London Ranger District (606–864–4163) can be helpful about trails on the east side of the Cumberland River outside the state park.

34 Dog Slaughter Falls

Highlights: A walk from Cumberland Falls to a far smaller but delightful waterfall downstream, and a return on trails noted for their wildflowers.

Location: Cumberland Falls State Resort Park, 20 miles southwest of Corbin.

Type of hike: Day hike; loop.

Total distance: 7.2 miles.

Difficulty: Moderate.

Best months: Spring, early summer.

Maps: State park visitor guide; Map 6 from the London District of the Daniel Boone National Forest; USGS Cumberland Falls.

Finding the trailhead: From exit 25 off Interstate 75 near Corbin, take U.S. Highway 25W south for 7 miles and turn right (west) onto Kentucky Highway 90. In 7.5 more miles, KY 90 passes the entrance to the Cumberland Falls State Resort Park lodge and begins a steep, winding descent to the Cumberland River. At the bottom of the hill—0.6 mile from the lodge entrance—turn right at the sign for the park gift shop. The trail begins in front of the gift shop. GPS: 36 50.367 N 84 20.723 W.

Dog Slaughter Falls

Parking and trailhead facilities: You'll find lots of parking space, as well as rest rooms, water, a snack bar, and a gift shop.

Key points:
  0.1   Cumberland Falls.
  2.8   Dog Slaughter Falls.

The hike: This hike takes you from the state park overlooks at Cumberland Falls down the Cumberland River to a 15-foot-high waterfall on Dog Slaughter Creek. In comparison to its mighty neighbor, Dog Slaughter Falls is a mere trickle—but it's a lovely trickle in a picturesque setting of rocky cliffs and big boulders. There's another difference as well. The Cumberland Falls viewing area is paved with concrete and full of people. At the pint-sized falls, chances are it will just be you.

To return from the falls, you can retrace yours steps along the Cumberland. This stretch of the river has lots of rapids and sandy beaches that make the trip enjoyable a second time. The loop hike described here, however, returns through the park interior on trails noted for their wildflowers. Park

Cumberland Falls are visible from the overlook at the start of the hike to Dog Slaughter Falls.

naturalist Bret Smitley says that violets, trilliums, and irises are plentiful in season. But be aware that the interior route is longer and more difficult. If you're tired or it's not wildflower time, you might consider taking the level riverside trail. In summer when the leaves are out, there are no good views from the ridgetops along the interior trails.

From the gift shop, there are two sidewalks going north. Take the one closer to the river; it goes to a series of overlooks with good views of Cumberland Falls and signs explaining the area's geological and human history. At the fifth and last overlook, turn around and go back toward the gift shop until you come to a concrete ramp to your left. Take this and, at the end, turn left and begin walking north. This is Moonbow Trail, which runs downstream 10.6 miles to where the Laurel River flows into the Cumberland. (See Options.) Moonbow Trail carries the numerical designation of 1 in the park trail list. It used to be 2, and the change can be confusing because there is still plenty of old written trail information floating around. To make matters even more confusing, the Moonbow is also the long-distance Sheltowee Trace National Recreation Trail (100). The name *Moonbow* has long been associated with the falls because on full-moon nights, a moonbow can be seen in the mist generated by the plunging river.

The turn onto the Moonbow is at mile 0.3. Initially, you are above the river. Shortly, however, after passing two separate entrances to the park's Wildflower Loop Trail (12), Moonbow Trail makes a sharp left and descends on wooden steps to just above the river. The large boulders between the trail and the water make a good place to stop and watch the fast-moving Cumberland. Not to disturb your reverie, but the building on the bluff above you is the park sewage treatment plant. If you look for it, you will see a pipe discharging liquid—fully treated, I was told—into the river.

At mile 0.8, after crossing a rock area at the base of a cliff, the trail comes to the first of a series of nice beaches. At mile 1, you pass the first of two entrances to Rock House Trail (7); just a few feet into that trail, a trickle of water cascades off a tall cliff, providing a refreshing shower on a hot day. For the next little while, the Moonbow alternates between rocky stretches over outcroppings and flat, low areas with heavy vegetation. At mile 1.7, it passes the beginning of Cumberland River Trail (2), which you will take later on your return route.

For now you continue to follow the Moonbow across more nice beaches as well as a small stream on a bridge. Then, where the river makes a distinct turn to the west, the trail turns east along a large stream. This is Dog Slaughter Creek, and in just a few feet you come to the junction with the USDA Forest Service's Dog Slaughter Trail (414). Take it to your right. After a climb of 0.2 mile over rocks along a cliff face, you reach the base of Dog Slaughter Falls. Be careful; the large rocks lining the pool at the bottom of the falls are slippery. Ease yourself onto them and enjoy a great rest spot. The rocks are slick enough that after a dip, I needed the aid of a conveniently placed tree trunk to hoist myself out of the water. From the falls, Dog Slaughter Trail heads east about 4 miles in the Daniel Boone National Forest and reaches Forest Road 195 a little less than a mile from KY 90.

When you're ready to move on, retrace your steps to the mouth of the creek and take Moonbow Trail back to its junction with Cumberland River Trail (2). From here on you meander over ridges in the park's interior. Turn left onto Cumberland River Trail and climb on switchbacks to the east and then the south. At mile 4.5, the trail turns left to make a long trek east to KY 90 and then south to the river. You, however, turn right onto Anvil Branch Trail (11) and begin winding southward. You eventually descend to cross a small, pretty stream with mossy logs at mile 5.2, and then climb toward KY 90. Just before reaching the road, the trail turns north and descends to a dead end at Rock House Trail (7). Turn left onto Rock House, shortly crossing a brook and then turning right onto Wildflower Loop Trail (12). Wildflower Loop follows a long cliff face west and then north before crossing the park road leading to the sewage plant. From there you descend to Moonbow Trail at mile 7. The gift shop is 0.2 mile to your left on a path parallel to the one you took along the falls overlooks at the beginning of the hike.

Options: For a one- or two-night backpack trip, you can continue on Moonbow Trail from Dog Slaughter Creek to the Mouth of Laurel boat ramp on KY 1277. The total distance from Cumberland Falls is 10.6 miles. There are two overnight shelters along the trail, at about 5 and 7 miles from the falls. There is no easy way, however, to devise a loop route back to the falls, so you would have to arrange a shuttle.

35 Eagle Falls

Highlights: Great cliffside views looking down on Cumberland Falls, plus a visit to beautiful Eagle Falls.
Location: Cumberland Falls State Resort Park, 20 miles southwest of Corbin.
Type of hike: Day hike; partial loop.
Total distance: 2.2 miles.
Difficulty: Moderate.
Best months: Any month.
Maps: State park visitor guide; USGS Cumberland Falls.

Special considerations: During high water, the side trail to the base of Eagle Falls may be impassable. If in doubt, check with park personnel (606–528–4121).

Finding the trailhead: From exit 25 off Interstate 75 near Corbin, take U.S. Highway 25W south for 7 miles and turn right (west) onto Kentucky Highway 90. In 7.5 more miles, KY 90 passes the entrance to the Cumberland Falls State Resort Park lodge and begins a steep, winding descent to the Cumberland River. Continue west across the river and pull into the parking area on the right shoulder; it's 0.3 mile from the end of the bridge. The trailhead is just up the hill from the parking area and on the same side of the road. GPS: 36 50.209 N 84 20.734 W.

Parking and trailhead facilities: There are designated spaces for six cars and room for six more to squeeze in. No facilities are available immediately at the trailhead, but rest rooms, water, and a snack bar are found at the state park gift shop next to the main Cumberland Falls viewing area, 0.6 mile east on KY 90.

Key points:
    0.0   Eagle Falls Trailhead.
    0.3   Side trail to CCC shelter.
    0.6   Side trail to falls.
    0.8   Base of falls.
    1.0   Junction with Eagle Falls Trail.
    1.7   Junction with closed trail.

The hike: This is a short hike, but beware: It's not an easy one. It has more ups and downs per mile than most walks. It also has more scenic rewards. Hundreds of years ago, according to a history of the area by Jeannie McConnell, Eagle Falls was sacred to the Indians, and it's easy to see why. Though just a thin ribbon of water, Eagle Creek plunges an impressive 44 feet onto the rocky Cumberland River shoreline, creating a scene that is Mother Nature at her most pleasing. As a bonus, the hike takes you past several overlooks that offer the best views of Cumberland Falls to be found in the park.
    From the north side of KY 90, take Eagle Falls Trail (9) and head north, paralleling the Cumberland River. Almost immediately the trail begins

Eagle Falls

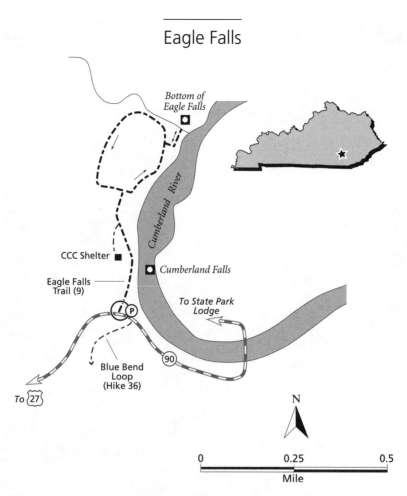

climbing, and you are soon looking down on the swirling river just before it tumbles over Cumberland Falls. In a few more minutes, you are directly above the falls. From this vantage point, more so than from the main falls-observation area across the river, you can actually feel the power of the falling water.

The striking views continue as you climb. At mile 0.3, a trail branches off to your left, rising sharply on steps to a shelter built in the 1930s by the Civilian Conservation Corps. The shelter is supposed to provide an overlook across the river, but the view is limited by vegetation. The climb (about 0.1 mile) is good exercise, but otherwise not worth the effort. This side path used to be part of a separate park trail (10) that tied in with Eagle Falls Trail. Because of a private commercial development that included the construction of a chairlift to the top of the nearby ridge, the park closed the trail. However, some TRAIL 10 signs remain and can be confusing. The chairlift operation, which is just beyond the shelter, apparently fell on hard times and was closed as of this writing.

Continuing north on Eagle Falls Trail, you soon come to a fork and the beginning of the loop portion of the hike. Turn right at the fork and at mile

Eagle Falls cascades down 44 feet into the Cumberland River.

0.6, after a brief descent, make a sharp right onto a side trail. This side trail, which is marked with a sign for Eagle Falls, descends toward the river on a series of wood-and-stone stairways steep enough that there is a cable to use as a banister. At the bottom, you are on the boulder-lined riverbank. The trail here isn't marked; just follow the river downstream, and at mile 0.8 you come to the bottom of Eagle Falls. This is a fine spot for a picnic; the creek water makes a nice pool before flowing into the river, and large rocks provide plenty of good reclining opportunities.

When you're ready to continue, retrace your steps to the main Eagle Falls Trail (9) and go right. The trail descends gently and, at mile 1.1, reaches Eagle Creek above the falls. Though you can't see the water cascading over the rocks, you are now at the top of the falls. From here the trail follows the creek upstream to another falls, this one small but also picturesque. After making your way through a patch of rhododendrons, you leave the stream and begin climbing to the south, steeply in places. On the way up, the trail jogs around a couple of cliffs before reaching the ridgetop at mile 1.5. From there it's a short, mostly level walk to the junction with old Trail 10, now closed. Turn left (southeast) at the junction, and in another 0.1 mile you are back at the fork where the loop began. Turn right and retrace your steps down to the parking area.

Options: Hike 36 starts just across KY 90 from the parking area.

36 Blue Bend

Highlights:	An easy walk along a serene Cumberland River stretch upstream of the falls.
Location:	Cumberland Falls State Resort Park, 20 miles southwest of Corbin.
Type of hike:	Day hike; loop.
Total distance:	4.3 miles.
Difficulty:	Easy.
Best months:	Any month.
Maps:	State park visitor guide; USGS Cumberland Falls.

Finding the trailhead: From exit 25 off Interstate 75 near Corbin, take U.S. Highway 25W south for 7 miles and turn right (west) onto Kentucky Highway 90. In 7.5 more miles, KY 90 passes the entrance to the Cumberland Falls State Resort Park lodge and begins a steep, winding descent to the Cumberland River. Continue west across the river and pull into the parking area on the right shoulder; it's 0.3 mile from the end of the bridge. The trailhead is just up the hill from the parking area and across the road. GPS: 36 50.195 N 84 20.755 W.

Parking and trailhead facilities: There are designated spaces for six cars and room for six more to squeeze in. No facilities are available immediately

Blue Bend

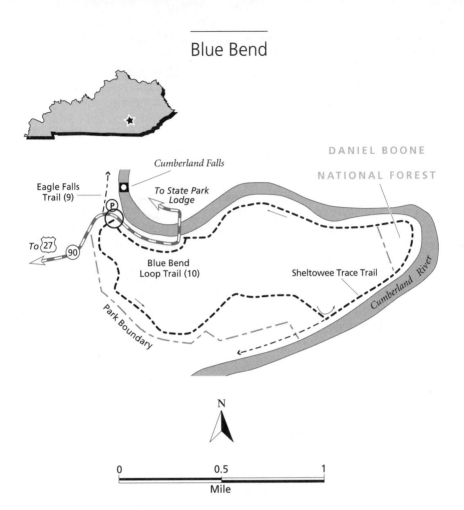

at the trailhead, but you'll find rest rooms, water, and a snack bar at the state park gift shop next to the main Cumberland Falls viewing area, 0.6 mile east on KY 90.

Key points:
- 0.0   Blue Bend Loop Trailhead.
- 0.4   Sharp left turn.
- 1.8   Sheltowee Trace Trail and Cumberland River.
- 3.9   KY 90 bridge.

The hike: The Cumberland River above the falls is wide, smooth, and peaceful, an altogether different stream from the fierce, boulder-strewn flow below the falls. This hike takes you along the serene Cumberland—from its sharp westward turn, known as Blue Bend, to the KY 90 bridge just above the falls. This stretch of just over 2 miles is perfect for the early-evening hours or any other time you feel like taking a quiet, relaxing stroll. Delightful rest spots dot the riverbank and invite wading. But be careful: Park personnel warn that despite the river's surface calm, the current can at times be swift.

Backcountry camping is not allowed on park property. The very tip of the bend is within the Daniel Boone National Forest, where camping is permissible if your site is more than 300 yards from a trail and 200 feet from a stream. However, the national forest boundary is not well marked.

To reach the river, you first take the state park's Blue Bend Loop Trail (10 on new park maps), which starts on the south side of KY 90 opposite the parking area. Marked with blue paint on trees and the letters BB on signposts, the trail follows an old roadbed as it climbs steadily but easily to the south. At mile 0.4, it reaches a clearing and makes a sharp turn left (east). You are now on the top of the ridge, and from here the hike is almost entirely level. From KY 90 to the riverbank, the distance is just under 2 miles.

Although designated a state nature preserve, the terrain in this first segment is unspectacular. The ridgetop was logged in the early 1990s, and small trees and brush predominate. In some spots the vegetation threatens to obscure the trail, and you have to keep a close watch. Also, the remnants of old roads can be confusing. After passing a metal gate at mile 0.8, the trail splits in two, and when I took the walk, there was no sign to show which way to go. It took a couple of minutes of exploration to locate a blue blaze next to the left-hand fork a short distance beyond the split. There's another potential problem at mile 1.2; a signpost directing a right turn around a marshy area is easily missed.

Continuing east, you reach a sign announcing the long-distance Sheltowee Trace Trail in another 0.6 mile. The Sheltowee, which runs north–south through much of the state, begins following the Cumberland just south of the park. At mile 1.8, after a sharp but brief descent to the southeast, Blue

The Cumberland River is wide and peaceful upstream of the falls.

Bend Loop Trail dead-ends into the Sheltowee at the riverbank. You turn left onto the Sheltowee and begin following the Cumberland downstream toward the KY 90 bridge, officially Gatliff Bridge, the name used on the trail signs.

The first thing that struck me about the river here was its utter silence. In stark contrast to the roar of the falls, the water glided past with all the noise of a soaring bird. The second thing I noticed was the gnarled tree stubs along the bank—evidence of old beaver activity. At mile 2.5, I found a group of large shoreline rocks perfect for sitting and enjoying the scene. If you want a softer perch, there's a small beach just beyond the rocks.

As you head west, the river seems to gradually pick up steam. The trail also becomes a bit rougher as it passes along a tall cliff. Shortly before reaching the bridge at mile 3.9, the trail veers away from the river, crosses a ravine, and climbs steeply up stone steps. You briefly parallel the river's course from on high before the trail ends at the KY 90 bridge. If you walk out on the bridge, you get a good view of the rapids that form just upstream.

The Sheltowee follows the bridge across the river, but you take KY 90 back to your car, an uphill walk of 0.4 mile. Be careful on the highway. The shoulder is nonexistent in places, and cars come barreling down the big hill at high speeds. If you have children with you, take their hands.

37 Natural Arch

Highlights:	One of Kentucky's largest sandstone arches, plus attractive streams and woodlands.
Location:	Natural Arch Scenic Area in the Daniel Boone National Forest, 14 miles west of Cumberland Falls State Resort Park and 23 miles south of Somerset.
Type of hike:	Day hike; loop.
Total distance:	5.5 miles.
Difficulty:	Easy.
Best months:	Any month.
Maps:	USGS Nevelsville; Natural Arch Scenic Area map from the Somerset District of the Daniel Boone National Forest.
Permits and fees:	A $3.00 day-use fee is charged for cars parked in the Natural Arch Scenic Area.

Special considerations: Two miles into the hike, the trail crosses Cooper Creek, a good-sized stream that can be impassable in high water. If in doubt, check with the Somerset Ranger District.

Finding the trailhead: From the intersection of Kentucky Highway 90 and U.S. Highway 27, about 20 miles south of Somerset, take US 27 south for 0.5 mile and turn right (west) onto KY 927. In 1.7 miles, turn right onto a gravel road that dead-ends in 0.2 mile at a parking lot. The trailhead is the asphalt walkway at the north end of the lot. GPS: 36 50.522 N 84 30.756 W.

Natural Arch

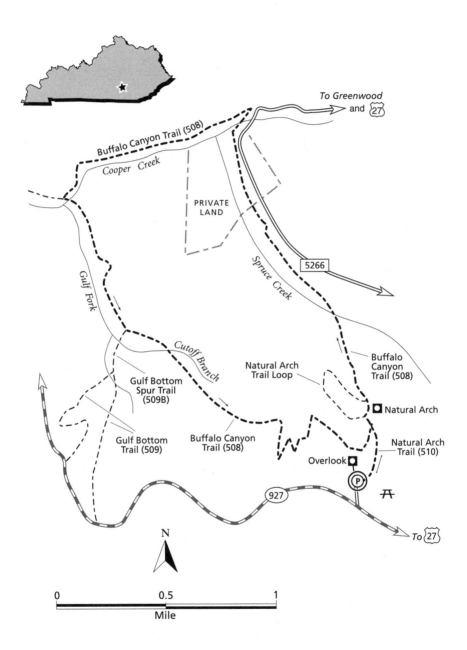

Buffalo Canyon Trail (508)

Cooper Creek

PRIVATE LAND

Gulf Fork

Spruce Creek

5266

To Greenwood and 27

Cutoff Branch

Natural Arch Trail Loop

Buffalo Canyon Trail (508)

Gulf Bottom Spur Trail (509B)

Gulf Bottom Trail (509)

Buffalo Canyon Trail (508)

Natural Arch

Natural Arch Trail (510)

Overlook

P

927

To 27

N

0   0.5   1
Mile

Parking and trailhead facilities: You'll find space for about thirty cars, plus a large picnic area with tables, rest rooms, and water.

Key points:
0.0   Natural Arch Trailhead.
0.4   Natural Arch.
0.9   Spruce Creek crossing.
1.3   Left on FR 5266.
2.0   Cooper Creek crossing.
3.0   Cooper Creek second crossing.
3.7   Gulf Bottom Spur Trail.

The hike: Natural Arch is either 50 feet (in height) by 90 feet (in length) or 60 by 100, depending on what publication you consult. The Forest Service generally cites the former figures, but whatever the exact dimensions of this sandstone arch, it is definitely one of Kentucky's largest. (Natural Bridge, in comparison, is 65 feet by 78 feet.) It's also one of the most impressive, and in 1961 it and 945 surrounding acres were given special protection as a scenic area. This hike makes a loop through the arch and along the area's perimeter on a series of paths and forest roads left over from the days when homesteaders farmed the stream bottoms. Even if there were no arch, it would be a walk well worth taking, through a lovely forest and along several attractive streams. In some places, including a parcel adjacent to the parking lot, numerous trees were downed in 1994 by a severe ice storm. The damage is still evident but does not overshadow the scenic rewards. I took the hike on a rainy July day, and consider it one of the most pleasing in this part of the state. The scenic area is restricted to day use, and this hike is designated a day hike. However, backcountry camping is allowed east of Forest Road 5266 and north of Cooper Creek, making an overnight trip possible. Roughly, the scenic area's boundaries are FR 5266, Cooper Creek, and KY 927.

The hike starts on the asphalt walkway at the end of the parking area on your right. But if you want a panorama of where you will be going, first take the concrete walkway at the center of the parking lot. In less than 0.1 mile, it delivers you to an overlook with a fine vista of the arch and scenic area. Returning to the parking lot, you take the asphalt walkway, which is Natural Arch Trail (510). It heads north on the ridgetop to another observation point, this one with more limited views. From here you descend on a series of log-and-stone steps to an intersection at mile 0.2 with Buffalo Canyon Trail (508), also known as 5-Mile Loop Trail. This is the path you take through the scenic area; it's well marked with white diamonds. There is no Buffalo Canyon in the area, at least none that Forest Service personnel know of, and the origin of the trail name seems to be lost to history.

At the intersection, turn right and follow the combined Natural Arch/Buffalo Canyon Trail, still paved, to near the base of the arch at mile 0.4. Here Natural Arch Trail turns left to make a short loop (about 0.5 mile) northeast around the arch. You take Buffalo Canyon Trail to your right and climb to the base of the arch. This is a spot to linger over. Like other sandstone arches, Natural Arch was formed as water and weather eroded away softer rock,

Buffalo Canyon Trail travels through Natural Arch.

leaving the harder top strata behind. The tall surrounding cliffs add to the otherworldly beauty of the site. Is this the state's biggest arch? Wilson Francis, naturalist at Natural Bridge State Resort Park, says the question is unresolved. That's because arches vary in size and shape, and there's no agreement on how to measure them. By height? By span? By size of the opening? Certainly Natural Arch is one of the largest arches in Kentucky. For the national title, there does seem to be agreement: Utah's Rainbow Bridge is, at 290 feet tall and 275 feet long, the largest natural bridge not just in the United States but also in the world, according to the National Park Service.

When you're ready to move on, follow Buffalo Canyon Trail, now a dirt path, through the arch, and bear left along the cliff wall. Heading north, you immediately pass the other end of the Natural Arch Trail loop on your left, and begin descending through an area full of downed trees, victims of the 1994 storm. Gradually the forest becomes more robust and inviting. At mile 0.9, the trail crosses Spruce Creek, and at mile 1.3 it dead-ends into FR 5266. Go left on this pleasant, little-used gravel road. The houses you pass on your left are on a privately owned parcel within the national forest.

At mile 2, the road reaches Cooper Creek and fords the stream on concrete ribs; as the sign notes, this crossing may not be passable in flooded conditions. Immediately on the other side of the creek, FR 5266 turns right (east) toward the community of Greenwood on US 27. You turn left onto an old dirt road and head west, with Cooper Creek on your left, flowing toward the Cumberland River. Disregard the small road coming in on your left and continue west through the pines. At mile 3, shortly after curving south, the trail forks. You take the left prong, which immediately crosses Cooper Creek and begins climbing to the east and then southeast—the first uphill since the arch. The trail is now following Gulf Fork upstream.

At mile 3.7, after leveling off, the trail passes the north end of Gulf Bottom Spur Trail (509B). This spur follows Gulf Fork south and connects with Gulf Bottom Trail (509), which climbs up the surrounding cliffs to reach KY 927 at an overlook 1.4 miles west of where your car is parked. The area between here and the highway is known as Great Gulf. Continuing southeast, Buffalo Canyon Trail climbs and crosses Cutoff Branch before coming to Chimney Arch at mile 4.6. This arch, surrounded by a cliff, is about 30 feet in height and makes an interesting rest stop. From the arch, you follow the ridgetop for a short distance before descending and then traversing another damaged area. At mile 5.3, after a series of ups and downs and sharp turns to avoid cliffs, the trail meets Natural Arch Trail and the start of the loop. Turn right, climb the steps, and you are back at your car at mile 5.5.

38 Three Forks of Beaver Creek

Highlights: An overlook above the Beaver Creek Wilderness and a descent to the creek bottom where the stream's three forks meet.
Location: Beaver Creek Wilderness in the Daniel Boone National Forest, 19 miles south of Somerset.
Type of hike: Day hike or one-night backpack; partial loop.
Total distance: 3.3 miles.
Difficulty: Easy.
Best months: Any month.
Maps: USGS Hail; Daniel Boone National Forest map of the Clifty and Beaver Creek Wilderness Areas; Somerset District map of Trails 512 and 512A.

Finding the trailhead: From the intersection of Kentucky Highway 90 and U.S. Highway 27, about 20 miles south of Somerset, take US 27 north for 4.1 miles and turn right onto gravel Bauer Road (Forest Road 50). At the fork in 2.3 miles, bear right onto Bowman Ridge Road (FR 51). In 0.7 mile, turn into the parking area on your right at the THREE FORKS OF BEAVER TRAIL sign. The trailhead is on the southeast side of the lot. GPS: 36 54.365 N 84 26.943 W.

Parking and trailhead facilities: There's space for about twenty cars, but no facilities.

Key points:
```
0.0   Three Forks Loop Trailhead.
0.8   Intersection with other half of loop.
1.0   Overlook.
1.8   Beaver Creek.
1.9   End of trail.
```

The hike: The Beaver Creek Wilderness, the smaller of Kentucky's two federal wilderness areas (the other is the Clifty Wilderness in the Red River Gorge), encompasses 4,791 acres strung along Beaver Creek and its three forks: Hurricane, Middle and Freeman. This hike heads first to an overlook on the edge of the wilderness area above the spot where the three forks meet, and then descends into the wilderness area to the junction itself. The Beaver Creek area, which was acquired by the Forest Service in the 1930s and given wilderness status in 1979, is by no means untouched by the hand of humankind. The old roadbeds that crisscross the area are evidence of the coal mining, logging, and homesteading that used to take place here. (For thousands of years before that, the creek valley and its steep cliffs were home to Indians.) Nevertheless, this Cumberland River tributary is remote enough to make you feel sufficiently removed from civilization, and the junction of the three forks is a spot of quiet beauty. In length, this walk is definitely a day hike. But the creek bank offers good camping opportunities, making this a nice overnighter, especially for families with small children.

Three Forks of Beaver Creek

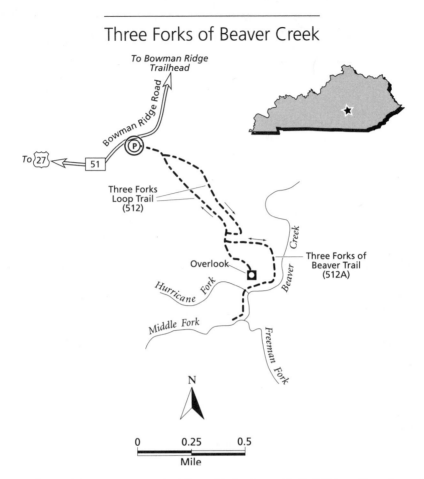

To Bowman Ridge
Trailhead

Bowman Ridge Road

To 27 ← 51

P

Three Forks
Loop Trail
(512)

Beaver Creek

Overlook

Three Forks of
Beaver Trail
(512A)

Hurricane Fork

Middle Fork

Beaver Creek

Freeman Fork

N

0   0.25   0.5
Mile

From the parking area, you take Three Forks Loop Trail (512) and head south-east. The trail is actually two separate paths that parallel each other to make a narrow loop. You can take either path; I chose the one on the left—the longer of the two—for the outbound leg of the hike, and followed the other on my return trip. The left-hand path descends gradually through a forest of hard-woods and pines, and at mile 0.5 passes a natural lookout point on your left with limited views into the Beaver Creek drainage. The path then weaves west and, at mile 0.8, intersects the other half of the loop coming from the parking area. Here you take a left and walk south, following the sign indicating a wildlife-viewing area ahead. Just past the intersection, there's an old roadbed to your left; ignore it for now and continue south, sloping gently down to a stone-fenced observation point at mile 1. From here there are excellent vistas south and west across the Beaver Creek valley. You can't see the stream itself, but you can see the cuts in the forest floor made by the three forks flowing toward their meeting point.

From the overlook, retrace your steps to the old roadbed. This is Three Forks of Beaver Trail (512A), which descends to Beaver Creek. Turn right onto the trail. In 0.1 mile, you pass a sign marking the wilderness area boundary.

Here the roadbed narrows and becomes steeper and, in places, overgrown. Continue downhill and, at mile 1.8, reach the creek bank at the point where Hurricane Fork flows into the main stream. It's a lovely spot, with a small sandy area and an inviting pool for wading. The trail now becomes harder to see, but it crosses Hurricane Fork and follows Beaver Creek upstream for about 0.1 mile to the spot where Freeman Fork flows into Middle Fork. This is a quiet site full of pine trees and rhododendron—and flat spots for tenting. Don't forget that the Forest Service requires backcountry campsites to be 200 feet away from any water source.

At the intersection of Freeman and Middle Forks, the trail disappears altogether, and it's time to turn around and retrace your steps up to the ridgetop. Some Forest Service maps show a trail continuing to follow Middle Fork upstream all the way to FR 839 near the community of Greenwood on US 27. In fact, there is no path. Following Middle Fork upstream requires bushwhacking, and unless you have strong backwoods skills, don't try it. A heavy snowstorm in 1998 felled numerous trees along Middle Fork, making it hard, if not impossible, to navigate the stream bottom. It would also be difficult to find your way from the stream up the ridge to FR 839. I started at FR 839 and tried to work my way north along the stream to the spot where the three forks meet—and gave up. If you want to walk along Beaver Creek, try Hike 39.

From the creek bank, return on Three Forks of Beaver Trail to the intersection, taking the other leg of Three Forks Loop Trail north to the parking lot. This leg is an old dirt-and-grass road. Before reaching the parking lot, it jogs northeast around a field created for animal habitat by Forest Service personnel. When I took the hike, a lack of directional signs made the final

Wading pools form along Beaver Creek.

0.2 mile confusing. Remember to turn right at the habitat field and you should have no trouble.

Options: For a longer walk along Beaver Creek, see Hike 39.

39 Bowman Ridge

> **Highlights:** A walk along the banks of isolated Beaver Creek.
> **Location:** Beaver Creek Wilderness in the Daniel Boone National Forest, 19 miles south of Somerset.
> **Type of hike:** Day hike or one-night backpack; loop.
> **Total distance:** 3.4 miles.
> **Difficulty:** Easy.
> **Best months:** Any month.
> **Maps:** USGS Hail; Daniel Boone National Forest map of the Clifty and Beaver Creek Wilderness Areas; Somerset District map of Bowman Ridge.

Special considerations: The path along Beaver Creek is subject to over-growth and can be difficult to follow in places. It's advisable to check with the Somerset District on current conditions. And be sure to bring a compass.

Finding the trailhead: From the intersection of Kentucky Highway 90 and U.S. Highway 27, about 20 miles south of Somerset, take US 27 north for 4.1 miles and turn right onto gravel Bauer Road (Forest Road 50). At the fork in 2.3 miles, bear right onto Bowman Ridge Road (FR 51). After 2.4 miles, turn into the parking area on your left just before the road dead-ends. The trailhead is at the parking area's north end. GPS: 36 55.265 N 84 25.855 W.

Parking and trailhead facilities: There's space for eight cars, but no facilities.

Key points:
0.0   Bowman Ridge Trailhead.
0.2   Right turn at junction.
0.9   Beaver Creek.
2.0   Turn at Big Bend.
3.2   Trail junction.

The hike: Clear, shallow Beaver Creek is lined with lush vegetation and wading spots, a perfect place to enjoy nature and solitude. This hike takes you along a 1.1-mile stretch of the stream about 3 miles before it empties into the Cumberland River. The Forest Service developed this loop route in the late 1990s by connecting several existing paths and old roads. Most of the loop is within the Beaver Creek Wilderness, where trails are generally left to take care of themselves. The walk down the ridge to the creek bottom and back up is mainly on old roads that are easy to follow. The path along the creek, however, is faint in some places and nonexistent in others. That's not a problem as long as you're following the stream. But finding your way

Bowman Bridge

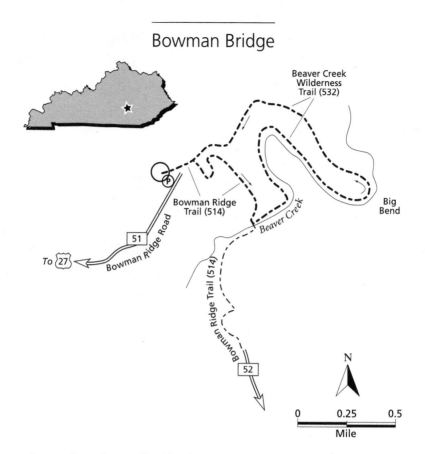

from the creek to the roadbed leading up the ridge and back to your car can be difficult. At least it was for me when I took the hike. The turn was completely unmarked, and I spent a few anxious minutes trying to figure out just where I was—a process aided considerably by GPS. I have included detailed instructions so the same won't happen to you. This is an enjoyable walk, however, even with the trail's disappearing act.

Bowman Ridge Trail (514) initially follows an old road as it heads northeast from the parking area. However, almost immediately you jog around a gate and bear right off the road onto a path running downhill to a fork at mile 0.2. The left-hand prong leading northeast is Beaver Creek Wilderness Trail (532), which you will take later in the hike. For now, you stay on Bowman Ridge Trail, which turns right (southeast) and broadens again into an old road. After passing the wilderness boundary marker, you curve first north and then southeast and southwest as you descend gently to the creek at mile 0.9, coming out on a wooden-floored bridge.

Bowman Ridge Trail crosses the bridge and ends 0.7 mile on the other side at FR 52 on Swain Ridge. Instead of crossing the bridge, however, you turn left and begin following the creek downstream toward the Cumberland River. This creek-bank route used to be called Middle Ridge Trail (518), but it's now part of Beaver Creek Wilderness Trail (532). When I hiked the route,

An old wooden bridge spans Beaver Creek at the junction of Bowman Ridge and Beaver Creek Trails.

there were signs with both designations at the bridge. Just downstream from the bridge, you pass a nice little beach. There are also a number of well-used camping spots, some obviously in violation of the required 200-foot distance from a stream. The forest includes pines and hardwoods; ferns dot the floor.

At one point, the trail multiplies into three paths, all paralleling the creek. It doesn't matter which you take; they eventually merge back into one. When the creek turns north, the trail moves away from it but then returns. The creek then makes a sharp bend south, creating a lovely pool and resting spot at the bend. It is when you are following the creek south that the path begins fading in and out of existence. Continue to keep the stream on your right. As you near what's called Big Bend—where the creek turns north again—the trail runs along the base of a cliff. It then veers left (away from the stream) and comes into a wildlife clearing at mile 2 (GPS 36 55.201 N 84 24.797 W). This is where you leave the creek for good.

After I reported my trouble finding the turnoff point, a Somerset District ranger told me he would make it more obvious. But just in case it's still not obvious enough, here's what you do: Go to the far end of the clearing (the east end) and turn left (north). You immediately come to an embankment lightly covered with vegetation. Walk up the embankment about 20 feet; you should find the beginning of an old roadbed heading uphill. That's the continuation of Beaver Creek Wilderness Trail (532), which you take up the ridge, going initially northeast and then northwest.

After reaching the ridgetop, the trail dips into a saddle and begins a series of shallow climbs and descents as it turns west and then southwest and leaves the wilderness area. There used to be a coal mine to the east of the trail on the ridgeside, and the area is full of old roads. But signs for Trail 532 show which turns to make, and at mile 3.2 you arrive at the junction with Bowman Ridge Trail (514). Bear right and you are back at your car at mile 3.4.

Big South Fork

From its origins in northern Tennessee, the Big South Fork of the Cumberland River cuts a deep gorge through the Cumberland Plateau as it flows north to join the main stem of the Cumberland in Kentucky near Somerset. Despite heavy logging and coal mining in the first half of the twentieth century, the rugged terrain of Big South Fork today makes one of the finest hiking areas in the state. The vistas along the gorge are dramatic, and the land is dotted with beautiful creeks, waterfalls, and sandstone arches. Long isolated by the river and gorge, the area still retains the rustic feel of the frontier. You can easily walk miles without seeing another soul.

Prodded by Kentucky and Tennessee lawmakers, Congress in 1974 created the Big South Fork National River and Recreation Area to give the stream and shoreline special protection and to encourage use by visitors. Run by the National Park Service, the 125,000-acre Big South Fork area is a cross between a national park and a national forest. It offers fewer creature comforts than a park but has a greater focus on hiking, camping, horseback riding, rafting, kayaking, and other outdoor activities than a typical national forest. Altogether, the Big South Fork area has more than 150 miles of hiking trails. The larger portion is in Tennessee, but the Kentucky section has a number of beautiful walks.

A $5.00 permit is required for backcountry camping within the National Park Service area. The permit covers up to six people and is good for an entire trip however many nights that may be. Permits can be purchased at either of two Big South Fork visitor centers: the Kentucky center located south of Whitley City on Kentucky Highway 92 (606-376-5073) or the Tennessee center located 14 miles west of Oneida on Tennessee Highway 297 at Bandy Creek (931-879-3625). The Kentucky center is open 9:00 A.M. to 5:30 P.M.; the Tennessee center is open 8:30 A.M. to 6:00 P.M.

The following Big South Fork hikes are all in Kentucky, although not entirely within the boundaries of the National Park Service–administered recreation area. Some of the trails are on adjacent Daniel Boone National Forest land administered by the Stearns Ranger District (606-376-5323). Backcountry camping permits are not required in the national forest. The terrain itself is indistinguishable between the recreation area and national forest, but the painted trail blazes used in the two do differ—generally a red arrowhead in the recreation area and a white diamond in the national forest.

A couple of cautionary notes: First, although the Big South Fork area is administered by the park service, hunting is allowed in accordance with state seasons. Second, the region was hard hit in 1998 by two severe storms that destroyed wide swaths of national forest land. As a result, a number of Big South Fork trails maintained by the Stearns District—including portions of the Sheltowee Trace National Recreation Trail—had to be closed and won't be reopened for years, if ever. Check with the Stearns District if you plan to use any trails not included in the following hikes. Two helpful books—*Hiking the Big South Fork* by Brenda G. Deaver, Jo Anna Smith, and Howard Ray Duncan, and *100 Trails of the Big South Fork* by Russ Manning—are sold at the Kentucky visitor center.

40 Yahoo Falls

Highlights: Kentucky's highest waterfall, and a walk along Big South Fork.

Location: Big South Fork National River and Recreation Area, near Whitley City and just north of the Tennessee line.

Type of hike: Day hike or one-night backpack; loop.

Total distance: 8.5 miles.

Difficulty: Moderate.

Best months: Any month.

Maps: USGS Nevelsville and Barthell; Stearns District map of Yahoo Arch Trail (602); Trails Illustrated map of the Big South Fork area.

Permits and fees: A $5.00 permit is required for backcountry camping in the Big South Fork National River and Recreation Area.

Finding the trailhead: From the intersection of U.S. Highway 27 and Kentucky Highway 478 at Whitley City, take US 27 north for 1.8 miles and turn left (west) onto KY 700. Continue straight at an intersection with KY 1651 and, in 3 miles, park on the right shoulder at the sign for Yahoo Arch Trail (602). GPS: 36 45.396 N 84 30.730 W.

Parking and trailhead facilities: There's space for three cars, but no facilities. If there's no room at the trailhead, go 100 yards west and park on the left shoulder.

Key points:
0.0   Yahoo Arch Trailhead.
0.8   Yahoo Arch.
1.7   Yahoo Falls.
2.0   Big South Fork.
3.6   Alum Ford Campground.

The hike: This hike starts and ends in the Daniel Boone National Forest, but most of the walking is in the Big South Fork National River and Recreation Area. The main attraction is the 113-foot drop that Yahoo Creek takes just before it flows into Big South Fork. This is said to be the highest waterfall in Kentucky. Be warned that Yahoo Creek is not a big stream, and in rainless periods it can dry up completely. Even so, the hike is worthwhile. You follow Big South Fork for 4.3 miles, and the trail along the riverbank crosses several scenic tributaries as they empty into the bigger stream. A

Yahoo Falls

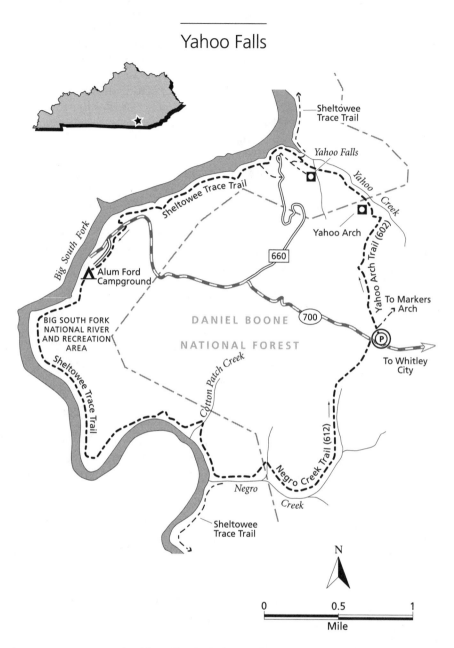

pleasant campground—Alum Ford—is located just about halfway through the loop. It has tent sites, picnic tables, and portable toilets but no treated water supply or other facilities. There is a $5.00-per-site fee.

From KY 700, Yahoo Arch Trail (602) heads northwest on an old roadbed across a level ridgetop. You immediately pass a side trail on your right leading 0.5 mile to minor Markers Arch. Continuing northwest on Yahoo Arch Trail, you have a few limited views east and west through the thin forest of hardwoods and evergreens. After descending on switchbacks and stone steps, you come first to a weathered rock outcropping to the left of the trail and then, at mile 0.8, to Yahoo Arch. The arch is 17 feet high and 70 feet wide and, with the surrounding cliff, makes an interesting rest stop.

Continuing on Yahoo Arch Trail, you follow the base of the cliff and pass from the national forest into the Big South Fork National River and Recreation Area. There is no boundary marker, but you notice the change because the white triangle blaze used by the USDA Forest Service suddenly gives way to the red arrowhead favored by the National Park Service. The trail curves more to the west and descends on switchbacks to a fork of Yahoo Creek, which you follow downstream toward Big South Fork. The forest here is fuller and more pleasing than on top of the ridge. At mile 1.5, you come to a fork in the trail and a sign indicating that the Yahoo Falls parking lot is straight ahead.

This is the beginning of the Yahoo Falls Scenic Area with its slightly confusing system of color-coded loop trails. There are three loops through the area, each marked by yellow, green, or blue arrowheads. You can, of course, explore all three, but here's my suggestion for a direct yet scenic route. At the sign, take the right-hand fork (marked with a yellow arrowhead). This trail descends and then heads west along the base of a cliff—the same cliff over which Yahoo Creek makes its 113-foot plunge. At mile 1.7, you walk behind the falls and beneath a tall rock overhang. A sign located on the other side of the falls explains how this kind of rock shelter is formed, and how it was used for shelter by Native Americans thousands of years ago.

Before reaching the falls, you pass a turnoff for the blue trail, which would take you down to another fork of the creek. After the falls, you pass a green-trail turnoff that descends farther into the gorge. Continuing on the yellow trail, you come to a fork at mile 1.9. Here the yellow trail bears left and climbs to the parking area. You, however, bear right onto Sheltowee Trace National Recreation Trail and follow Yahoo Creek to Big South Fork. The Sheltowee is a north–south route approximately 260 miles long through Kentucky; it ends just south of the state line in Tennessee's Pickett State Park, adjacent to the Big South Fork area. *Sheltowee* means "big turtle," the Indian name for Daniel Boone, and thus the trail is blazed with the outline of a turtle. This stretch also serves as part of the green loop and is marked with green arrowheads as well.

Taking the Sheltowee, you reach Big South Fork at mile 2 and curve left to begin following the river upstream. You quickly cross a wooden bridge spanning a beautiful rocky drainage area festooned with rhododendrons and ferns. The cliff towering above on your left adds to the feeling of isolation. Just past the bridge, the green trail turns off to your left to ascend to the Yahoo Falls parking area. The Sheltowee soon jogs briefly away from the river to cross another streambed. Note the sign indicating that you have now left the no-hunting zone around Yahoo Falls. The park service forbids hunting near a number of Big South Fork attractions, but even so you have to be careful. The large bullet hole through the NO HUNTING sign near Alum Ford Campground suggests that some people are less than slavish when it comes to heeding the prohibition.

Yahoo Falls spills over this 113-foot cliff, except during dry periods.

As you walk along Big South Fork, you cross a number of small streams flowing into the river through interesting rock formations, several producing delightful waterfalls in the process. Initially, the Sheltowee stays close to the river, and although there are no established side trails down to the water, you can easily reach the riverbank if you wish. The trail, however, then turns away from the stream, and at mile 3.4 comes out onto KY 700 shortly before the road dead-ends into the river at the Alum Ford boat ramp. You turn right onto KY 700 and follow it a short distance to a gravel road branching off to your left. Take the gravel road up the hill and reach Alum Ford Campground at mile 3.6. The boat ramp and river are directly below you but difficult to see.

The gravel road ends at the campground, and the Sheltowee once again becomes a forest path as it continues following Big South Fork southward. Periodically the river and trail veer away from each other, at times putting the water completely out of sight. The walking is generally level, although there is a good climb at mile 5.6. After a pronounced jog inland, the Sheltowee crosses Cotton Patch Creek at mile 5.9, and at mile 6.3 it meets Negro Creek Trail (612), an old name that is jarring today. In *Hiking the Big South Fork,* the authors say that the origin of the name is uncertain, but a local historian believes an African-American family—a rarity in this part of Kentucky at the time—lived at the mouth of the creek in the 1800s.

The Sheltowee crosses Negro Creek and continues south along the riverbank, but you turn left onto Negro Creek Trail and head east, paralleling the creek. At first the walking is level, but shortly you begin climbing through evergreens. As the trail turns north and crosses a branch of the creek, it passes over several old dirt roads that might be confusing. Keep a close lookout for the trail's white diamond markings.

Winding along the ridgeside, Negro Creek Trail follows the creek's main stem north, sometimes climbing steeply. At mile 8.1, beneath a power line, you reach the base of a rock outcropping. Using footholds chipped into the rock, climb the outcropping; at the top, turn left onto the gravel road in the power-line clearing. The thankfully brief part of the hike that remains is not what you would call scenic. Avoiding discarded sofas and tires, follow the gravel road north to KY 700, which you reach at mile 8.5. Your car is a minute's walk to your right (east).

41 Blue Heron

Highlights:	Overlooks from the gorge rim above Big South Fork, and a visit to a re-created coal-mining camp.
Location:	Big South Fork National River and Recreation Area, near Whitley City and just north of the Tennessee line.
Type of hike:	Day hike or one-night backpack; loop.
Total distance:	6.6 miles.
Difficulty:	Moderate.
Best months:	Any month.
Maps:	USGS Barthell; National Park Service map of Blue Heron trails; Trails Illustrated map of the Big South Fork area.
Permits and fees:	A $5.00 permit is required for backcountry camping in the Big South Fork National River and Recreation Area.

Finding the trailhead: From the intersection of U.S. Highway 27 and Kentucky Highway 92 south of Whitley City, take KY 92 west past the Big South Fork National River and Recreation Area visitor center and, in 1.3 miles, turn left (south) onto KY 1651. In 0.4 mile, turn right onto KY 741; in another 0.7 mile, turn right onto KY 742. Take KY 742 west for 5.2 miles and bear left at the fork, following the sign to the overlooks. In 0.4 mile, pull into the parking area on the left of the road at the sign for Blue Heron Loop Trail parking. GPS: 36 40.633 N 84 31.839 W.

Parking and trailhead facilities: There's space for several cars. No facilities are available at the trailhead, but you'll find rest rooms, water, a telephone, and a seasonal snack bar at the Blue Heron visitor complex, which is 2.5 miles away by road. Also, water, showers, electricity, and telephone are available at Blue Heron Campground just north of KY 742.

Key points:
- 0.0   Blue Heron Loop Trailhead.
- 0.7   Devils Jump Overlook.
- 1.4   Blue Heron Overlook.
- 2.1   Entrance to Blue Heron Mining Camp.
- 2.8   Side trail to Devils Jump.
- 4.4   Laurel Branch.

The hike: Blue Heron was a coal-mining town built in 1937 on the banks of Big South Fork by the Stearns Coal and Lumber Company. Disappointed with production, Stearns closed the mining operation in 1962, and the town was abandoned. Now, as a major attraction of the Big South Fork National River and Recreation Area, Blue Heron has been re-created to give visitors an idea of what life was like in the self-contained company towns that once dominated the coal-mining economy of eastern Kentucky. This loop hike starts

Blue Heron

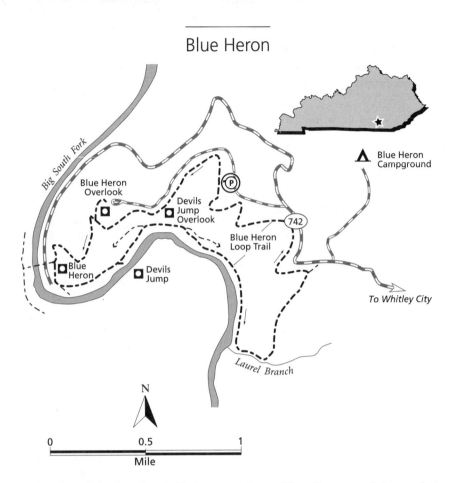

on the rim of the Big South Fork gorge above Blue Heron and descends to the town. From there you follow the river past a narrow, rocky stretch called Devils Jump before climbing back up the ridge.

Unfortunately, except for the huge coal tipple, none of the original Blue Heron buildings survived. As a result, the re-creation is dotted with new metal-frame structures that are supposed to represent the church, company store, school, homes, and other buildings that no longer exist. I found the modern appearance of these so-called ghost structures disconcerting. Instead of an old coal camp, I had the feeling I was walking through a bunch of fast-food restaurants. Nevertheless, the recorded first-person accounts of Blue Heron life by former residents are authentic and interesting, and the full-sized mockup of a mine opening is also well done. Because the tour of Blue Heron is self-guided, how much time you spend there is entirely up to you. Distance-wise, the Blue Heron visit is only a small fraction of the total hike. Most of the walking is in the woods and along the river bottom.

From the parking area on the west side of KY 742, take the path heading west into the woods. It immediately dead-ends into Blue Heron Loop Trail, which is marked by red arrowheads. Turn right and go north through a forest of hardwoods, evergreens, and mountain laurel. For about the first mile,

A "ghost" structure stands sentry at the Blue Heron mining camp.

the trail parallels KY 742, which comes into and out of view on your right. The road ends at the Blue Heron Overlook.

Where the dirt path turns into pavement, there is an unmarked fork. You take the left prong and reach the Devils Jump Overlook at mile 0.7. Below, you see the river and the narrow rocky stretch of rapids known as Devils Jump. In their book *Hiking the Big South Fork,* the authors say the name may stem from the 1800s when men who floated logs downstream—known as raft devils—had trouble with this dangerous section. At one point, the Corps of Engineers wanted to build a dam at Devils Jump, a proposal that helped stimulate support for legislation to protect the gorge area.

From the lookout, return to the fork and take the other prong, which passes in front of the overlook parking area. The walking surface changes back to dirt as the trail reenters the woods near a sign that tells you that you're heading toward something called Cracks in the Rock. Walking northwest and then west, you follow the base of a cliff on your right; the edge of the gorge is on your left. After a sharp right turn around the end of the cliff, you come to a side trail to your right. It climbs in a little more than 0.1 mile up to the Blue Heron Overlook. The climb is not difficult, but the view is similar to the one you had from the Devils Jump Overlook.

Continuing on the main loop trail, you descend gently to the beginning of a long, steep set of wooden steps that take you down a large rock. Be careful here; the steps can be dangerous, especially for small children. Just beyond the bottom of the stairway, you come to Cracks in the Rock—a huge rock with holes cut by nature through three of its sides. The trail goes through the rock and begins winding its way down to Blue Heron.

You reach the entrance to the mining town at mile 2.1. A free pamphlet is available to help guide you. You can take either one of the two paved walkways that go south through the exhibits. The walkway on your left takes you to the mine opening and tipple, the one on your right to various "ghost" structures with cutout figures and buttons that activate the recorded oral histories. At one, for example, a woman's voice explains that as a girl she entertained herself by reading all of the Nancy Drew books. You also learn that courtship consisted of walking a member of the opposite sex home from church. The train station and more exhibits are located below the tipple near the parking lot. Blue Heron can be reached by car by taking the right-hand prong of the fork on top of the ridge.

Just south of the tipple, the paved path forks. You go left, following a sign marking the continuation of Blue Heron Loop. Heading south, you pass the snack bar and picnic pavilion, descend concrete steps, cross the parking lot, and come to a fork at mile 2.4. The right prong is a gravel path leading a short distance down to the river. You go left on a dirt path that parallels the river and quickly comes to a sign telling you that Devils Jump is 0.4 mile ahead and Laurel Branch 1.7 miles. Following the riverbank but staying slightly above it, you pass several side trails down to the water's edge. For the best view of Devils Jump, take the second side trail, which you reach at mile 2.8. It leads to large rocks that offer nice spots for watching the water.

Back on the main trail, continue along the riverbank for a short distance until the trail forks. You go right and climb north away from the river through a cleared area. At mile 3.1 you reach the bottom of a flight of wooden steps that take you up to a broad bench in the ridge. This bench once carried a rail line used in the mining operation; it now serves as a horse path, which you take to your right (east). There are good views of the river below, and the black you see in the cliffside is testament to the mining that once went on here. At mile 3.3, the loop trail leaves the horse path, dropping off to your right and crossing an attractive rocky area.

After passing over several small wooden bridges, the trail returns to the riverside and broadens into what appears to be an old roadbed. There are several nice resting spots above the water. At a cleared area with a fire ring, the trail turns away from the river and climbs east to a sign at mile 4.3. The sign points straight ahead to Laurel Branch, an attractive creek just 350 feet away. Blue Heron Loop Trail turns left at the sign and takes a series of steps and switchbacks up the ridgeside. Winding your way generally northward, you reach the top of the ridge and enjoy a level stroll with limited views as you near KY 742.

At mile 5.2, just before reaching KY 742, the trail forks; the right-hand prong goes north to the road, coming out near the entrance to Blue Heron Campground. You turn left and parallel KY 742 back to the hike's starting point, which you reach at mile 6.6.

Options: See Hike 42 for another walk in the Blue Heron area. Also, for a change of pace, how about a train excursion? In season you can ride the Big South Fork Scenic Railway from the attractive little town of Stearns to Blue

Heron. For the cost and schedule of the three-hour, round-trip run, call (800) 462–5664. Stearns, which was built by the Stearns company as headquarters for its now-defunct coal-and-lumber business, is located just off KY 92 a mile west of US 27.

42 Big Spring Falls

Highlights: An overlook from the west side of the Big South Fork gorge, and a beautiful waterfall.
Location: Big South Fork National River and Recreation Area, near Whitley City and just north of the Tennessee line.
Type of hike: Day hike or one-night backpack; out-and-back.
Total distance: 7.2 miles.
Difficulty: Moderate.
Best months: Any month.
Maps: USGS Barthell; National Park Service map of Blue Heron trails; Trails Illustrated map of the Big South Fork area.
Permits and fees: A $5.00 permit is required for backcountry camping in the Big South Fork National River and Recreation Area.

Finding the trailhead: From the intersection of U.S. Highway 27 and Kentucky Highway 92 south of Whitley City, take KY 92 west past the Big South Fork National River and Recreation Area visitor center and, in 1.3 miles, turn left (south) onto KY 1651. In 0.4 mile, turn right onto KY 741; in another 0.7 mile, turn right onto KY 742. Take KY 742 west for 5.2 miles and bear right at the fork, continuing 2.5 miles to the parking lot at the re-created Blue Heron mining town. The hike starts above the parking lot at the east end of the tipple and bridge. GPS: 36 40.109 N 84 32.883 W.

Parking and trailhead facilities: There's unlimited parking space, along with a snack bar (open seasonally), rest rooms, water, a telephone, and soft drink machines. A campground with showers and electricity is located at the top of the gorge just north of KY 742.

Key points:
0.0   East end of the Blue Heron tipple-bridge.
0.5   Three West Creek.
1.6   Catawba Overlook.
2.2   Dick Gap Falls.
3.6   Big Spring Falls.

The hike: The center of activity in the Blue Heron mining town was the tipple, where raw coal was dumped, sorted, and loaded into waiting rail cars for shipment. Connected to the tipple was a bridge that allowed motorized trams to bring coal from mines on the west side of Big South Fork as well

Big Spring Falls

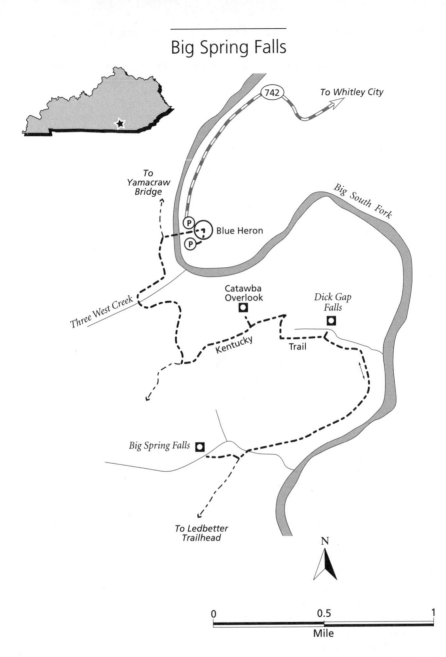

To Whitley City

742

To Yamacraw Bridge

Big South Fork

P 🚩 Blue Heron
P

Three West Creek

Catawba Overlook

Dick Gap Falls

Kentucky Trail

Big Spring Falls

To Ledbetter Trailhead

N

0   0.5   1
Mile

as on the east side. This massive tipple-and-bridge structure, standing about 100 feet above the river, was considered leading-edge technology when it was built in the 1930s. Today it is open to pedestrian use, permitting access to hiking trails across the river from Blue Heron. (See Hike 41 for more about the Blue Heron mining community.) This hike follows a scenic west-side route called Kentucky Trail, first to an overlook and then to two waterfalls on Big South Fork tributaries. The first falls is uncertain in rainless periods, but the second is likely to be flowing even in the driest of weather.

As you walk across the bridge to the river's west side, take in the various exhibits that help explain how the mining operation worked. I found the old mine maps on the left wall of the bridge particularly interesting. At the far end of the bridge, turn left and head south on a broad, dirt roadbed cut into the side of the ridge. This was the tram road for the old mining operation, and is now part of the Kentucky Trail, a 27-mile north–south route through the Kentucky portion of the Big South Fork National River and Recreation Area. The trail runs from Yamacraw (KY 92) Bridge, located 8 miles north of Blue Heron, to the Peters Mountain Trailhead, 19 miles to the south.

At the west end of the bridge, the trail sign tells southbound hikers they are headed toward the Ledbetter Trailhead and Oil Well Branch, both farther south than this hike goes, and to the Catawba Overlook, which is your first destination. The trail curves west, and you follow the base of a cliff on your right as you gradually climb up Three West Hollow, passing through a lovely grove of evergreens. Veteran Big South Fork ranger Howard Ray Duncan explains that the hollow was named for the number three mine opening, which was on the west side of the river. Turning south, you cross Three West Creek at mile 0.5, and on the other side climb initially southeast, then northeast, and finally south. There are limited views of the Blue Heron community below. At mile 1, after reaching the base of a tall cliff with a rock shelter, you climb a set of steep wooden steps. At mile 1.2, the trail merges briefly with a horse path coming in from your right. After a few steps, the foot trail leaves the horse path, branching left into a pleasant area of rocks and rhododendrons.

A pedestrian bridge links the Blue Heron mining camp with hiking trails across the Big South Fork River.

At mile 1.6, you reach a short side trail that descends to a wooden platform. This is the Catawba Overlook, named for a type of rhododendron. To the north you have a good view of the cliff lining the ridgetop above the Blue Heron community. You also see the Devils Jump and Blue Heron Overlooks visited in Hike 41 as well as the Blue Heron bridge you just crossed. Leaving the overlook, Kentucky Trail heads northeast and then drops south toward a small stream flowing out of an area known as Dick Gap. Along the way, you pass over an unusual bridge. Instead of a stream, it crosses the trunk of a downed tree that has continued to live despite its horizontal attitude. Just after the tree bridge, you descend a flight of wooden steps and, at mile 2.2, come to a sign pointing left to Dick Gap Falls. I was at the falls in a dry period, and there wasn't so much as a drip of water. Nevertheless, the abundance of ferns, rhododendrons, and moss-covered rocks made this a delightful spot.

From Dick Gap Falls, you descend gently, with the streambed on your left, and at mile 2.5 run into an old road running along the ridgeside high above Big South Fork. To your left the road is blocked off. That stretch used to be part of Kentucky Trail but is now considered unsafe because of unstable coal waste, according to the authors of *Hiking the Big South Fork*. Turning right, you follow the road south and then west over level terrain. At mile 3.3, shortly after passing a small pile of coal on the left of the trail, you cross Big Spring Creek on a bridge.

From the bridge, the path climbs to a fork. Turn right and, at mile 3.4, you come to a sign pointing right to a side trail that leads to Big Spring Falls. Head west on this side trail; at mile 3.6, shortly after the trail mounts a boardwalk, you reach a fenced observation area. Just beyond, you see water falling over a massive cliff approximately 90 feet high and into a ravine blanketed with rhododendrons and ferns. From this pleasant scene, retrace your steps to the Blue Heron parking lot.

Options: You can easily lengthen the trip by continuing south on Kentucky Trail, but you will have to either arrange a shuttle or retrace your steps. Sheltowee Trace National Recreation Trail parallels Big South Fork just north of Kentucky Trail, and it used to be that you could use the Sheltowee to make a loop route. However, two severe storms in 1998 closed that portion of the Sheltowee, and Forest Service personnel don't expect it to be reopened anytime soon. Check with the Stearns District of the Daniel Boone National Forest for the Sheltowee's current status.

43 Buffalo Arch

Highlights:	A walk, mainly on a level ridgetop, to a large, graceful arch.
Location:	Daniel Boone National Forest, just north of the Tennessee line.
Type of hike:	Day hike; out-and-back.
Total distance:	4.4 miles.
Difficulty:	Easy.
Best months:	Any month.
Maps:	USGS Barthell SW (Tenn./Ky.) and Sharp Place (Tenn./Ky.); Stearns District map sheets for Parker Mountain Trail and Buffalo Arch Trail.

Special considerations: Just before reaching the trailhead, you must drive on a narrow, gravel forest road that fords two small, bridgeless streams. Signs warn motorists not to attempt to cross the streams in high water. If the weather has been rainy, check with the Stearns District before setting out.

Finding the trailhead: From U.S. Highway 27 south of Whitley City, take Kentucky Highway 92 west for 6 miles to Yamacraw Bridge over Big South Fork. At the far end of the bridge, turn left onto KY 1363 and go south for 11 miles. Here the pavement ends and the road forks; you go right on Forest Road 564. In another 1.2 miles, turn left onto FR 137, following the sign for the Hemlock Grove picnic area and Great Meadows Campground. In 7 miles—after passing the picnic and campground sites and fording the two small streams with warning signs—park on the left shoulder across the road from the Parker Mountain Trailhead (634) sign. Your total driving distance from Yamacraw Bridge is 19.2 miles. GPS: 36 36.228 N 84 44.433 W.

Parking and trailhead facilities: There's room for three cars on the shoulder. No facilities are available, but Great Meadows Campground, 3 miles north on FR 137, has rest rooms and (from mid-April to mid-November) water.

Key points:
- 0.0 Parker Mountain Trailhead.
- 0.5 Top of ridge.
- 1.8 Buffalo Arch Trail.
- 2.2 Buffalo Arch.

The hike: Buffalo Arch is 18.5 feet high and, at its base, 81 feet wide. Indians hunting buffalo used to stand on top to look for their prey, hence its name. Or so the story goes. What is definite is that this is a large, impressive sandstone structure that makes a rewarding destination. The arch, located at the end of a cliff, slopes gracefully west, sheltering a wide swath of ground beneath its span. In his book *The Historic Cumberland Plateau*, author Russ Manning likens this arch to "a flying buttress holding up the hillside"—an apt description. This is a remote corner of the state, but this hike is surprisingly easy. Most of the walking is on top of a level ridge.

Buffalo Arch

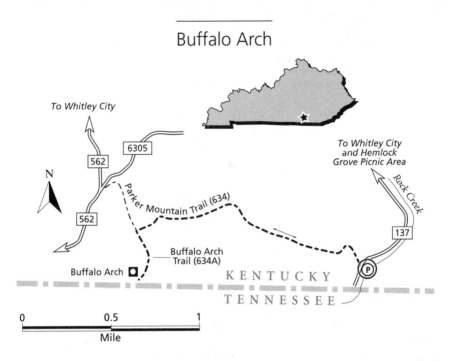

From FR 137 just north of Rock Creek, you take Parker Mountain Trail (634) north and begin climbing up the Rock Creek valley wall. You immediately notice a large number of downed trees, the victims of two severe storms in 1998—a heavy snow that winter and a tornado in spring. The damage throughout this section of the national forest was significant, and you will see more of it as you make your way to the arch. You also see the results of a massive effort to clean up the mess and repair the trail. It will be years before the scars are healed but, thankfully, this hike does not suffer appreciably from them.

The narrow dirt path, marked by white plastic diamonds, curves west as it continues climbing the ridgeside, providing views to the east and south. After reaching the base of an attractive, fern-sprouting cliff, you climb stone steps to the southwest and wind your way up a break in the cliff wall. Next is a metal stairway, which takes you up to a good view of the valley to the south. Continuing to climb, but more gradually, you head northwest and reach the top at mile 0.5.

From here on, the trail is generally flat, most of the ups and downs slight enough to be unnoticeable. The ridgetop woods are pleasant enough but without remarkable features. At mile 1.8, the trail comes into a clearing and meets a dirt road. Parker Mountain Trail follows the road to your right and heads north toward FR 6305 about 0.4 mile away. You, however, turn left onto the road and head south. The turn marks the beginning of Buffalo Arch Trail (634A), which immediately leaves the clearing and goes into the woods, sloping down gently. After curving right, the road comes to a fork and you bear right. After the fork, the trail narrows once again into a path, turns west, descends, and reaches the arch at mile 2.2.

Buffalo Arch spans 81 feet at its base.

Options: See Hike 44 for a walk in this same corner of the national forest. Great Meadows Campground, located nearby on Rock Creek, is an exceptionally nice camping spot. The two sections—one on each side of FR 137—have a total of eighteen tent sites; there's no electricity.

44 Gobblers Arch

> **Highlights:** A forest walk with a good variety of ridges and hollows, and a stop at a sizable arch.
> **Location:** Daniel Boone National Forest, near the Tennessee line.
> **Type of hike:** Day hike or one-night backpack; loop.
> **Total distance:** 4.8 miles.
> **Difficulty:** Moderate.
> **Best months:** Any month.
> **Maps:** USGS Bell Farm; Stearns District map sheets for Gobblers Arch and Mark Branch Trails.

Finding the trailhead: From U.S. Highway 27 south of Whitley City, take Kentucky Highway 92 west for 6 miles to Yamacraw Bridge over Big South Fork. At the far end of the bridge, turn left onto KY 1363 and go south for 11 miles. Here the pavement ends and the road forks; you go right on Forest Road 564. In another 1.2 miles, turn left onto FR 137, following the sign for the Hemlock Grove picnic area and Great Meadows Campground. In 2.6

Gobblers Arch

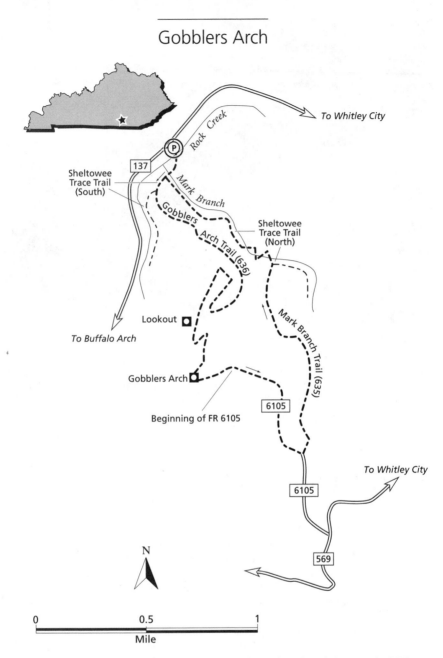

To Whitley City

Rock Creek

137

Sheltowee
Trace Trail
(South)

Mark Branch

Gobblers Arch Trail (636)

Sheltowee
Trace Trail
(North)

Lookout

To Buffalo Arch

Mark Branch Trail (635)

Gobblers Arch

Beginning of FR 6105

6105

To Whitley City

6105

N

569

0   0.5   1
Mile

miles, park at the picnic area, which is on the left side of the road. GPS: 36 38.697 N 84 42.682 W.

Parking and trailhead facilities: You'll find space for about twenty cars, along with rest rooms, picnic tables, and a pavilion.

Key points:
- 0.0   Hemlock Grove picnic area.
- 0.1   Sheltowee Trace Trail.
- 0.2   Gobblers Arch Trailhead.
- 2.0   Gobblers Arch.
- 2.2   Forest Road 6105.
- 2.8   Mark Branch Trail.
- 4.1   Sheltowee Trace Trail.

The hike: Gobblers Arch is a squat, solid structure 50 feet wide at the base and just under 12 feet in height. It lacks the grace of Buffalo Arch (Hike 43) and instead personifies brute strength. It could be a linebacker for the Green Bay Packers. This loop (cobbled together from several trails) does take you to Gobblers Arch, but its real attraction is the variety of terrain and forests it lets you sample along the way.

The Hemlock Grove area was damaged by severe storms in 1998, and more than a year later the picnic grounds were still in the process of reconstruction. So it's possible the beginning of this loop route will in the future be better marked and easier to find than it was when I was there. But in case it isn't, here's how you get started.

From the parking area, walk southwest through the picnic grounds to Rock Creek and ford it. This is a substantial stream and there's no bridge; if it's been raining, you may get your feet wet. Once you're on the other side, continue southwest, and at mile 0.1 (from the parking area) you come into a field with a sign for Sheltowee Trace National Recreation Trail. Brush along the creek bank may make the field difficult to see, but don't give up. I had trouble until I found an old farm track, barely visible, leading from the stream to the field.

The Sheltowee is a long-distance trail that starts at the north end of the Daniel Boone National Forest and passes through Hemlock Grove on its way to its ending point in Tennessee's Pickett State Park, 15 miles to the southwest. From the trail sign, take the Sheltowee west—but not for long. At mile 0.2, you turn left (south) onto Gobblers Arch Trail (636) and begin a climb from the Rock Creek valley floor up the ridge. Initially the incline is gentle, but it soon becomes steep. On the way up you see the remains of numerous trees felled by the 1998 storms.

At mile 0.5, you come to a rock outcropping and begin paralleling the base of the ridgeside cliff, first going south and level, then southwest and up a small, inviting ravine lined with evergreen trees and rhododendrons. Near the top of the ridge, the trail turns northeast before curving again to the south. At mile 1.4, you come to a lookout with good views to the west across the Rock Creek valley. The lookout, located just to the right of the trail, makes a nice rest spot, but be sure to watch small children carefully.

At mile 2, after winding through several drainages, you reach Gobblers Arch, a perfect place for lunch. The trail proceeds through the arch opening and climbs to the top of the ridge that houses the arch. From there you go northeast over level terrain until you meet FR 6105. This is where Gobblers Arch Trail ends.

Gobblers Arch Trail passes through 12-foot-high Gobblers Arch.

You follow FR 6105 south for 0.6 mile to Mark Branch Trail (635), which will take you north back toward the picnic grounds. FR 6105 starts out as a wide, pleasant forest path but grows into a full-fledged gravel road by the time you leave it at the top of a slight rise. The left-hand turn onto Mark Branch Trail is marked by a sign, but both the trail and sign are far enough off the road that you could miss them if you're not on the lookout. FR 6105 continues south to FR 569, which connects with roads leading to Yamacraw Bridge and Whitley City.

Mark Branch is a small stream that runs into Rock Creek at the Hemlock Grove picnic area. But the trail of that name doesn't reach the stream for 1.3 miles. From FR 6105, Mark Branch Trail winds northward, taking you through several lovely hollows and across a number of small streambeds, which may be dry. At mile 3.7, the trail begins its descent toward Mark Branch, gradually at first and then steeply. At mile 4.1, just before reaching the stream, Mark Branch Trail dead-ends into the Sheltowee.

To your right (southeast), the Sheltowee is blocked off because of damage from the 1998 storms. This is one of several Sheltowee sections closed indefinitely because of the multitude of downed trees and scarcity of federal cleanup dollars. To your left, however, the Sheltowee is open, and that's the way you go. You immediately cross Mark Branch, recross it twice in rapid succession, and in another 0.1 mile cross it again. Heading north with the stream below you, descend gently, and at mile 4.7 reach the open field where you found the Sheltowee Trace Trail sign at the beginning of the hike. Retrace your steps across Rock Creek; you're back at your car at mile 4.8.

45 Lick Creek

Highlights:	A walk along a picturesque stream to a striking waterfall.
Location:	Daniel Boone National Forest, near Whitley City.
Type of hike:	Day hike or one-night backpack; out-and-back.
Total distance:	5.6 miles.
Difficulty:	Easy.
Best months:	Any month.
Maps:	USGS Whitley City and Barthell; Stearns District map sheets for Lick Creek and Lick Creek Falls Trails.

Finding the trailhead: From U.S. Highway 27 in Whitley City, take Kentucky Highway 478 west for 0.1 mile to the stop sign, turn left onto KY 1651, and in 0.9 mile turn right onto Forest Road 622, which is the first paved road after the school bus lot. Park on the side of the road 100 feet from KY 1651 near the gated dirt road and Lick Creek Trailhead sign. Be careful not to block the gate. GPS: 36 42.925 N 84 28.869 W.

Parking and trailhead facilities: There's room for three or four cars, but no facilities.

Key points:
- 0.0   Lick Creek Trailhead.
- 1.0   Dirt road ends, path begins.
- 1.2   Bottom of second metal stairway.
- 2.2   Lick Creek Falls Trailhead.
- 2.8   Lick Creek Falls.

The hike: Lick Creek, a tributary of Big South Fork, is a picturesque stream lined with interesting rock formations and full of pleasant pools. This hike descends into the Lick Creek valley, follows the stream a short distance, and then climbs along a feeder stream to a beautiful waterfall named for the creek.

Most of the hike is on Lick Creek Trail (631), which starts in a residential area not far from the center of Whitley City. From FR 622, the trail initially follows a dirt road. Heading south at first but turning to the northwest, the road crosses a flat ridgetop that has been timbered. This makes for easy walking but not particularly attractive scenery. After the first half mile, however, the forest becomes more substantial, and there are limited views to the east.

At mile 1, just after starting to descend, the dirt road narrows into a path. It then turns left (west) and goes down a set of stone steps. Next you negotiate a metal stairway followed by a second, bringing you at mile 1.2 to the base of a cliff. The trail follows the cliff north, and along the way passes beneath a number of impressive rock overhangs. Children especially will like these interesting rock formations. At one point, you feel as if you're in a tunnel; a cliff flanks you on one side, a huge boulder on the other.

Lick Creek Trail passes alongside cliff faces and beneath rock overhangs.

Lick Creek

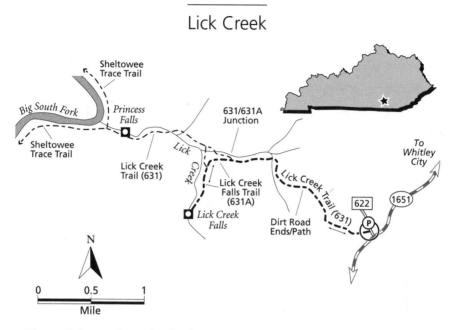

The trail descends gradually and, after following stone steps around a large outcropping, crosses a small tributary and comes to Lick Creek. The banks of this lovely stream are covered with tall evergreen trees and rhododendrons. You should have no trouble finding a nice lunch spot here.

You follow the creek downstream and, at mile 2.2, come to a side trail branching off to your left. Although there may be no sign identifying it— there wasn't when I was there—this is Lick Creek Falls Trail (631A), and you take it. Meanwhile, the main trail continues to follow Lick Creek to Sheltowee Trace National Recreation Trail a little more than a mile away. The Sheltowee, a long-distance trail through the Daniel Boone National Forest, runs along Big South Fork.

Climbing south, Lick Creek Falls Trail comes to a fork at mile 2.4. The right-hand prong, which goes back down to Lick Creek Trail, is for hikers continuing to the Sheltowee after visiting the falls; that way they don't have to completely retrace their steps. You bear left at the fork and at mile 2.8, after following the base of a tall cliff, reach the falls. The water comes down over a V-shaped overhang, making it possible to walk behind the falls without getting wet. The entire area seems to be dripping with water. Lush ferns and mossy rocks cover the bottom of the narrow ravine. From the falls, retrace your steps to your car.

Options: For a longer hike, continue on Lick Creek Trail to Sheltowee Trace Trail, which connects north to the Yahoo Falls area. (See Hike 40.) Just before reaching the Sheltowee, Lick Creek Trail passes Princess Falls, named for Princess Cornblossom, a Cherokee princess in the late 1700s. The one-way distance of the full Lick Creek Trail, including the detour to Lick Creek Falls, is 4 miles.

46 Laurel Creek

Highlights: A stroll along a lovely, easily accessible stream.
Location: Daniel Boone National Forest, south of Whitley City.
Type of hike: Day hike or one-night backpack; out-and-back.
Total distance: 8.8 miles.
Difficulty: Easy.
Best months: Any month.
Maps: USGS Whitley City; Stearns District map sheet for Laurel Creek Trail.

Finding the trailhead: From Whitley City, take U.S. Highway 27 south for 2 miles and turn left (east) onto East Appletree Road. Disregard the numerous side streets and, in 2.2 miles, just after the road surface changes from pavement to gravel, park on the shoulder by the sign for Laurel Creek Trail. GPS: 36 42.906 N 84 25.851 W.

Parking and trailhead facilities: There's room for about five cars, but no facilities.

Key points:
0.0   Laurel Creek Trailhead.
0.5   Laurel Creek.
4.4   Kentucky Highway 478.

The hike: Even in the driest weather, you can count on finding water flowing in Laurel Creek. The banks of this robust stream make a refreshing walk

Laurel Creek

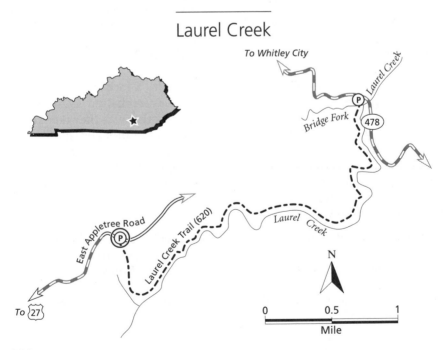

Wildflowers, ferns, and rock outcroppings line Laurel Creek.

any time of year. There are numerous wading spots as well as an abundance of wildflowers, ferns, rhododendrons and interesting rock outcroppings.

Located only minutes off US 27, the trailhead is unusually easy to reach. Some may not see this as an attribute. At the north end of the hike, there is apt to be traffic noise from KY 478. And midway along the creek, a power line passes overhead several times, each passing accompanied by a clearing that interrupts the forest. Despite these distractions, I felt far from civilization.

This hike is entirely on Laurel Creek Trail (620), which runs between East Appletree Road and KY 478. The trail doesn't intersect any roads or other trails, and so there is no way to avoid retracing your steps. Either end of the trail will do just fine as the starting point. For no good reason, these directions are from the southern trailhead.

From the south side of East Appletree Road, the trail heads south on an old dirt road across a ridgetop timbered in the 1980s. As with Hike 45, this initial stretch is not attractive, though it does offer vistas of mountain ridges to the southeast. You descend gradually at first and then more steeply. At mile 0.5, just after leaving the cut area and entering a forest of evergreens and mountain laurel, you come to Laurel Creek. Turn northeast and follow it downstream, the trail now narrowed into a path.

Unlike the other streams encountered on hikes in this section of the book, Laurel Creek does not flow into Big South Fork. Instead, after mingling with other creeks, its waters make their way into the main stem of the Cumberland River south of Cumberland Falls. Not only was the Laurel Creek watershed hit by the 1998 storms that damaged so much of this part of the Daniel Boone National Forest, but it also suffered a wildfire in 1999. You see the scars, including some blackened splotches, but hopefully will feel that the stream retains enough beauty and solitude to overcome those negatives.

Except for a few gentle ups and downs, the trail follows the creek's gradual descent—so gradual it's undetectable. On this hike there are no obvious features to point out, like a waterfall or sandstone arch. But at mile 1.7, a tall cliff towering above the trail and a pooling in the creek make a particularly nice rest spot. There's another at mile 2.8, where tall pines line the creek bank. I found the middle third of the creekside hike the prettiest.

Just before reaching KY 478, the trail crosses a bridge and climbs wooden steps to a gravel parking area on the south side of the highway. This is the end of the trail. Turn around and return to your car the same way you came.

Central Kentucky—North

The northern half of central Kentucky is a beautiful area. It includes the famous Bluegrass region—the gently rolling countryside surrounding Lexington where thoroughbreds romp on exquisite lawns in front of handsome old mansions surrounded by gleaming white fences. Yes, these perfect scenes really do exist—and you will see some of them as you drive to the hikes outlined below. This part of Kentucky has a number of parks and wildlife areas that offer quiet walks through moderate terrain. These public areas, however, are relatively small in size, and consequently the following are all day hikes of fairly short duration. For the most part, this is easy walking along stream bottomlands and low-lying ridges.

47 Middle Creek: Two Loops

Highlights: Wooded ridges with wildflowers and some limited views across the Ohio River valley.
Location: West of Florence.
Type of hike: Day hike; two separate loops.
Total distance: 3.4 miles (each loop 1.7 miles).
Difficulty: Easy.
Best months: Any month.
Maps: USGS Rising Sun and Lawrenceburg (Ind./Ky.); Kentucky State Nature Preserves Commission maps of the Boone County Cliffs and Dinsmore Woods Nature Preserves (office 502–573–2886).

Special considerations: These two short loops are near each other but in separate nature preserves, making a short drive necessary to get from one loop to the other. Also, pets are not allowed in the preserves.

Finding the trailhead: From exit 181 off Interstate 75 at Florence, take Kentucky Highway 18 west. For the first loop, turn left in 10.9 miles onto Middle Creek Road; 1.7 miles farther, park on your left in the gravel lot for the Boone County Cliffs State Nature Preserve. The loop starts at the lot. GPS: 38 59.603 N 84 47.068 W. For the second loop, return to KY 18, turn left, and in 0.3 mile turn left again into the parking area for Middle Creek Park. The second loop, in the Dinsmore Woods State Nature Preserve, starts on the north side of KY 18 directly across from the park entrance. GPS: 38 32.850 N 82 50.515 W.

Parking and trailhead facilities: The first loop has room for five cars, but no facilities. At the second loop, you'll find room for two dozen cars and a portable toilet.

Middle Creek: Two Loops

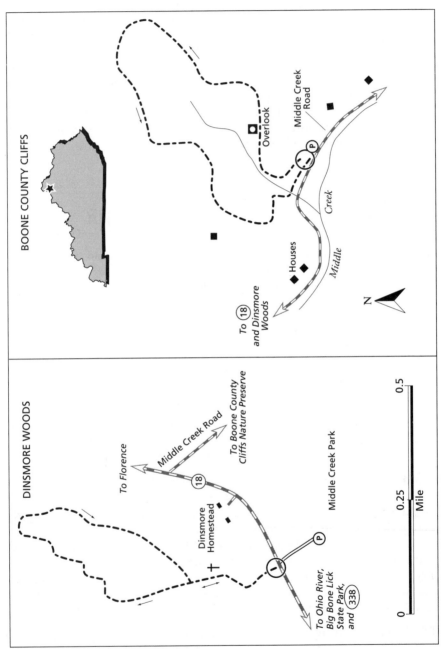

BOONE COUNTY CLIFFS

Middle Creek Road

Overlook

P

To 18 and Dinsmore Woods

Houses

Middle Creek

N

DINSMORE WOODS

To Florence

Middle Creek Road

To Boone County Cliffs Nature Preserve

18

Dinsmore Homestead

Middle Creek Park

P

To Ohio River, Big Bone Lick State Park, and 338

0   0.25   0.5

Mile

Key points:

The hike: Together, these two short loop walks in the rolling Middle Creek area of Boone County make a pleasant, leisurely half-day escape from the urban bustle of northern Kentucky. Both are easy rambles up wooded ridges covered with wildflowers and offering views—though limited by the surrounding trees—across the Ohio River into Indiana. Unfortunately, the two walks must be interrupted by a 2-mile drive because they are in separate preserves with no connecting trail. The two preserves are jointly managed by The Nature Conservancy and the Kentucky State Nature Preserve Commission.

The first loop is in the Boone County Cliffs preserve, a seventy-four-acre wooded tract bordering Middle Creek, a lively little stream that empties into the nearby Ohio River. The trail climbs a ridge above the creek, circles the head of a ravine, and descends along a brook that flows into Middle Creek just south of the parking lot. A sign at the parking lot explains the area's geological background.

From the sign, walk northwest to the little feeder stream, follow it north for a short distance, and then climb the log steps to the east. At mile 0.2, you come up to a level ridgeside spot that provides an overlook across the Ohio River valley, though the views are partially obstructed. Continuing up, you pass one of several old side trails that have been closed to prevent erosion.

After rounding the head of the ravine, the trail turns southwest, initially staying on the level ridgetop. At mile 1.4, you descend and cross the small Middle Creek tributary just north of Middle Creek Road. Follow the road east, and you are back at the parking lot at mile 1.7.

The second loop is in Dinsmore Woods, a 106-acre preserve that includes mature maple, oak, and ash trees. The tract was once part of a farm belonging to a prominent Boone County family, the Dinsmores, and has never been logged commercially. The nineteenth-century Dinsmore homestead, separately administered by a private foundation, is adjacent to the preserve and open to the public.

From the preserve sign on the north side of KY 18, you take a narrow dirt path ascending northwest. After curving northeast, you come to a level area that includes the walled Dinsmore family cemetery, and then climb north to the beginning of the loop at mile 0.3. Continuing to climb, you reach the ridgetop at mile 0.5, where there are limited views west across the Ohio. In March, here and at other spots along the trail, the ground is white with spring beauties.

After winding along the ridge, the trail curves east and descends partway down the hillside toward KY 18 before turning south and following a level contour. You have views across the Middle Creek valley. You also have noise

Dinsmore Woods Trail goes up a wooded ridge near Middle Creek.

from the considerable truck traffic on the highway below. At mile 1.2, you circle back to the beginning of the loop, and from there retrace your steps to the KY 18 trailhead at mile 1.7.

Options: Big Bone Lick State Park, which has several short hiking trails, is just a few miles south via KY 18 and KY 338.

48 Quiet Trails State Nature Preserve

Highlights:	An unspoiled spot on the banks of the Licking River, and good views of the rolling river valley.
Location:	North of Cynthiana.
Type of hike:	Day hike; loop.
Total distance:	2 miles.
Difficulty:	Easy.
Best months:	Any month.
Maps:	USGS Claysville; Quiet Trails map from the Kentucky State Nature Preserves Commission (502–573–2886).

Special considerations: Pets are not allowed in the preserve.

Finding the trailhead: From Cynthiana, take U.S. Highway 27 north about 10 miles and turn right onto Kentucky Highway 1284. Drive 2.8 miles to the town of Sunrise. At the four-way stop, go straight on gravel Pugh's Ferry Road; in 1.8 miles, turn right into the small parking area for the nature preserve. GPS: 38 33.409 N 84 13.627 W.

Parking and trailhead facilities: There's room for six cars, but no facilities.

Key points:
    0.0   Deep Hollow Trailhead.
    0.3   Licking River.
    1.9   Vista.

The hike: The name of this small preserve along the Licking River may sound a bit trite, but it's accurate. These 165 acres, tucked away in the rural northeast corner of Harrison County, are tranquil indeed. Most of the preserve is former farmland donated to the state in the early 1990s. From the fields, you get good views of the Licking River valley. This hike also takes you to a pretty riverside spot that was once the site of a trading post for river travelers. Now it's just you and the fish.

From the parking area, go through the gate. To your left is a box that should have trail maps and a sign-in sheet. Half a dozen trails weave through the preserve, and this loop uses three of them. First is Deep Hollow Trail, which starts just inside the gate on your right.

Deep Hollow Trail heads south and then east as it follows the preserve boundary downhill toward the river. Initially you are on a mowed grass path, a line of young hardwoods to your right. But you soon enter more mature woods on an old roadbed that follows a drainage area downhill. Disregard the connector trail that goes off to your left into the preserve interior. At mile 0.5, after crossing a small drainage, Deep Hollow Trail ends at its intersection with Challenger Trail. Note the old fence made of stones placed vertically instead of horizontally, an arrangement said to be more stable.

Quiet Trails State Nature Preserve

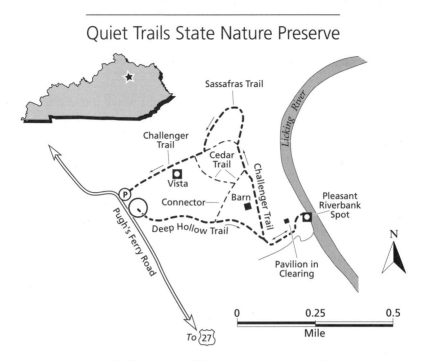

Turn right onto Challenger, and head east with a good view of a beautiful rolling pasture in the distance. If you pass a sign on your right for Cypress Trail, disregard it; that trail is no longer maintained. At mile 0.7, you enter a large clearing with a rickety-looking pavilion, outhouse, and picnic table. This is the site of the trading post and more recently a scout camping area. Continue east, keeping the woods on your right, and go through the tall grass, where you find a set of wooden steps down to the river. There are rocks along the water where you can sit and watch the stream lazily on its way to meet the Ohio River at Covington. The nature preserve map shows a short trail running north along the river, but it was overgrown when I was there.

Return to the clearing and backtrack to the Deep Hollow Trail intersection, where you turn right onto Challenger Trail. Follow Challenger uphill to the north, passing a barn on your left and, a little farther on, the entrance to Cedar Trail. Continue on Challenger until, at mile 1.5, you reach the top of the hill. Immediately on your right is the beginning of Sassafras Trail, a short loop through an attractive ravine.

Turning right onto Sassafras, you quickly come to a wire fence marking the preserve boundary and turn left (west). After jogging across a bridgeless drainage, you come to a wooden bridge over a seasonal stream, a delightful spot. From there you climb and, at mile 1.8, rejoin Challenger Trail next to a small animal-observation hut that looks across a grassy field.

Turn right onto Challenger and follow the trail, now a well-defined farm road, west past the other end of Cedar Trail and then past a small pond. Just after the pond, a sign points left to Prairie Vista. From this vantage point in

The rolling Licking River valley can be seen from Challenger Trail.

an open field a few steps off the trail, you enjoy a wonderful view south-east across the Licking River valley. From the overlook, you can either return to the trail or simply walk west through the field. Either way, the parking lot is just ahead at mile 2.

49 Kleber Wildlife Management Area

Highlights:	A pleasant walk on an old roadbed along a modest creek with a short side trip to a hilltop vista.
Location:	North of Frankfort.
Type of hike:	Day hike; out-and-back.
Total distance:	4.6 miles.
Difficulty:	Easy.
Best months:	Spring or fall.
Maps:	USGS Switzer and Stamping Ground; Kleber Wildlife Area map (office 502–535–6335).

Special considerations: State officials have discussed building a shooting range for state police at Kleber, a development that could affect all or part of the hiking route. Before heading out, call the Kleber office for current conditions.

Kleber Wildlife Management Area

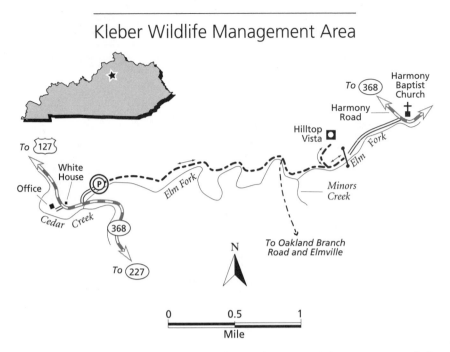

Finding the trailhead: From Frankfort, take U.S. Highway 127 north for about 15 miles and turn right (southeast) onto Kentucky Highway 368. In 5 miles, you come to a metal building on your right, which is the office for the wildlife area, and a white farmhouse on your left. Go 0.1 mile farther and turn left onto the narrow gravel road, which ends in 0.2 mile at a gate. Park near the gate, which is where the hike begins. GPS: 38 21.634 N 84 46.736 W.

Parking and trailhead facilities: You'll find space for about six cars, but no facilities.

Key points:
- 0.0   Trailhead.
- 1.6   Rock ford across Elm Fork.
- 1.9   Left turn onto old farm track leading up to hilltop field.

The hike: The state's John A. Kleber Wildlife Management Area covers 2,575 acres of hills and bottomlands in rural Owen and Franklin Counties about halfway between Frankfort and Owenton. The rolling terrain is covered with a mixture of brush, grassland, and woods—a habitat that attracts a variety of birds along with deer, raccoons, and groundhogs. For the most part, this hike follows an old roadbed along a little stream called Elm Fork. It's all fairly level, except for a short detour up a grassy hilltop to enjoy a 360-degree view of the rolling countryside. There is nothing spectacular about the creek or the scenery along it, and in hot weather this is likely to be sticky, buggy territory. But in spring and fall, this is a delightful walk along a quiet country

Near its eastern end, the Kleber Trail leaves the woods and meanders through fields.

road. The wildlife area is named for a Frankfort resident who left money in his will to help the state buy the initial acreage in the early 1950s.

From the gate, go east on the old two-track dirt road, which is an extension of the gravel road you took in from KY 368. Beyond the gate, travel is restricted to foot and horseback. On your right, between you and the creek, is a field covered with grass, scrub bushes, and small trees; on your left is a cedar forest. The vegetation lining both sides of the road, however, soon becomes more substantial and attractive. As you head upstream, the road veers alternately toward and away from the creek, putting you one minute on the bank and the next on a wooded ridge above the stream. At both mile 1 and 1.3, the road climbs a good way from the creek.

At mile 1.6, you pass a line of rocks lying across the creek to make a ford. On the other side a path goes up the bank and heads south to Oakland Branch Road near the hamlet of Elmville on KY 368—a distance of about 1.5 miles. Continuing east on the creekside roadbed, you pass the mouth of Minors Creek and come into an area of open fields. For a nice break from the bottomland, take the old farm track that veers off to your left at mile 1.9 (GPS 38 21.723 N 84 44.893 W). The rough roadbed climbs steadily northwest and then northeast for 0.2 mile to a treeless hilltop field with a grand view of the ridges that surround the Kleber area. This is an especially nice spot at sunset.

After returning to the creekside road, you continue east and at mile 2.5 come to a gate that marks the eastern end of the hike. Beyond the gate, a rough gravel road leads 0.4 mile to Harmony Road and Harmony Baptist Church, an attractive white structure built on land donated for the church in 1851. Between the gate and Harmony Road is a shooting range open to the public. At the gate, turn around and take the creekside road back to your car, which you reach at mile 4.6.

50 Buckley Wildlife Sanctuary

Highlights: A good mix of open fields and wooded areas, along with a small, beautiful pond.
Location: South of Frankfort.
Type of hike: Day hike; loop.
Total distance: 2.4 miles.
Difficulty: Easy.
Best months: Any month.
Maps: USGS Frankfort East; Buckley Wildlife Sanctuary map (859–873–5711).

Special considerations: Pets are not allowed.

Finding the trailhead: The sanctuary is 6.5 miles from the intersection of Interstate 64 and U.S. Highway 60 at Frankfort. Going east on US 60, just past the interstate, turn right onto Kentucky Highway 1681, and in 2.5 miles turn left onto KY 1659. In 1.6 more miles, turn right onto KY 1964, and in

Buckley Wildlife Sanctuary

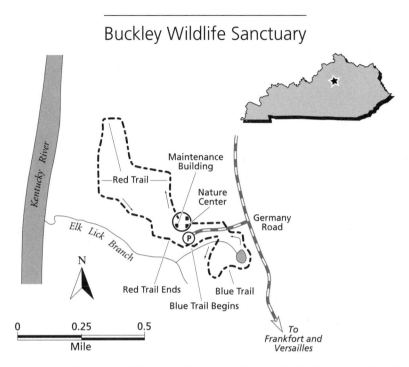

another 1.1 miles turn right onto Germany Road. Take Germany Road 1.3 miles and turn left at the BUCKLEY WILDLIFE SANCTUARY sign. Drive to the end of the road and park in the gravel lot. The trailhead is just north of the lot, up the incline. (Coming from Versailles on US 60, turn left onto KY 1685 and follow the signs to the sanctuary.) GPS: 38 08.167 N 84 51.340 W.

Parking and trailhead facilities: There's space for several dozen cars, along with water and rest rooms.

Key points:
- 0.0   Red Trailhead.
- 1.4   Blue Trailhead.
- 2.1   Pond.

The hike: The trails on this small, privately owned preserve near the Kentucky River are geared to families. The distances are short, the terrain level, and the interpretive materials easy to understand. So for families with little ones, this is a perfect place for an afternoon hike. But even if you don't have children—or maybe you just want to get away from some—these 374 acres can provide a couple of hours of pleasant walking. You will find a good mix of woods and open fields, and a lovely little pond near the end of this 2-mile loop.

This hike combines the sanctuary's two longest trails—the Red and Blue—into one loop, although they can easily be separated since both start and end near the parking lot. Hikers are expected to pay an admission fee, currently $3.00 for adults, $2.00 for children. It's an honor system; you put the money

The cattail-lined pond is near the end of the Blue Trail.

in the well next to the parking lot. For each of its trails, the sanctuary has a written guide explaining plants and environmental conditions you see along the way. You can borrow a copy to take with you on the hike. Copies are kept at the end of the message board next to the well.

The sanctuary was founded in the 1960s when a Lexington woman, Mrs. Emma E. Buckley, set aside this farm as a memorial to her late husband. The handsome beige farmhouse near the parking lot, now the Emma E. Buckley Center, is the sanctuary's nature center and gift shop. The grounds and trails are closed on Monday, Tuesday, and holidays.

This hike starts with the Red Trail, which begins on the rise north of the parking lot beyond a large maintenance building. The trail, marked by red-painted cutouts of a fox, heads north on a broad dirt path into a thin forest along the edge of a field. You soon emerge into an open field and follow a fence west before turning north along a tree line separating two fields.

After again turning west, the trail descends slightly and enters more mature woods. At mile 0.6, it turns to begin a long leg south, initially on the edge of the field and then in the woods. You are now on the opposite side of the field you were walking north along several minutes ago. The Kentucky River is below you on your right; you can't see the stream through the trees, but as you move south you can see the palisades.

The trail winds south and then east through the woods above the Elk Lick Branch, joining a section of the White Trail—a third loop—before ending on the northwest edge of the parking lot at mile 1.4. Skirting the lot's south side along the woods, you quickly come to the other end of the White Trail and the beginning of the Blue Trail.

Following the Blue Trail, you descend southeast into the woods and take a power-line clearing east a short distance before turning south and crossing a fork of Elk Lick Branch. You then wind eastward and come to the south end of an acre-and-a-half pond lined with cattails. The trail guide says the pond also has ducks and muskrats. I didn't see any, but even without them it's a delightful spot, the highlight of the hike.

Continuing to the pond's north end at mile 2.1, you climb easily to the north and then follow a power-line clearing west to the sanctuary's entrance road. You go west a few steps along the road and then cross it to continue west along a tree line. At mile 2.4, you come to a grass lawn east of the nature center and near the redbrick home of the sanctuary manager. Your car is just a few steps away.

51 Raven Run Nature Sanctuary

Highlights:	A wooded walk to a Kentucky River overlook and into a scenic creek gorge.
Location:	About 30 minutes south of downtown Lexington.
Type of hike:	Day hike; loop.
Total distance:	3.9 miles.
Difficulty:	Easy.
Best months:	Any month.
Maps:	USGS Coletown; Raven Run Nature Sanctuary Trail map (859–272–6105).

Special considerations: Pets are not allowed.

Finding the trailhead: From exit 99 off Interstate 75, take U.S. Highway 25/421 (Old Richmond Road) north toward Lexington; after 5 miles, turn left onto Jacks Creek Road. Stay on Jacks Creek Road through several sharp turns and a change in its numerical designation, and in 5 miles turn left at the sign for Raven Run Nature Sanctuary. In 0.4 mile, turn right into the visitor parking lot; only employees are allowed to drive beyond this point. From the lot, take the paved walkway 0.2 mile northwest, then northeast, to the sanctuary office. The trail starts at the gate just north of the office. GPS: 37 53.378 N 84 23.740 W.

Parking and trailhead facilities: You'll find space for about fifty cars; picnic tables and rest rooms at the parking lot; and nature displays and a drink machine at the sanctuary office.

Key points:
- 0.0 Red Trailhead.
- 1.0 Kentucky River Overlook.
- 2.0 Old grist mill site on Raven Run.

Raven Run Nature Sanctuary

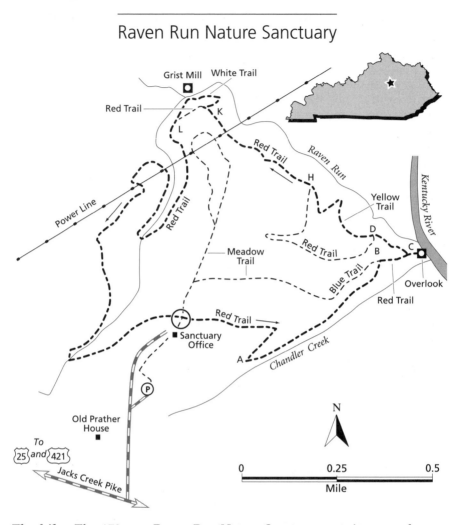

The hike: The 470-acre Raven Run Nature Sanctuary gets its name from a scenic creek that meanders through southeastern Fayette County and empties into the Kentucky River just below a 100-foot bluff. The area was originally settled and farmed two centuries ago; a house built by the Prather family in the late 1700s on a Revolutionary War land grant still stands. Today, run by the Lexington-Fayette County government, the sanctuary is exactly that—a delightful wooded area where you can get away from almost all signs of urban life. It has deer, wild turkeys, more than 300 species of wildflowers, and a well-developed system of trails totaling about 8 miles. For the most part, this hike follows the longest trail—the Red Trail—in a counterclockwise loop that takes you to the bluff overlooking the Kentucky River and then down into the Raven Run gorge at the site of a nineteenth-century gristmill. A trail map available at the office includes information about the mill and other historical points along the way. (To make it easier to read, the map in this book purposely excludes some of the shorter trails.)

The Kentucky River Overlook provides commanding views.

At the gate just north of the sanctuary office, turn right (east) and follow the sign for the overlook. Following a fence built of fieldstones in the 1800s, the dirt path soon begins a gentle descent through a young forest, then makes a sharp right turn followed at mile 0.3 by a sharp left turn. At the latter, there's a trail marker labeled A. Like the other lettered markers you will see throughout the hike, this one shows how many miles remains to complete the circuit—3.6. The mileage figures on the two sides of each marker differ, because each side shows the remaining distance for that direction of the loop.

From A, the trail follows the ravine made by Chandler Creek on its way to the Kentucky River. At marker B, the Blue Trail intersects on your left; you continue to follow the Red Trail, which curves right and comes to a set of stairs. At the bottom, you come to C and a short side trail leading right to a rock outcropping at mile 1.0. This is the Kentucky River Overlook, and it would be hard to find a better rest spot. The view of the river below makes you feel like a soaring bird. Just to the north you see the mouth of Raven Run. In fall the trees covering the riverside cliff make a handsome tapestry of oranges, yellows, and browns.

Returning to C, you take the Red Trail west as it follows the level ridgeline above Raven Run to D, where the Red Trail goes left and the Yellow Trail descends right into an attractive area of wildflowers. This is a worthwhile detour, the first of two on the hike. Following the Yellow Trail, you come down to a quiet stream at mile 1.2 and then climb north to rejoin the Red Trail at H. The Yellow Trail, apparently little used, is faint, but there are enough yellow blazes on the trees to keep you from getting lost. Because of this and the upcoming detour, the mileage figures you see on the Red Trail markers will at times be slightly off from your actual mileage.

From H, the Red Trail is level as it continues along the ridge near the top of the Raven Run gorge. At mile 1.9, after passing beneath a power line, you come to K. Here the Red Trail goes left and the White Trail descends right into the gorge—another detour worth taking. Following the White Trail, at mile 2 you reach the banks of Raven Run and the stone foundation of a grist mill built in 1820, said to be typical of the mills that once operated in the Kentucky River valley. Here Raven Run, which is the sanctuary's eastern boundary, flows over rocks, making this a beautiful spot to stop and rest. Concerned about liability and littering, the sanctuary does not allow wading or picnicking along the creek. As of this writing, construction of a creekside observation deck is being planned for this location.

From the creek, the White Trail makes a short climb back up the gorge to rejoin the Red Trail at L The Red Trail, which you take from here on, goes south, passes beneath the power line a second time, and, at mile 2.5, crosses a branch of Raven Run. From here you follow the streambed northeast to another meeting with the power line. At mile 3, after crossing beneath the power line twice more and turning southwest, you skirt a meadow and drop down to cross the same branch of Raven Run that you crossed less than a mile earlier. You now head northeast and, at mile 3.9, arrive at the gate, completing the loop. Turn right for the sanctuary office and parking lot.

52 Kentucky River Palisades

Highlights: The banks of the Kentucky River beneath towering palisades that line both sides of the stream.
Location: Tom Dorman State Nature Preserve, south of Nicholasville.
Type of hike: Day hike; loop.
Total distance: 2 miles.
Difficulty: Moderate.
Best months: Any month.
Maps: USGS Wilmore.

Finding the trailhead: From Nicholasville, take U.S. Highway 27 south for about 10 miles and, after crossing the Kentucky River, turn right onto Kentucky Highway 1845. Go 0.9 mile and turn right onto the narrow road by a small church. Drive another 0.7 mile—making sure to go straight at the fork—and park in the gravel lot at the end of the road. GPS: 37 45.914 N 84 37.628 W.

Parking and trailhead facilities: There's space for twenty cars, but no facilities.

Key points:
- 0.0 Palisades Trailhead.
- 0.9 Knight's Ferry Trail.
- 1.0 Kentucky River.

The hike: In the early evening the tops of the Kentucky River Palisades gleam in the setting sun. This is a good hike anytime, but it's especially nice

The Palisades rise dramatically above the north side of the Kentucky River.

Kentucky River Palisades

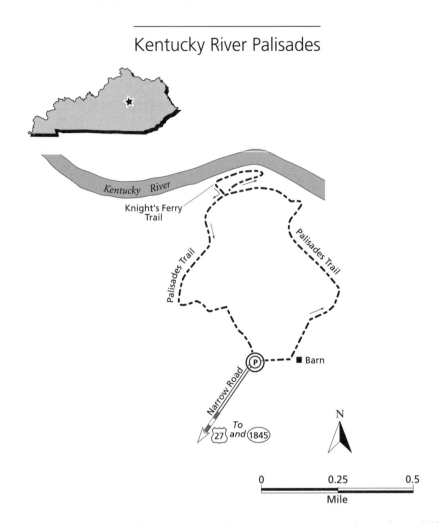

when the last rays of the day are lighting up the 200- and 300-foot cliffs that line the river. This short hike takes you from the top of the gorge on the river's south side down to what used to be a ferry landing, although nothing is now left except the remains of a house. Most of the walking is on old roadbeds, and despite the elevation change, the grades are not severe. Originally this approximately 365-acre area was called the Palisades State Nature Preserve. It was renamed in 1999 to honor a former director of the Kentucky River Authority.

One end of the loop starts at the west end of the parking lot, the other at the east end. You can take either; the west half of the hike is a bit steeper. These directions start from the east end. The trail is not blazed, but it is well trod and easily followed.

Going east on an old roadbed, you come quickly to a barn, where you turn northeast onto a grass path and enter a forest of young trees. As the trail curves north, the woods become more mature. You are descending, gradually at first. But when the trail, now an old dirt road, turns west, the going gets steeper. It's at this point that you also get your first good view of the palisades along the opposite shore. At mile 0.9, just after the grade becomes gentle once again, you come to a sign on your right for Knight's Ferry Trail, which loops to the river and rejoins Palisades Trail a few steps farther west.

Turning right onto Knight's Ferry Trail, you immediately pass stone ruins that were once the home of a family who ran the ferry and farmed these bottomlands, according to a state nature preserve official. The trail winds east and comes to the riverbank at mile 1. It then turns west to parallel the river for a short distance before returning to Palisades Trail.

Back on the main trail at mile 1.2, you continue west for only a few steps before turning left and beginning the climb up the side of the gorge. The trail is steep at first but tapers off. When it turns southwest, you even enjoy a level stretch. You dip down twice to cross drainages before the final up-hill push, which gets you to the west side of the parking lot at mile 2.

53 Central Kentucky Wildlife Management Area

Highlights: Fields and wooded areas full of birds, small game, and flowering plants.
Location: South of Richmond.
Type of hike: Day hike; loop.
Total distance: Any distance you choose; there are no set trails.
Difficulty: Easy.
Best months: Autumn (definitely not July and August).
Maps: USGS Moberly and Bighill.

Special considerations: This is a do-it-yourself hiking area. There are no established trails; you compose your own route on mowed paths and horse tracks.

Finding the trailhead: From Richmond, take U.S. Highway 421 south for about 9 miles; at Kingston, turn left onto Dreyfus Road. Go 2 miles and turn right onto gravel Old Muddy Creek Road. The wildlife area extends south for about a mile on both sides of the road. To hike the 2.2-mile route I took, go 0.4 mile south and turn right into the parking area. GPS: 37 37.775 N 84 12.095 W.

Parking and trailhead facilities: There's room at the parking area I used (one of several along Old Muddy Creek Road) for half a dozen cars; no facilities.

The hike: Marcia Schroder, manager of this 1,690-acre state wildlife area, says fall is her favorite time of year here, and it's easy to see why. The grasses and stalks that cover the fields are golden brown, and the trees that line them are rich in oranges and yellows. And—of no small importance—there are no

Central Kentucky Wildlife Management Area

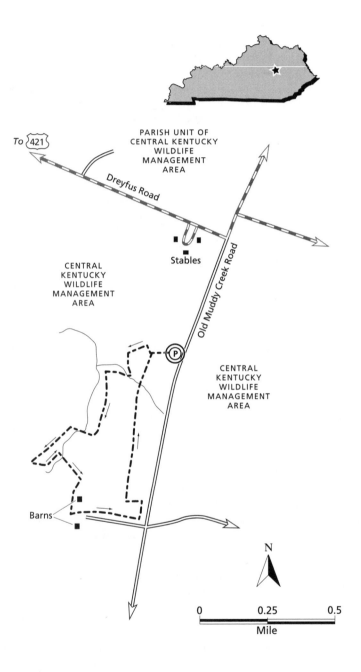

PARISH UNIT OF
CENTRAL KENTUCKY
WILDLIFE
MANAGEMENT
AREA

To (421)

Dreyfus Road

Stables

CENTRAL
KENTUCKY
WILDLIFE
MANAGEMENT
AREA

Old Muddy Creek Road

P

CENTRAL
KENTUCKY
WILDLIFE
MANAGEMENT
AREA

Barns

N

0   0.25   0.5
Mile

bugs. Bugs are one reason you don't want to come in the heat of summer. Another is that there are no mowed swaths through the fields, so hiking is difficult.

The mowing, which starts in late August, produces a labyrinth that lets you go just about anywhere in the wildlife area you want. On a gorgeous afternoon of deep October colors, I walked to two picturesque barns near the south boundary. With a GPS, I pinpointed the barns before I started out. Then, following mowed paths, horse tracks, and tree-lined streambeds, I worked my way toward them from the parking area, a round-trip of 2.2 miles.

I had a great time, and have included a map of my route as an example of what you can do here. The terrain is flat and without points of special note. The enjoyment here is walking, watching for wildlife, and soaking up the sounds and smells of rural central Kentucky.

One piece of advice: Supposedly the soil in this wildlife area doesn't drain well and the ground gets soggy. I was there in a dry spell, and the clumps of dried dirt were hard as rock—and tough on feet. I was glad I was wearing boots.

The Central Kentucky Wildlife Management Area is used heavily for dog trials. On my walk I came nose to nose with a cute little beagle, followed closely by his owner and the trial judges, all on horseback and all looking much more serious about the proceedings than did the beagle. Hunting for doves, squirrel, deer, and some waterfowl is allowed.

At the information stand, there are free copies of a list of birds seen at the wildlife area—from common wrens to rare hawks and waterfowl. The stand is located next to the stables on the right side of Dreyfus Road, just before the turn onto Old Muddy Creek Road (office 606–986–4130).

An old barn stands near the south boundary of Central Kentucky Wildlife Management Area.

54 Berea Forest

Highlights:	Five overlooks with striking views of rolling central Kentucky farmland.
Location:	East of Berea.
Type of hike:	Day hike; loop.
Total distance:	6.7 miles.
Difficulty:	Moderate.
Best months:	Any month.
Maps:	USGS Bighill; Indian Fort Mountain Trails map from Berea College forestry office (859-985-3587).

Special considerations: Save this hike for a clear day; the views are terrific.

Finding the trailhead: From exit 76 off Interstate 75, take Kentucky Highway 21 east through the city of Berea. In 4.3 miles from the interstate, turn left at the sign for Indian Fort Theatre and park in the lot. The trail starts at the north end of the lot at the wooden gate. GPS: 37 33.260 N 84 14.470 W.

Parking and trailhead facilities: You'll find a large parking lot with space for dozens of cars, but no facilities. A sign warns that at dusk the lot is locked and cars towed.

Key points:
0.0	Trailhead.
1.4	East Pinnacle.
2.7	Eagles Nest.
3.3	Buzzards Roost.
4.3	Devils Kitchen.
4.5	Indian Fort Lookout.
5.4	West Pinnacle.

The hike: Located in the town of the same name, Berea College is a highly rated liberal arts school that gives a tuition-free education to promising youngsters from Appalachia. In fact, inability to pay is a requirement for admission; students work, instead. In addition to the pleasant campus, the college owns some 8,000 acres of forestland, much of it donated in the early 1900s to give the college timber income and forestry demonstration sites. Included in these holdings is Indian Fort Mountain, a popular hiking area full of cliffs and overlooks. It's a tradition that on one beautiful day each autumn, the college cancels classes and the students troop out to Indian Fort Mountain for hikes and fellowship. The area is open to the public, but camping is not allowed. This hike takes you to the most impressive of the observation points.

Indian Fort Mountain is crisscrossed by many trails, a good number unmarked by signs. Also, be aware that the college map of the area includes trails that are no longer maintained. From the north end of the parking lot, head north on the asphalt walkway through an area used for outdoor crafts fairs. You quickly come to Indian Fort Theatre, an amphitheater, on your

Berea Forest

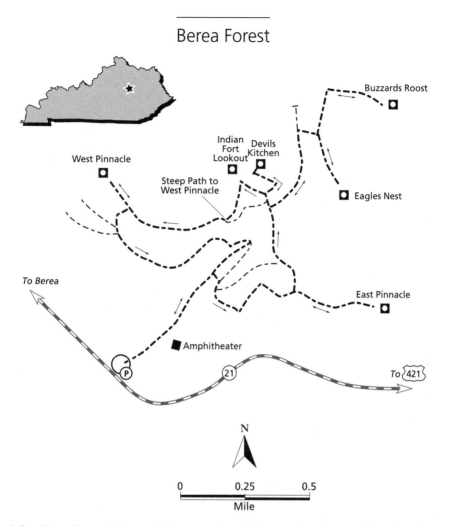

West Pinnacle

Indian Fort Lookout

Devils Kitchen

Steep Path to West Pinnacle

Buzzards Roost

Eagles Nest

East Pinnacle

To Berea

To 421

Amphitheater

P

21

N

0   0.25   0.5
Mile

right. Here the path turns into gravel and dirt, and a sign explains that humans roamed this area in the period from 100 B.C. to A.D. 400. The forest is oak-hickory with pines and yellow poplars. Much of this land was farmed at one time, and the hardwoods are tall but thin. At mile 0.4, after climbing gently along a streambed on your left, you turn right onto a narrower, steeper dirt path. This junction, the first after the amphitheater, was not marked when I took the hike; the college has a hard time keeping signs in place. Almost immediately after turning, you come to a second junction, and again you take a right. This is rapidly followed by a third junction and right turn.

Following the level contour south, then east, and finally north, the trail passes through woods badly burned in a 1987 arson fire. You also see scars from a less severe 1999 blaze. At mile 1, the trail dead-ends into another path; you turn right and climb to the southeast. When you reach a stand of small pines, there are views to the east; a number of rock outcroppings make inviting rest stops. I did a double take when I spied what appeared to be a goat

Central Kentucky farms are visible from the trail in the Berea Forest.

scampering along the rocky ledge. Sure enough, the college forester later confirmed that several feral animals had taken up residence. At mile 1.4, the trail ends on a large outcropping named East Pinnacle. The commanding views east across the knobs and north across the flat Bluegrass make this a spot to enjoy.

From East Pinnacle, retrace your steps for 0.4 mile to the last junction. But instead of turning left the way you came, continue straight (north). Climbing, you reach a well-marked intersection at mile 2.1 where a large sign points left to Indian Fort Lookout and right to Eagles Nest and Buzzards Roost. You will eventually go to Indian Fort Lookout, but for now turn right and head north to Eagles Nest. Traversing a level stretch of thin woods, you come to an unmarked fork at mile 2.4; take the right prong heading east. (The left prong is no longer maintained and eventually peters out in brush.) You quickly come to another unmarked junction and again take a right. Walking south through pines, you come out on a high, rocky bluff at mile 2.7. This is Eagles Nest. There are lots of boulders to climb on, but if children are along, watch them carefully; it's straight down.

From Eagles Nest, retrace your steps to the last junction and continue north. The trail curves east and follows a rocky ridgetop to still another overlook at mile 3.3. This is Buzzards Roost, and from it you see the knobs below woven together by a quilt of tidy farm fields. From here you return to the well-marked intersection with the large sign, taking the broad dirt path northwest toward Indian Fort Lookout. When the path forks, you go right and immediately see a side trail on your right marked DEVILS KITCHEN, which is a large rock shelter about 0.1 mile off the main trail. To reach it, follow the side trail down the ridgeside and then west along the base of the cliff.

After returning to the main trail, you continue northwest, crossing over the top of the cliff that holds Devils Kitchen. The trail forks a couple of times; each time you bear right. At mile 4.5, you come out on Indian Fort Lookout—a broad outcropping with fine views to the northwest. A number of paths snake across this well-used area and can be confusing. But simply follow the cliff edge southward, keeping the drop-off on your right, and you soon come to another overlook, this one with good views looking south. Here it's easy to get stumped, because the trail to West Pinnacle—your next destination—is hard to find. The only path immediately visible goes northeast back toward Indian Fort Lookout, which you don't want. But if you closely examine the boulders on the west edge of the overlook, you will find a steep dirt path—almost a chute—cutting down through the rocks on the west side of the cliff. This is what you take (GPS 37 33.834 N 84 14.077 W). You will need both hands, but it's not dangerous, and you quickly reach the bottom.

Heading west on a dirt path, level at first, you soon climb up one side of a wooded peak and down the other. After passing a narrow side trail leading off to your left, you make your way northwest over a rocky section and, at mile 5.4, come to a mushroom-shaped tower of rock called West Pinnacle. There is a way to get on top, although at first you may not think so. Midway up the west side of the huge rock, there's a ledge. Put your feet on the ledge and, holding the top of the rock with your hands, inch your way to the middle of the west side. There you will find a large hole running down the rock that looks as if it were made by a giant corkscrew. Bracing your body against the inside of the hole, you can push yourself up and come out on the flat top of West Pinnacle. You will feel like a true climber. Children should not try it on their own, however; a fall could cause serious injury.

From here, retrace your steps to the narrow side trail you passed shortly before reaching West Pinnacle. Take this trail, now on your right, and descend initially west and then south to a wider path. Turn left onto this wider path; almost immediately you come to another trail and again turn left. Heading south and then east, this trail takes you through a level stretch of large hardwoods before intersecting two trails at mile 6.2, both going southwest. You turn right onto the trail farther to your right, which is the main route back to the parking lot. You soon pass the unmarked trail to East Pinnacle that you took at the beginning of your hike. Continuing southwest past the amphitheater, you are back at your car at mile 6.7.

55 Shakertown at Pleasant Hill

Highlights: A walk from Shakertown down to the Kentucky River, partially on a roadbed built by the Shakers in the early 1800s.
Location: The Shaker village of Pleasant Hill, northeast of Harrodsburg.
Type of hike: Day hike; out-and-back.
Total distance: 3.4 miles.
Difficulty: Easy.
Best months: Any month.
Maps: USGS Wilmore; Shakertown map (office 800-734-5611).

Special considerations: Shakertown is a restored village owned by a private nonprofit educational organization, and a fee is charged for admission. As this is written, visitors are allowed to hike to the river free of charge but should be aware that most of the grounds are for paying guests.

Finding the trailhead: From Harrodsburg, take U.S. Highway 68 northeast for 7 miles and turn left at the Shakertown entrance directly across from Kentucky Highway 33. Park in the first lot. Directions for this hike start from the information booth just north of the lot. GPS: 37 49.078 N 84 44.418 W.

Parking and trailhead facilities: There's room for numerous cars; rest rooms are found near the parking lot; restaurant and hotel accommodations are available nearby in the Shaker village.

Key points:
0.0   Beginning of gravel path.
0.3   East end of the village.
0.7   Gate to the 1826 roadbed.
1.4   Stairway down to the road.
1.7   River landing.

The hike: The Shakers were members of a religious sect that began in England in the early 1700s and came to America about the time of the Revolution, settling first in New York and then spreading to other states. The Pleasant Hill community, located on a plateau above the Kentucky River, started in 1805 and grew to 500 people before dying out in the early 1900s. It was a fate not too surprising given the group's teachings against marrying and having children. Nonetheless, the Shakers—the name comes from their movements during religious observance—were an industrious lot, and this handsomely restored village is a testament to their talents. Some fifteen buildings are open on the self-guided tour; admission ranges from $10.00 for adults to $3.50 for children.

Among other things, the Shakers were successful traders, and they moved their wares to the marketplace on the Kentucky River. This hike follows the route the Shakers took to get their goods from the hilltop village down to

Shakertown at Pleasant Hill

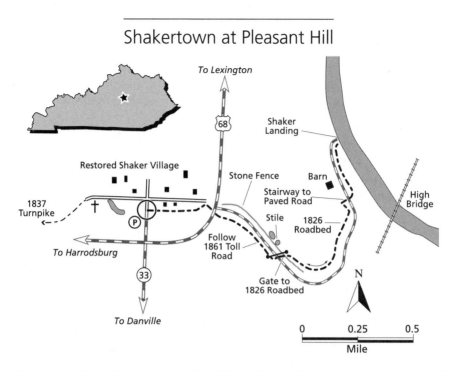

To Lexington

68

Shaker Landing

Restored Shaker Village

Stone Fence   Barn

Stairway to Paved Road

1837 Turnpike

Stile   1826 Roadbed

High Bridge

P

To Harrodsburg

Follow 1861 Toll Road

Gate to 1826 Roadbed

N

33

To Danville

0   0.25   0.5

Mile

the river landing. It's an easy, delightful stroll that alternates between a paved country lane and the rocky path that the Shakers cut out of the cliffside in 1826. At the river, there is a Shaker-built barn with exhibits, and a paddleboat that (for a fee) will take you on a one-hour river excursion.

From the parking lot, go north to the information booth and take the gravel path running east behind the main (admission-required) village street. You quickly come to another parking lot, where you take a paved road and continue east past a field that may be growing tobacco or other traditional crops. At mile 0.3 from the information booth, you reach the east end of the village. There you let yourself through an interesting gate contraption and walk southeast toward US 68. Just before the highway, you navigate a second, similar gate.

After crossing the highway, you take the narrow road on the other side and go downhill (southeast.) Though paved, the road is little used and pleasant. An old stone fence lines the left side, and rolling farmland is all around. This was originally a toll road built by the Shakers in 1861 as a replacement for the more rudimentary version they constructed in 1826.

In the stone fence near two small ponds, there is a stile—farm lingo for steps over a fence. You are supposed to cross the stile and take a path that leads to the 1826 roadbed. When I took this hike, however, the other side of the fence was overgrown and impassable. So I continued down the road a short distance, and at mile 0.7 climbed over a locked farm gate. On the other side was the start of the path, which parallels the paved road all the way to the river.

An old stone fence lines the 1861 toll road built by the Shakers.

Initially the path is a mowed swath through a grassy field lined with wild-flowers. But after passing the ruins of a stone building, it narrows and runs along the base of a rocky cliff. This is the roadbed dating back to 1826. The cliff is on your left, and the paved road on your right far below. The drop-off to the road is severe enough in certain spots that you will want to take the hands of small children.

As the path turns sharply left and parallels the Kentucky River, you get a good view of the beautiful, tall palisades that line the river. You also get a good view of a railroad bridge spanning the river gorge high above you. Built in 1877, this is High Bridge, a well-known landmark.

At mile 1.4, you come to a metal stairway that takes you down to the paved road. Following it, you soon pass an 1866-built barn that contains exhibits on the Shakers' river activities. After passing the foundation of a Shaker ware-house, you come to the river landing at mile 1.7. If it's not out on a sight-seeing trip, the sternwheeler *Dixie Belle* will be tied up here. (Tickets for the riverboat can be purchased at the landing.) Return to Shakertown the same way you came.

Options: Shakertown also allows nonpaying hikers to walk the 1837 Turn-pike—a gravel road extending west from the west end of the village. Walk-ing northwest from the parking lot, you reach the start of the turnpike near the village cemetery. Aditionally, in 2000 Shakertown began developing new trails on property farther removed from the village.

Central Kentucky—South

The southern half of central Kentucky is dominated by public parks, and the following hikes explore the best of the offerings—three state parks built on the banks of man-made lakes and the national park land above Mammoth Cave. These areas are larger and not quite as tame as the public tracts available in the northern half of central Kentucky. Consequently, these hikes are longer and a bit more demanding than those in the previous section. You should find the walking entirely enjoyable.

56 Green River Lake

Highlights:	A walk up, down, and across the low ridges bordering Green River Lake, with stops along the shoreline.
Location:	Green River Lake State Park, south of Campbellsville.
Type of hike:	Day hike; loop.
Total distance:	6.1 miles.
Difficulty:	Moderate.
Best months:	Any month.
Maps:	USGS Campbellsville; state park trail map (office 270–465–8255).

Finding the trailhead: From Campbellsville, take Kentucky Highway 55 south for 4 miles and turn left (east) onto Kentucky 1061. In 1.2 miles—where KY 1061 makes a sharp right turn—go straight on Robin Road. In 0.4 mile, turn right into the lot marked for trailhead parking. (From the south, turn right onto KY 1061 off KY 55 when you're 14 miles north of Columbia.) GPS: 37 16.962 N   85 20.774 W.

Parking and trailhead facilities: There's space for three dozen cars. No facilities are available at the trailhead, but you'll find drinking water, rest rooms, and a campground nearby in the state park. The park entrance is 0.3 mile farther east on KY 1061.

Key points:

0.0	Trailhead.
1.2	Lakeshore.
3.5–3.7	Lakeshore at South Point.

The hike: The Green River is one of Kentucky's major streams. In the 1960s, as part of the flood-control plan for the Ohio and Mississippi Rivers, the Corps of Engineers dammed the Green just south of Campbellsville, 300 river miles from where it empties into the Ohio near Henderson. The resulting 8,200-acre

212

Green River Lake

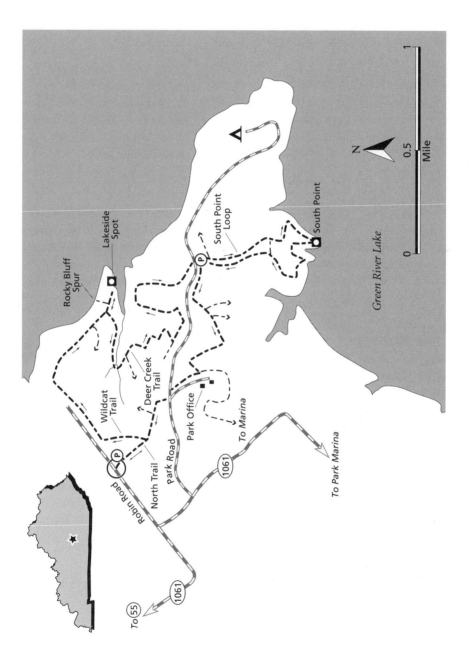

reservoir snakes 25 miles through low-lying ridges in the rolling farmland of Taylor and Adair Counties. This hike loops through the 1,331-acre park developed by the state in the early 1970s on the west side of the lake at one of its widest sections.

The park terrain is not spectacular, but this is an enjoyable walk through a good mix of easily maneuvered ridgetops and bottomlands, including visits to two attractive lakeside spots. The park has lots of birds as well as deer and wild turkeys. The ridgetops were farmed before the reservoir was built, and so are now thinly wooded with cedars and young hardwoods. But more mature growth covers the low-lying areas around the lake.

Park personnel and volunteer groups of hikers, equestrians, and mountain bikers have developed an ambitious system of trails totaling nearly 30 miles. Indeed, there are so many trails going in so many directions, it can all be a bit confusing. When I visited, park ranger David Goode was working to update the trail signs and park map, steps that will definitely help. But you should have no trouble following this loop route, which uses a number of different park trails.

From the southeast corner of the parking lot, head southeast into the low-lying woods on an old roadbed covered with wood chips. This first stretch is part of North Trail, one of the main loops through the park. At mile 0.2, you turn left on a narrower path called Wildcat Trail, which goes north at first and then northeast. There are no blazes, but the path is well worn and impossible to lose. Disregard the unmarked trail joining on your left, and another on your right. After curving southeast, you pass Ranger Trail leading off to your right; disregard it as well.

At mile 1, as you begin to descend gradually, you come to a fork, which was unmarked when I was there. Continue straight ahead, and in a few more steps you come to another fork, this one with a sign. The left prong, marked ROCKY BLUFF SPUR, goes to a small bluff overlooking the lake, but I took it only far enough to drop down to the lakeshore on an old roadbed. This quiet, rocky spot on an isolated inlet is well worth the modest climb down and up.

After your waterside rest, retrace your steps to the fork and follow the other prong, which leads to what is called Devils Canyon, a dramatic name for a scenic but shallow ravine. Going west, with the lake below on your left, you drop into the ravine, and at mile 1.7 cross two clear, rock-bottomed streams just before they join together for their final dash to the lake. This is another pretty spot, though rainfall and the lake's level will affect the streams' robustness.

From the streams, you climb steeply up the ridgeside to a trail junction. Here Eagle Ridge Trail goes right, and you turn left onto Deer Creek Trail. For the next mile, you remain at a fairly constant elevation as the trail follows the ridge contour first south, then north, and once again south. This last leg brings you at mile 2.9 to the park road just across from a small parking lot.

Cross the road and, on the south side of the parking lot, find two trails going into the woods. Take the one on your left to begin a loop south to the lakeshore; the loop returns to the parking lot on the trail to your right. A few steps from the lot, you come to a fork and go right on South Point Loop.

(The left prong, labeled WINDY RIDGE LOOP goes to the park campground and boat ramp.)

Going south, the South Point Loop trail is initially level, but at mile 3.3 begins to descend. At mile 3.5, you reach the lakefront, though you are on a cliff above the water. Turn right and parallel the shoreline south. At mile 3.7, you arrive at a point of land with flat rocks that go down to the water just like steps. This is a fine spot for sunning, and you have a view south to the dam.

From here the trail leaves the shore and heads north and west as it winds around two inlets. You then climb back up the ridge, curve north, and reach the small parking lot at mile 4.8. From this lot, take the path going west along the south side of the park road. Initially on the open shoulder, the path soon turns into the woods at a sign identifying this as the trail connecting the campground at the east end of the park with the marina at the west end near the dam. Although continuing to parallel the road, you hardly know it's there. This is another nice stretch.

After veering from the roadside, the trail passes the two ends of a loop trail that goes south on a ridge. Continue past them. At mile 5.4, you leave the campground-marina trail and take a short side trail right to the park office and maintenance buildings. There you turn right and follow the driveway to the main park road. Cross the road and, on the other side, take the path going northwest through the field. The path quickly runs into an old roadbed—the same one you took at the hike's start. Following the roadbed northwest, you pass a right turn for Ranger and Eagle Ridge Trails; a little farther on you pass the Wildcat Trail turnoff that you took earlier. You reach your car at mile 6.1.

Rocky ledges form steps to Green River Lake at South Point Loop.

57 Lake Cumberland

Highlights: A ridgetop walk along Lake Cumberland, plus stops at the shoreline and an overlook high above the lake.
Location: Lake Cumberland State Resort Park, southwest of Somerset.
Type of hike: Day hike; loop.
Total distance: 3.8 miles.
Difficulty: Easy.
Best months: Any month.
Maps: USGS Jamestown; state park's *Visitors Guide* (park 270–343–3111).

Finding the trailhead: From exit 62 off the Cumberland Parkway at Russell Springs, take U.S. Highway 127 south for 13 miles and turn left onto the state park entrance road marked by a sign for Lure Lodge, the park's main overnight facility. Drive 5 miles and park in the lot by the lodge. From the south, starting at Kentucky Highway 90, take U.S. 127 north for 16.5 miles and turn right onto the park road. GPS: 36 55.755 N   85 02.431 W.

Parking and trailhead facilities: There's unlimited parking space. Rest rooms, drinking water, a restaurant, and overnight accommodations are available at the lodge; the park campground is nearby.

Key points:

0.0	Trailhead next to activities center.
0.8–1.4	Lakeside ridgetop.
2.8	Lakeshore.
3.6	Overlook.

The hike: This hike is a lot like walking through a city park, because you are never far from roads, buildings, and cars. But this loop route offers something you won't find in many other parks of any kind: a huge lake. With a length of 101 miles and a shoreline totaling 1,255 miles, Lake Cumberland is one of the largest man-made bodies of water in the eastern United States. This stroll through Lake Cumberland State Resort Park takes you along an unspoiled ridge overlooking the 52,250-acre reservoir at one of its widest points. You then meander through the park's developed area to a rock outcropping at the water's edge, and end up at a commanding lake overlook. You're in one of the state's most popular parks, so don't expect wilderness. What you do get is a chance to see and enjoy one of the state's premier attractions.

Lake Cumberland was created by damming the Cumberland River. Work on the project started in the early 1940s in response to devastation from the river's all-too-frequent flooding. The Wolf Creek dam, completed by the Army Corps of Engineers in 1951, is 240 feet high and slightly more than a mile long. US 127 runs on top of the dam 4 miles south of the state park road. Lake Cumberland is deep—200 feet in some spots—and as a result it ranks as the largest man-made lake east of the Mississippi in terms of water

Lake Cumberland

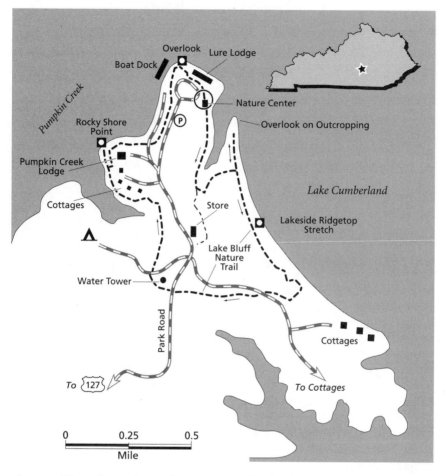

volume, although not in surface acreage. In the latter category, for example, Kentucky Lake and Lake Barkley in western Kentucky are both bigger.

The 3,117-acre Lake Cumberland State Resort Park was built in the early 1950s to take advantage of what was then the new reservoir. This hike is entirely on the park's Lake Bluff Nature Trail, which starts just south of Lure Lodge next to the nature center. Go down the steps in front of the nature center, turn right at the bottom, then left, and descend more steps. There you come to the first of a series of signs and plaques that you may appreciate the next time you play Trivial Pursuit. What is the Kentucky state tree? The answer, you learn on this hike, is the tulip poplar, the tallest hardwood species in North America.

From the nature center, the trail heads south above a small inlet of the lake. The trees here are young, but the area is attractive. After crossing a bridge over a drainage area and passing what may or may not be a waterfall, depending on rainfall, the trail forks. The right prong climbs to a store on the park road; you bear left to begin an easy climb up a ridge running

Lake Cumberland can be viewed from a ridge on the southwestern side.

along the main stem of the lake. On top, follow the sign pointing left a short distance to an overlook on a rock outcropping. Here you get a good view northeast across the lake as well as an inviting lunch spot. But be careful; you are high above the water, and there are no railings.

From the overlook, retrace your steps to the main trail and walk south on the wooded ridgetop along the water. This is the prettiest stretch of the hike. It ends at mile 1.4 with a turn right (west) away from the lake and a climb up to a park road leading south to cottages. You cross the road and, on the other side, follow it west, keeping watch for a NATURE TRAIL sign directing you away from the road and into the woods. At the sign, the trail descends to cross a shallow drainage; at mile 2.1, it crosses the main park road.

On the other side, the trail climbs northwest past a water tower and across the campground road. From here you go north into the woods, descend to cross another drainage, and at mile 2.6 come to an old road. A sign for Pumpkin Creek Lodge points left down the road, and you follow it. The lodge, named for the creek that it overlooks, was the park's original lodge; it is still used for guests.

Following the road, you pass between a finger of the Pumpkin Creek inlet far below on your left and park buildings above on your right. When the road comes to a fork, bear left and descend on shale and rock to the shoreline. How easy this descent is will depend on the water level. In dry periods the water may be too far below to reach. Still, this rock outcropping makes an enjoyable waterside rest spot.

Return to the fork and head north on the other prong. Disregarding a path up to the cottages, you walk along the side of the bank and round the promontory on which Pumpkin Creek Lodge sits. At mile 3.3, after climbing to a point near the lodge, the trail crosses the road to a large boat dock. You immediately climb up to the main park road and follow it to a sidewalk that leads to a fenced overlook on the bluff near Lure Lodge. You look down on the dock and have a good view of the lake. From the overlook, take the walkway east to the lodge and nature center at mile 3.8.

Options: The park has one other trail, Baugh Branch Trail, which runs 1.6 miles from the park road to a lake overlook. The trail starts 1.7 miles from the US 127 turnoff.

58 Dale Hollow Lake

Highlights:	A forested walk on a ridgetop jutting into the lake, with a side trip down to a secluded cove.
Location:	Dale Hollow State Resort Park, south of Burkesville and just above the Tennessee line.
Type of hike:	Day hike; out-and-back.
Total distance:	5 miles.
Difficulty:	Easy.
Best months:	Any month.
Maps:	USGS Frogue and Dale Hollow Reservoir SE (Tenn.); the state park's *Trail Guide* (park 270-433-7431).

Finding the trailhead: From the junction of U.S. Highway 127 and Kentucky Highway 90, north of Albany, go west on KY 90 for 10 miles, turn left (south) onto KY 449, and in another 4.5 miles turn left onto KY 1206. In 4 miles, you could enter the park—but continue instead for another mile on KY 1206, turning right at the sign for the Mary Ray Oaken Lodge. Go 0.9 mile and park in the lot at the end of the road near the lodge complex. The hike starts on the west side of the parking lot. (From Burkesville, take KY 90 east and turn right onto KY 449.) GPS: 36 38.339 N 85 18.000 W.

Parking and trailhead facilities: You'll find unlimited parking space; rest rooms, drinking water, a restaurant, and overnight accommodations are available in the lodge. The park's campground is off KY 1206.

Key points:
0.0	Entrance to Boom Ridge Trail.
0.5	Short Ridge Trail turnoff.
0.6	Brushy Ridge Trail turnoff.
0.9	Groce Ridge Trail turnoff.
1.4	Buck Ridge Trail turnoff.
1.5	State line.
1.7	Side trail to lakeshore.
1.9	Lakeshore.
2.7	Bluff at the end of Boom Ridge.

Dale Hollow Lake

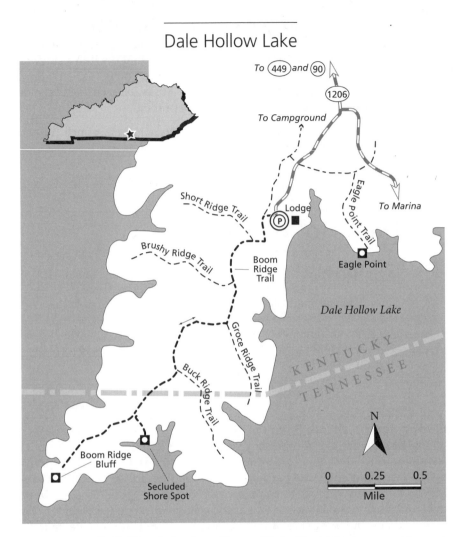

To (449) and (90)

(1206)

To Campground

Short Ridge Trail

Brushy Ridge Trail

Lodge

Eagle Point Trail

To Marina

Boom Ridge Trail

Eagle Point

Dale Hollow Lake

Groce Ridge Trail

Buck Ridge Trail

KENTUCKY
TENNESSEE

N

Boom Ridge Bluff

Secluded Shore Spot

0   0.25   0.5
Mile

The hike: Dale Hollow Lake State Resort Park, Kentucky's second largest, opened in 1978, and the lodge (named for a deceased state park official) didn't open until 1997. This hike follows an old roadbed that was around long before either. Along the way, you pass the remnants of one of the homesteads that years ago dotted these isolated hollows and ridgetops on the Kentucky–Tennessee border.

Dale Hollow Lake is a flood-control reservoir built by the Army Corps of Engineers in the early 1940s by damming the Obey River, a tributary of the Cumberland. The dam is near the Tennessee town of Celina. The shoreline around this 27,700-acre impoundment is largely undeveloped, and this hike takes you to a bluff at the tip of one of the isolated fingers of land that jut into the water. This peninsula is called Boom Ridge, and to get there you cross onto Corps property in Tennessee. You also pass the entrance to several side trails that follow small ridges shooting off Boom Ridge.

These side trails are not included in the 5.0-mile round-trip distance listed for the hike. The mileage does include a short, steep detour down to the lake shoreline. Otherwise the hike is entirely on the ridgetop, and it's about as flat a walk as you will find anywhere. Backcountry camping is not allowed in the state park, and only at designated sites on the Corps property in Tennessee.

From the west side of the parking lot—directly across from the main lodge entrance and next to a large glass-covered message board—a path goes about 50 feet up a small hill and into the woods. Just inside the trees, this little path dead-ends into Boom Ridge Trail. To your right, Boom Ridge Trail goes through scraggly woods and across mowed areas to the entrance to the park campground about 1.5 miles away. To your left, which is the way you go, it follows an attractive old dirt roadbed through a forest made up largely of beech, cedar, oak, and walnut that's home to a large number of deer.

Initially Boom Ridge Trail goes south, but it soon curves west. Disregard the first side trail you see on your left. The trail then turns northward briefly, and at that point a side trail spouts to your right and heads down Short Ridge for 0.5 mile. (All side-trail mileages are state park measurements.) Don't count on finding signs identifying these side trails; several were unmarked when I was there.

At mile 0.6, after once again heading south, the trail comes to Brushy Ridge Trail on your right (0.8 mile long), followed at mile 0.9 by Groce Ridge Trail on your left (0.6 mile long). You then head west again, passing the remains of a stone-and-brick foundation. Next, after the trail again curves back to the south, you come to Buck Ridge Trail on your left. This side trail is 0.2 mile long, according to the park. But I found that it went twice that distance before petering out on a bluff with a view south over the lake.

While the trees along the trail are generally young, there are definitely some senior citizens still around. At mile 1.5, a large beech stands guard just before the trail passes the boundary marker separating the state park from Corps property. This is also the line between Kentucky and Tennessee. The park trail map shows that just before the boundary, Wolf Ridge Trail branches north off the main trail. If such a trail still exists, I couldn't find it.

At mile 1.7, the trail curves southwest, and at this point (GPS 36 37.337 N 85 18.800 W) there is a short unmarked path down to the lakeshore. It's the best opportunity you'll have on the hike to get to the water—a welcome stop on a hot summer day. To reach the lake, go southeast instead of southwest, and at the edge of the ridge take the shale-covered path. The drop is extremely steep at first but quickly moderates. The "beach" is shale, but even so this secluded inlet makes a nice waterside picnic spot.

Retracing your steps up to the ridgetop, you are back on Boom Ridge Trail at mile 2.1 and making the turn southwest. From here on, the trail is more difficult to follow, in part because of storm damage. Also, for the most part it's now just a path, not a roadbed, and there are no blazes.

At mile 2.5 (GPS 36 37.197 N 85 19.104 W), the trail curves right (west). A large downed tree obscured the direction change when I took the hike,

The Dale Hollow Lake shoreline can be viewed from Eagle Point.

and I continued south before realizing my mistake. Shortly after the turn westward, the trail passes rock outcroppings on your right, and then makes another right turn before reaching the end of the ridgetop at mile 2.7. The lake is far below, and I had excellent views south across the water. That was autumn, however; the vista is no doubt diminished by summer foliage. From here, return to the lodge parking lot the way you came.

Options: The park's Eagle Point offers a spectacular overlook of the lake and several islands. To walk there from the lodge parking lot, take Boom Ridge Trail 0.7 mile north (toward the campground) and turn right onto a trail marked with red and blue squares. In 0.5 mile, turn right onto Eagle Point Trail, which reaches the lookout in another 0.5 mile.

59 Mammoth Cave Park Long Loop

Highlights:	Scenic hollows and ridgetops along the Green and Nolin Rivers.
Location:	Mammoth Cave National Park.
Type of hike:	One- or two-night backpack; loop.
Total distance:	15.7 miles.
Difficulty:	Moderate.
Best months:	Any month.
Maps:	USGS Rhoda; Trails Illustrated map of Mammoth Cave National Park; park brochure (office 270–758–2251).
Permits and fees:	A free permit, issued only at the park visitor center, is required for backcountry camping.

Finding the trailhead: Mammoth Cave National Park is off Interstate 65 about 25 miles north of Bowling Green and 85 miles south of Louisville. From the north, take I–65 exit 53 and go west on Kentucky Highway 70. In 3 miles bear right onto KY 255, and in 4.2 miles turn right onto the park's South Entrance Road. In 0.7 mile, turn left; continue 1.2 miles to the Green River ferry landing. (The visitor center is 0.6 mile farther north on the entrance road.) Coming from the south, take I–65 exit 48, go north on KY 255 to KY 70, and then turn right onto South Entrance Road. The two-minute ferry ride is free.

On the other side of the river, drive north and, in 6.2 miles, turn left onto KY 1827. In another mile turn left onto KY 728, and almost immediately left again onto Ollie Road. In 3 miles, where the road makes an abrupt right turn, go straight on gravel Houchins Ferry Road. After 0.1 mile, park in the lot on your right. The hike starts on the left side of the road. GPS: 37 14.647 N 86 11.449 W. (The little ferry does go on the blink at times, and flood conditions will also stop operations. If the ferry isn't running, get directions at the visitor center for the longer, nonferry route to the park's north side.)

Parking and trailhead facilities: There's room for about twenty-four cars, but no facilities. The park hotel, restaurant, and main campground are near the visitor center. A second campground is located on the south side of the Green River at the Houchins ferry landing.

Key points:
- 0.0 Wet Prong Trailhead.
- 0.5 Straight where the trail splits.
- 2.1 Bear right on McCoy Hollow connector.
- 2.6 Right on McCoy Hollow Trail.
- 4.3 Spur to McCoy Hollow Campsite.
- 7.4 Spur to Three Springs Campsite.
- 8.4 Houchins Ferry Road and First Creek Trailhead.
- 9.6 Spur to two First Creek Campsites.
- 11.6 Spur to Second Creek Campsite.

Mammoth Cave Park Long Loop

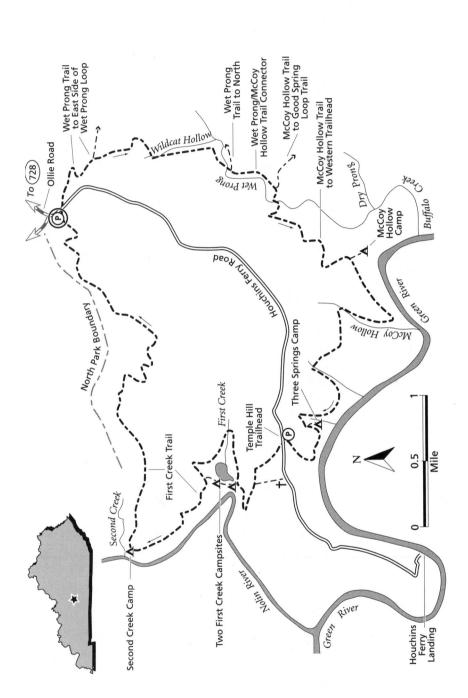

The hike: Mammoth Cave, the largest cave system in the world, has more than 350 miles of known underground passageways and possibly hundreds of more miles not yet discovered. Touring this subterranean limestone labyrinth, of course, is why most people come to the national park. Indeed, the visitor center has a kind of Grand Central Station feel to it as tourists rush to sign up for the popular cave trips, which are often sold out.

The park's 52,830 aboveground acres are also an attraction, but one less known. Established in 1941, the park covers scores of wooded hollows and ridges along the Green River. In spring especially, these little valleys are alive with creeks and waterfalls, punctuated by spreads of colorful wildflowers. Running across it all are some 70 miles of hiking trails.

Most of the trails, and all of the long ones, are located on the north side of the Green River—the park's undeveloped side. For a comprehensive description of the entire trail system, get *Guide to the Surface Trails of Mammoth Cave National Park* by Stanley D. Sides, a thin paperback sold at the visitor center. This hike uses four different trails to make a wide loop through a big chunk of the park's north side. It takes you by five of the park's twelve backcountry campsites, and so is a good backpacking route.

Hikers planning an overnight should be aware that backcountry camping is allowed only in the twelve designated campsites or on the banks of the Green and Nolin Rivers. Permits are required for both, and the campsite permits are site-specific, with each site limited to eight people per night. Which means that in busy periods, such as the schools' spring vacation week, you may not get your first choice. Advance reservations by telephone aren't allowed. I met some backpackers who came from Wisconsin only to find the campsites on their planned itinerary already taken. The earlier in the day you show up at the visitor center, the better your chances. The campsites are located in pleasant spots but are definitely primitive: a fire ring and enough level ground for several tents. All water must be treated. Many of the streams in the park are intermittent, and in dry periods it is smart to check with rangers beforehand on water availability.

From the parking area, you cross Houchins Ferry Road and go east on Wet Prong Trail. This loop trail is named for one of the two branches (Dry Prong is the other) of Buffalo Creek, a tributary of the Green. At mile 0.5, the trail splits into the two sides of the loop, one path going straight—this is the one you take—the other left. The entire Wet Prong loop is 4.9 miles, but you will take less than half of it.

Heading south, you are initially on the level ridgetop, but you soon make an easy descent into Wildcat Hollow, a lovely ravine covered with hardwoods. It has an intermittent stream, but if it's flowing, you'll pass a waterfall with a good-sized pool. The trail crosses the stream three times before settling on the west bank. You follow the stream south down the hollow until you meet and cross the larger Wet Prong at mile 2.1. There is no bridge, and in spring you may need a couple of minutes to find a dry route across on rocks. On the other side, about 20 feet upstream, Wet Prong Trail heads left for the loop's northbound leg, and you turn right onto the path headed south. This is a short connector trail between Wet Prong and McCoy Hollow Trails. This junction was marked with a confusing sign when I was there.

The connector climbs the stream bank and, after dipping to cross a couple of drainages, meets McCoy Hollow Trail at mile 2.6. To your left, less than half a mile away, the trail ends at Good Spring Loop Trail. (See Hike 60.) You, however, turn right and follow McCoy Hollow Trail toward its western trailhead on Houchins Ferry Road.

The trail descends and recrosses Wet Prong, which suddenly was no longer wet when I took the hike. Where did the water go? Underground. This part of the stream frequently flows below the surface. You then climb partway up the ridge on the west side of the stream and begin a winding route toward the Green River. The trail is blazed with blue metal rectangles nailed to trees, but they are few and far between, and in spots the narrow, leaf-covered path can be hard to see. At mile 4.3, after a pleasant level stretch on the ridgetop, you come to a sign depicting a tent and pointing left. Here a side path blazed with orange rectangles descends gently 0.1 mile to McCoy Hollow Campsite. It's on a bluff above the Green River, but the surrounding trees, even when leafless, make the river hard to see.

Back on the main trail, as you continue along the ridge, you have views across the river. Going southwest, you cross the top of a rock outcropping and turn right to begin a descent on long switchbacks into McCoy Hollow. At mile 5.6, you cross the stream in the hollow, then climb northwest to the top of the next ridge for a level segment. After turning northwest and descending into another hollow, the trail again turns south toward the river. You then repeat the process one last time—north up a hollow, across the stream, and south back to near the river. All of these hollows make delightful rest spots. In addition to waterfalls and wildflowers, you are likely to see deer and wild turkeys.

At mile 7.4—going south down the last hollow—you come to another campsite side trail, this one leading 0.1 mile to Three Springs Camp located just above a small stream. The main trail heads northwest between a cliff on your right and the river—colored the green you expect of pea soup—on your left. Soon, however, the trail turns up a ravine and climbs to a parking lot off Houchins Ferry Road at mile 8.4. The lot, called the Temple Hill Trailhead, marks the end of McCoy Hollow Trail and the start of First Creek Trail. The latter will take you back to your car.

First Creek Trail starts by the road at the west end of the parking area. Going northwest on the ridgetop, the trail is fairly level until it passes a side trail on your left to the Temple Hill cemetery on Houchins Ferry Road. It then descends gradually and, at mile 9.6, reaches First Creek Lake and a spur trail to First Creek Camp. Actually, there are two campsites here. First Creek Camp 1, which I found the more scenic of the two, is directly on the banks of the Nolin River; Camp 2 is nearer First Creek Lake. Note that this is the Nolin River, not the Green. The two come together just southwest of the campsite. The little lake has turtles and signs of beaver activity.

Staying level, the main trail makes a wide circle counterclockwise around the First Creek bottomland, crossing several small streambeds in the process.

The Nolin River flows alongside First Creek Camp.

The orange-marked side trail on your left goes back to First Creek Camp along the lake's western side. After a level stretch northwest above the Nolin River, the trail climbs easily, and at mile 11.6 comes to a short but steep side trail down to Second Creek Camp, located where Second Creek empties into the Nolin River.

The main trail turns east and climbs through holly and mountain laurel to the top of the ridge, where you have good views of the tree-covered ridges to the north. For the rest of the hike, the trail stays on or near the ridgetop. At mile 12.9, you cross an old dirt track and begin weaving between the park's northern boundary and the ravines and hollows to the south. Before the national park's creation, the land was occupied by some 600 families, mostly small farmers. Here you see road remnants and other evidence of the old homesteads.

At mile 14.9, the trail returns to the same dirt track you crossed earlier and follows it briefly along the park boundary line. The trail then bears right, crosses a couple of shallow ravines, and reaches the parking area and your car at mile 15.7.

Options: For a longer backpacking trip, combine this hike with the Hike 60 loop. It's easily done by taking McCoy Hollow Trail east from the McCoy Hollow connector trail.

60 Mammoth Cave Park Short Loop

Highlights: Quiet, wooded ridgetops.
Location: Mammoth Cave National Park.
Type of hike: Day hike or one-night backpack; loop.
Total distance: 7.9 miles.
Difficulty: Easy.
Best months: Any month.
Maps: USGS Rhoda; Trails Illustrated map of Mammoth Cave National Park; park brochure (office 270-758-2251).
Permits and fees: A free permit, issued only at the park visitor center, is required for backcountry camping.

Finding the trailhead: Mammoth Cave National Park is off Interstate 65 about 25 miles north of Bowling Green and 85 miles south of Louisville. From the north, take I-65 exit 53 and go west on Kentucky Highway 70. In 3 miles bear right onto KY 255, and in 4.2 miles turn right onto the park's South Entrance Road. In 0.7 mile, turn left; continue 1.2 miles to the Green River ferry landing. (The visitor center is 0.6 mile farther north on the entrance road.) Coming from the south, take I-65 exit 48, go north on KY 255 to KY 70, and then turn right onto South Entrance Road. The two-minute ferry ride is free.

After crossing the river, take the park road north for 2.2 miles and turn left onto the compacted-gravel road for Maple Springs. In 0.4 mile, bear left onto the road marked MAPLE SPRINGS GROUP CAMPGROUND AND GOOD SPRING CHURCH TRAILHEAD; in another 0.6 mile, turn left onto the loose-gravel road, which dead-ends in 0.5 mile at the Good Spring United Baptist Church. Park by the church. The hike starts in front of the building. GPS: 37 12.535 N 86 08.807 W.

Parking and trailhead facilities: There's room for twelve cars, but no facilities. The park hotel, restaurant, and main campground are found near the visitor center.

Key points:
0.0   Good Spring Loop Trailhead.
0.6   Trail to Turnhole Bend on the Green River.
1.2   Spur trail to Waterfall Campsite.
2.8   Spur to Bluffs Campsite.
4.3   Collie Ridge Trail.
6.0   Right turn south off Collie Ridge Trail.

The hike: This hike, which follows the park's Good Spring Loop Trail, runs through attractive Green River valley scenery and terrain similar to what is encountered on Hike 59. The big difference is distance. For hikers who don't have time for a one- or two-night backpack trip, this is a good way to explore the undeveloped north side of Mammoth Cave National Park. This hike

Mammoth Cave Park Short Loop

is also a bit easier, because it stays largely on the ridgetop. The route takes you near three of the park's twelve backcountry campsites. See Hike 59 for information about backcountry camping.

Good Spring Loop connects with a number of other major park trails, including McCoy Hollow, Sal Hollow, and Collie Ridge Trails. So it's easy to expand your hike beyond these 7.9 miles if you wish. For a comprehensive look at the entire trail system, see *Guide to the Surface Trails of Mammoth Cave National Park* by Stanley D. Sides, sold at the park visitor center. Be aware that as this is written, the park is planning to overhaul its trail layout; in the coming years some trails are certain to be changed, a few even eliminated. Check at the visitor center for current conditions.

The Good Spring United Baptist Church, established in 1842, was an important gathering place for the local community before the park's establishment in 1941. It is still used today by descendants of the former landowners for reunions, weddings, and funerals. From this handsome white-clapboard building, you can take Good Spring Loop Trail either way;

the following describes a clockwise route. The trail is marked with blue rectangles, but only sporadically. It's well trod, however, and difficult to lose. The various junctions you pass present the only real opportunity for getting off track.

From the front of the church, the trail heads southwest and crosses two small drainages before turning northwest and climbing gradually. At mile 0.6, you pass a trail on your left that goes south about 2.5 miles into the Green River's Turnhole Bend. Continuing northwest with little elevation change, you reach the Waterfall Campsite spur trail at mile 1.2. The campsite, located 0.2 mile off the main trail, is in a lovely, secluded spot. In spring, at least, there is a small waterfall nearby.

The main trail turns southwest, descends briefly to cross a drainage, and climbs back up to follow the level ridgetop running above the Dry Prong of Buffalo Creek. At mile 2.4, you pass the western end of Sal Hollow Trail, which starts at Maple Springs Road. Just beyond this junction, Sal Hollow Trail intersects Buffalo Trail, another east–west route. Turning northwest and following the ridge, you come to the Bluffs Campsite spur trail at mile 2.8. This campsite is 0.2 mile off the trail next to a large rock overhang and a small waterfall—a pleasant setting.

Continuing northwest and level, the main trail passes over the rock cliff above Bluffs Campsite; here you have views south across the Green River valley. Descending gradually along the base of a rock outcropping loaded with wildflowers and ferns, you come into a broad bottomland, cross a streambed, and begin a steep climb back up the ridgeside.

Backcountry camping can be found at Waterfall Campsite.

At mile 4.3, Good Spring Loop Trail intersects McCoy Hollow and Collie Ridge Trails. Here there are two left turns and one right. The sharp left is Collie Ridge Trail, and will take you to Collie Ridge Campsite 0.3 mile west. The next left is McCoy Hollow Trail, and leads to the longer loop route described in Hike 59. Good Spring Loop Trail, combined with northbound Collie Ridge Trail, turns right to begin a long, flat stretch northeast on the top of the ridge.

At mile 5.4, you pass an old trail on your right—still shown on some maps but now closed—that used to provide a shortcut back to the Good Spring Trailhead at the church. You continue northeast. At mile 6, Good Spring Loop Trail makes a sharp right turn, leaving Collie Ridge Trail and heading south. You descend into the Dry Prong valley and cross the stream.

On the other side you climb the ridgeside, following a small creek upstream. Just before a wooden bridge that takes you across the creek, named Mill Branch, you pass an old track that goes east a short distance to Raymer Hollow Trail. On the other side of Mill Branch, climb steeply and come up to the Good Spring cemetery at the back of the church. Rounding the east side of the church, you reach your car at mile 7.9.

Louisville Area

A number of good hiking opportunities surround Kentucky's largest city. The following walks are all within about an hour's drive of downtown—with the exception of the Yellowbank Wildlife Area, which is a little farther. Wooded ridges and hollows of moderate grade dominate the area, so you can expect gentle ups and downs. As a corollary, you can also expect few overlooks or dramatic views. What you will find are enjoyable rambles that take you far from the hurly-burly of urban life.

61 Taylorsville Lake

Highlights: Ridgetop fields with lots of birds and a good lake overlook.
Location: Taylorsville Lake State Park, east of Louisville.
Type of hike: Day hike; loop.
Total distance: 5.6 miles.
Difficulty: Moderate.
Best months: Spring and fall.
Maps: USGS Taylorsville and Mount Eden; Taylorsville Lake State Park map (office 502–477–8713).

Finding the trailhead: From Louisville, take Interstate 64 east for about 25 miles to exit 32 and go south on Kentucky Highway 55. In 9 miles, turn left onto combined KY 55/155; in another 5 miles, in the town of Taylorsville, turn left (east) onto KY 44. In another 5 miles, KY 44 turns left, while you continue straight on KY 248. In 2 more miles, at the sign for the state park information center and boat launch, turn right onto Park Road. In 1.1 miles, park in the small gravel area on the left side of the road at the sign for trailhead parking. GPS: 38 01.806 N 85 14.910 W.

Parking and trailhead facilities: There's room for about twenty cars. There are no facilities here, but you will find rest rooms and water 0.2 mile farther west at the park office/visitor center.

Key points:
0.0   West on Possum Ridge Loop Trail.
0.1   Little Beech Creek Loop Trailhead.
1.1   Rejoin Possum Ridge Loop Trail.
1.4   South on Salt River Vista Loop Trail.
3.3   Overlook at end of Possum Ridge.
4.6   East on Possum Ridge Loop Trail.

The hike: Taylorsville Lake is a 3,050-acre reservoir that the Corps of Engineers built by damming the Salt River, a medium-sized stream that originates

Taylorsville Lake

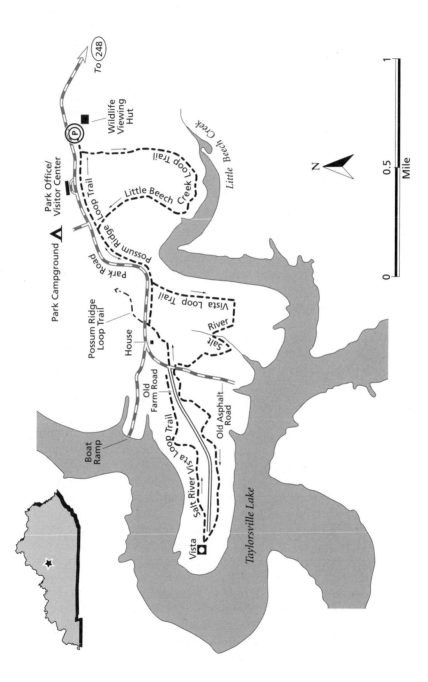

in central Kentucky and empties into the Ohio River west of Louisville at West Point. The name comes from the saltworks that pioneers operated along the banks in the early 1800s. Flood control was the lake's main purpose, but since its completion in 1983 this narrow, snakelike body of water has been a major attraction for Louisville-area boaters and anglers. The 1,232-acre state park, which includes a campground but no lodge accommodations, is on the northeast shore between the lake's Beech Creek and Little Beech Creek arms. The park has 16 miles of trails.

This hike combines three loop trails to make a large loop that takes you near the lakeshore and also to an impressive overlook above the intersection of Beech Creek and the main lake stem. There are several descents to the lakeshore, but the majority of the walking is relatively level along the top of Possum Ridge, a peninsula that juts out into the lake. All of this area was farmed before the river's impoundment, and much of the flat ridgetop remains as fields covered only by small cedars, shrubs, and grasses. As a result, this is prime habitat for birds, including wild turkeys. In summer the treeless environment can make hiking hot, if not entirely miserable. But in spring and fall, the open ridgetop offers delightful walking with lots of bird-watching opportunities.

From the parking area, which includes a hut for viewing wildlife, follow Possum Ridge Loop Trail west along the south side of Park Road. This 6-mile trail is the main walking route through the park but you are on it only briefly. In about 0.1 mile you turn left on the rock and mud path marked LITTLE BEECH CREEK LOOP. This trail, the first of the two loop routes, is also used for horseback riding, as its rough condition attests. Thankfully, the path gets narrower and smoother as you proceed. It's blazed, though not very often, with yellow arrows. Walking south and level on the top of Possum Ridge, you pass through a meadow sprouting low-lying cedars and hardwoods. At mile 0.4, the trail begins a quick descent toward Little Beech Creek but turns west before running into the water.

The trail then ascends partway up the ridgeside before dropping down once again near the lake. From there you make a steady climb north all the way back to the top of Possum Ridge near an attractive wildlife pond. Continue north and, at mile 1.1, rejoin Possum Ridge Loop Trail just south of Park Road across from the park campground. Turn left and follow the Possum Ridge Trail southwest for 0.3 mile to an old dirt roadbed that angles south parallel to the lake's Little Beech Creek arm far below on your left. This is the beginning of the Salt River Vista Loop Trail. Turn left on the Salt River Vista Loop Trail. It passes through a stand of lovely large hardwoods before reaching a small pond and turning west away from the lake. Here a side trail continues south 0.1 mile to a second pond surrounded by small cedars—a nice spot if you're in need of a rest. From the first pond, the main trail heads west and at mile 1.9 begins a steep descent to a creek. After crossing it, you climb back up the hillside. Walking north near the edge of the ridge, you come to a fork—unmarked when I was there. Bear left and descend gently on an old roadbed to a deteriorated asphalt road at mile 2.3. To your left the asphalt road descends to the lakeshore in about 0.2 mile.

You, however, turn right and then left as you continue to follow Salt River Vista Loop west.

With only minor ups and downs, you quickly come to the end of Possum Ridge and a lake overlook that makes a perfect lunch stop. This spot, which you reach at mile 3.3, is the most appealing of the hike, at least for my money. A mix of small and large trees draws numerous birds. Locals say it's an especially good place to see turkeys. There is also a fine view of the lake as well as a rickety old picnic table. The only blemish on the scene is the small piece of machinery—a sewer pump—located just below the overlook. The old dirt road that ends at the overlook used to connect the top of Possum Ridge to a bottomland farm, now under water.

This dirt road runs down the middle of Possum Ridge, and Salt River Vista Loop parallels it. If you have trouble following the loop eastbound away from the overlook—which I did—simply take the road instead. The eastbound leg, which is largely in the woods, was not well maintained or blazed when I was there. Whether you take the road or the trail, you come to the old asphalt road just south of Park Road. Here you take the trail across the asphalt road, circle behind a modern house facing Park Road, and at mile 4.6 once again rejoin Possum Ridge Loop Trail. To the left the Possum Ridge trail winds through the northern section of the park. You, however, turn right and take the trail east along Park Road. After passing the campground and office/visitor center, you reach the trailhead parking area and your car at mile 5.6.

The view from the bluff at the end of Possum Ridge looks across Taylorsville Lake.

62 Bernheim Forest

Highlights: Quiet ridgetops and hollows in a handsome
hardwood forest.
Location: South of Louisville.
Type of hike: Day hike; loop.
Total distance: 13.6 miles.
Difficulty: Moderate.
Best months: Late fall to early spring.
Maps: USGS Shepherdsville; Bernheim Forest map of
Millennium Trail (office 502–955–8512).
Permits and fees: Hikers using this trail—Millennium Trail—must
register at the Bernheim Forest Visitor Center, open
daily at 9:00 A.M. Because the forest closes at dark,
trail users are not allowed to start after 1:30 P.M. You
are asked to return to the center when you are
finished and sign out.

Special considerations: Bernheim Forest, a private nonprofit corporation, charges a $5.00-per-car admission fee on weekends and holidays. Admission is free Monday through Friday. The forest is open from 7:00 A.M. to sunset daily except Christmas and New Year's Day. Camping is not allowed.

Finding the trailhead: From Louisville, take Interstate 65 south for 25 miles to exit 112, turn left (east) onto Kentucky Highway 245, and in 1 mile turn right into Bernheim Forest. At the fork just past the entrance, bear right and follow the road for another 0.8 mile to the visitor center parking lot on your right. After registering at the center for Millennium Trail, drive back toward the forest entrance 0.2 mile and turn left onto the road marked by a sign for Guerilla Hollow. In 0.2 mile, bear right where the road turns into a one-way loop. In another 0.4 mile—just before the loop road curves sharply left—pull into the parking strip on your right by the picnic area. The hike starts 50 yards farther down the road on the right side near the chain gate. GPS: 37 54.574 N 85 39.966 W.

Parking and trailhead facilities: You'll find spaces for at least a dozen cars, along with a picnic table and cooking grills. The visitor center has vending machines and rest rooms.

Key points:
0.0 Millennium Trailhead.
1.2 Deer-fence gate into natural area.
1.7 Tower Hill Road.
3.8 Side trail to picnic table on ridgetop.
6.7 Ashlock Hollow Road, hike's halfway mark.
9.1 Beginning of 0.7-mile stretch on Yoe Trace Fire Road.
11.3 Ridge with limited views northeast.
13.2 Return gate into Bernheim's developed section.

Bernheim Forest

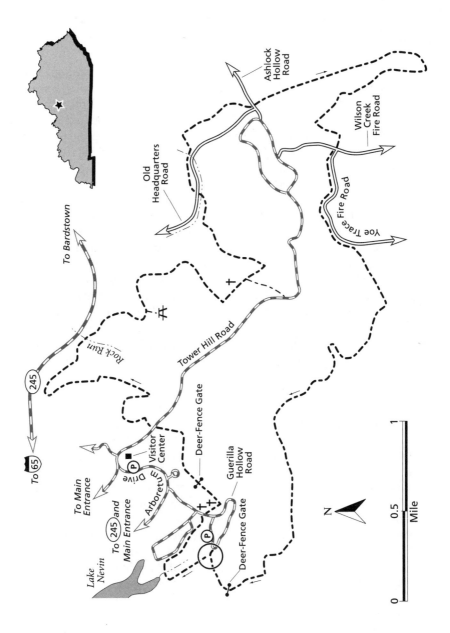

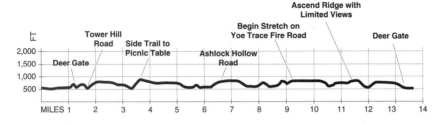

The hike: Isaac W. Bernheim (1848–1945) was a German immigrant who settled in Kentucky and became a successful whiskey distiller under the I. W. Harper brand. In 1929, full of gratitude for his good fortune, he established Bernheim Forest and dedicated it to the education and enjoyment of the Kentucky public. His gift has become one of the top outdoor attractions in the Louisville area. A small, carefully manicured section of Bernheim Forest—the part you drive through immediately after entering—consists of an arboretum, gardens, and lawn, all of it sprinkled with statues and other artworks. But most of the 16,000 acres are covered with wooded ridges and hollows, and it is this natural area that provides the best hiking. Most of the land was farmed before 1929, and so the forest is still not fully mature. In addition to art displays, the visitor center has educational materials.

For decades Bernheim Forest offered hikers only relatively short paths, most of them less than 2 miles. In the year 2000, however, Bernheim redesigned its trail system to add a 13.6-mile loop named, appropriately, Millennium Trail. It combines several old trail segments with three short road sections and a number of newly developed paths to take you into the forest's interior. The walk is a sequence of level legs along ridgetops and bottomlands interrupted by fairly short climbs and descents. So you can expect a good number of ups and downs but none strenuous.

You can also expect to see deer and, in season, lots of wildflowers. Oak, beech, and maple dominate the woods. The walk is most interesting after a rain when the little wet-weather streams that crisscross the hollows come alive, creating small, attractive waterfalls. If there has been no rain, you may not find even a drop of water; there are no permanent streams. In summer this can be a dry, hot environment—and a buggy one. On one Bernheim hike in early September, I was visited by a particularly nasty family of chiggers. Also, be aware that while in winter there are some limited views, you can see very little from the ridgetops when the leaves are out. What you get on Millennium Trail is a pleasant walk in the woods, not dramatic scenery.

The hike starts on the edge of Guerilla Hollow, so named because Confederate guerrillas supposedly operated out of it during the Civil War. Both Bernheim and the USGS map use the less common spelling of the word. The Millennium Trailhead sign is located about 50 feet from the road—on the other side of the chain fence, just across the small wet-weather streambed. The trailhead sign is purposely difficult to see from the road; Bernheim wants only registered hikers to know about it. The trail is designed to be hiked clockwise. In that direction you constantly pass the little yellow disks that mark the trail throughout. Keep a close lookout for them; otherwise, it's easy to stray onto one of the old footways that frequently intersect Millennium Trail. The reverse direction—counterclockwise—is marked by yellow triangles, but there are far fewer of them. Mileage signs are posted every 2 miles.

From the trailhead, you head northwest on an old double-track road that quickly peters out into a path. After passing the ending leg of the loop on your left, you cross a grass field and enter the woods. At mile 0.3, you come into a small meadow at the south end of thirty-two-acre man-made Lake Nevin, make a sharp right turn, and cross a feeder stream on a wooden bridge. On the other side a short climb takes you up to an old asphalt road now open only to cyclists and walkers; turn right (south) and follow this paved strip. Without the yellow disks, this initial part of the hike through Bernheim's developed section would be impossible to follow. In 0.3 mile, the trail makes a well-marked right turn off the asphalt strip, cuts through the woods, and at mile 0.9 crosses Guerilla Hollow Road just before the beginning of the one-way loop. On the other side of the road, you quickly come to the Magruder family cemetery. Archibald Magruder, a member of the Maryland militia during the American Revolution, was one of the area's original landowners, and the old tombstones make interesting reading.

From the cemetery, you briefly go southeast before making a sharp turn left (north) and starting to climb the first ridge of the hike. The small fenced plot you pass at the turn encloses what was a cemetery for the Magruders' slaves. At mile 1.2, you reach the ridgetop—and a gate in the wire-mesh fence designed to keep deer out of Bernheim's developed section. Go through the gate, turn left, and follow the fence northeast. Initially you descend into a hollow, then you climb again. At mile 1.7, after an easy downhill stretch, you cross Tower Hill Road, which takes motorists to the trailheads for most of Bernheim's short hikes and to an old fire tower that is open on weekends. At the road, you leave the deer fence behind and climb north to another ridgetop—and the trail's 2-mile marker.

Here pay special attention to the yellow disks. Just past the mileage sign, the trail turns sharply right (south)—away from a broader path that tempts you to continue straight ahead. Millennium Trail crosses over to the other side of the ridge and then turns north to follow the level ridgeline toward KY 245. At mile 2.5, you jog around a small clearing and begin following a pleasant old roadbed gently down and around the north end of the ridge. This is easy, delightful walking, marred only by the truck noise from the highway and the steady humming of a nearby distillery operation, one of a number that populate this part of Kentucky.

At mile 2.9, the trail leaves the old roadbed, turning sharply right into the woods. This turn—another that is easily missed—comes just before the road intersects a power-line clearing. From the woods, the trail parallels the clearing in a southeasterly direction before crossing the clearing and descending—at mile 3.3—to the often dry bed of a stream named Rock Run. KY 245 is just above you.

From intermittent Rock Run—which eventually drains into the Salt River, a tributary of the Ohio—you climb southeast through ferns and, at mile 3.8, reach the top of a ridge. Here a side trail to your right leads to an "overlook" named in honor of Robert Paul, Bernheim's first executive director. This level path ends in 0.1 mile at a little clearing—said to be Mr. Paul's favorite spot in the forest. You will find a picnic table built by the Boy Scouts, the only accommodation on the trail. But especially when the trees are full, you won't find much of a view; you just barely see the tops of distant ridges through the leaves. Returning to the main trail, you walk first east and then south to reach—at mile 4.9—the cemetery of the Jackson family, another of the early settlers. Just past the cemetery, an unmarked trail to your right leads a short distance down to Tower Hill Road. It comes out near a parking lot for Jackson-Yoe Loop, one of the short Bernheim hikes.

Continuing southeast, Millennium Trail comes to a fork and goes left; the unmarked right prong is another remnant of Bernheim's old trail system. You then wind northward, following a small drainage downhill to its intersection with a streambed. At the intersection, the trail turns right and follows the streambed east for a short distance. At mile 5.8, the trail crosses the streambed and, immediately on the other side, hits Old Headquarters Road. Turn right and follow this tree-shaded dirt-and-gravel road for 0.2 mile— to just beyond the spot where it crosses the streambed. Here the trail turns left into the woods and begins an easy climb to intersect gravel Ashlock Hollow Road on the ridgetop, just east of the loop end of Tower Hill Road. This spot—which is where Old Headquaraters Road also intersects Ashlock Hollow Road—marks the hike's halfway point.

Crossing Ashlock Hollow Road, you begin a long stretch to the south, initially on the level ridgetop and then dropping down into bottomland and crossing a series of wet-weather streambeds. The forest here is completely

A distant ridge can be seen in the winter in Bernheim Forest.

quiet—and in spring full of blooming dogwoods. You climb another ridge and, at mile 9.1—after descending to cross still another of Bernheim's ephemeral streams—come up to a gravel road just as it splits into two: Wilson Creek Fire Road going left (south) and Yoe Trace Fire Road heading right (west). The trail follows Yoe Trace for an easy, level stretch of 0.7 mile before turning off the road to your right and entering the woods.

The trail dips down to cross another drainage and, at mile 11.3, begins climbing the first of a series of four ridgetop knobs that in winter offer limited views northeast to the next ridgeline. You then descend southwest to cross Guerilla Hollow and climb up the other side of the hollow. At mile 13.2, after a short descent, you come once again to the deer fence—and a gate that lets you back into Bernheim's developed section. Go through the gate, turn right, and follow the grass-and-dirt track along the fence. At mile 13.5, the fence ends; in a few steps you run into the trail's beginning leg. Turn right onto the old double-track road. Almost immediately you are back at the trailhead near the loop road where you left your car.

Options: If you want a shorter hike, I suggest hiking the second half of the trail—from Ashlock Hollow Road to the start/finish point along Guerilla Hollow Road. The second half is 6.9 miles long and more removed from Bernheim's developed section and avoids the KY 245 truck noise. You will, of course, need a second car—leaving one on Guerilla Hollow Road and driving the other up to the parking area on Tower Hill Road near its intersection with Ashlock Hollow Road. The only other alternative is a road walk between the two spots—a distance of almost 4 miles.

63 Vernon-Douglas State Nature Preserve

Highlights:	A walk through mature second-growth forest to a ridgetop overlook with partially obstructed views.
Location:	South of Louisville.
Type of hike:	Day hike; loop.
Total distance:	3.7 miles.
Difficulty:	Moderate.
Best months:	Any month.
Maps:	USGS Nelsonville; trail map from the Kentucky State Nature Preserves Commission (office 502–573–2886).

Special considerations: Dogs, even on a leash, are not allowed.

Finding the trailhead: From Louisville, take Interstate 65 south for about 32 miles to exit 105. Go south on Kentucky Highway 61 and, in 4 miles in the town of Boston, turn right (west) onto combined U.S. Highway 62/KY 61. In 3.8 miles turn left (south) onto KY 583, and in 2 miles—immediately

Vernon-Douglas State Nature Preserve

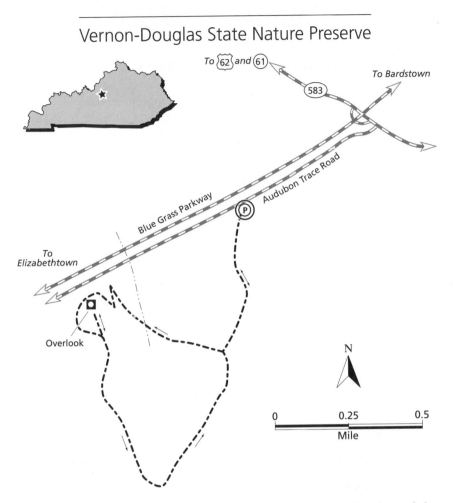

after passing over the Blue Grass Parkway—turn right (west) onto Audubon Trace. In 0.6 mile, turn into the gravel parking lot on the left side of the road. GPS: 37 44.023 N 85 42.475 W.

Parking and trailhead facilities: You'll find space for a dozen vehicles, but no facilities.

Key points:
- 0.0   Trailhead.
- 0.6   Beginning of loop.
- 1.0   Hall Hollow.
- 1.7   Overlook.
- 3.1   End of loop.

The hike: Central Kentucky is dotted with knobs, and this hike explores one of these large hills—one covered with mature second-growth hardwoods, mainly maple, beech, tulip poplar, oak, and hickory. Unlike Bernheim Forest, this 730-acre preserve is not well known. Most likely you will see no one else as you make your way through Hall Hollow and then climb up the ridge to the Pinnacle, the local name for a bluff overlooking the pastoral Younger Creek valley. The only intrusion on your solitude—and in some spots it definitely is an intrusion—is the swish-swish of traffic on the nearby Blue Grass Parkway. Even so, the attributes of this little preserve, including its many wildflowers, more than compensate for that one drawback. The Douglas family owned the land before donating it to the National Audubon Society in 1972. The Vernons owned it before the Douglases. Both families were careful to leave the land undisturbed. It has never been commercially logged, at least not in the last half century, according to the Kentucky State Nature Preserves Commission. The Audubon Society gave the property to the state in 1991.

The trail—the preserve has only one—starts at the south end of the parking lot at the gate in the fence. There were no signs or blazes identifying the trail when I was there, but the path was well-enough defined to be easily followed. Heading south, you cross several split-log bridges over small drainages before angling up a ridge known as Hall Hill. You don't go to the top but rather, at mile 0.6, come up to a saddle between Hall Hill and an unnamed hilltop just to the south. Here a signpost announces the beginning of a 2.5-mile-long loop through the preserve. You can go either way, but I suggest a counterclockwise approach.

Turning right (west) at the signpost, you descend gently on a broad path that no doubt at one time was a dirt road, and at mile 1 come down into Hall Hollow. After crossing a small creek on rocks, you begin climbing—initially northwest, but shortly making a sharp turn left, followed by a sharp

The winter sun prepares to set on the ridgetop in Vernon-Douglas State Nature Preserve.

turn right. The grade here is steep but eased considerably by a series of wood-and-dirt steps. Soon the path curves west and begins an almost-level slabbing of the ridgeside parallel to the parkway below. At mile 1.5, after turning southeast away from the parkway, you reach the top of the ridge.

Here the main trail turns right, but you turn left and follow a side path 0.2 mile north through pines and cedars to a bluff at the end of the ridge—a spot known locally as the Pinnacle. You look down on farms and houses lining the flats along Younger Creek. It's a peaceful scene, but the view is constricted by trees along the ridgetop. In summer the view is especially limited.

From the Pinnacle, return to the junction and take the main trail south along the ridgetop. The large trees make a pleasing canopy. As you near a farm field sprouting a tall communications tower, the trail curves east and then north to circle Hall Hollow. At mile 3.0, the trail begins descending; you are soon back at the signpost marking the beginning of the loop. From there you retrace your steps and reach the parking lot at mile 3.7.

64 Jefferson County Forest

Highlights: Pleasantly wooded ridges and hollows with limited views north toward the Ohio River and Indiana.
Location: South of Louisville.
Type of hike: Day hike; out-and-back.
Total distance: 13 miles.
Difficulty: Moderate.
Best months: Any month.
Maps: USGS Valley Station; Jefferson County Memorial Forest trail map (office 502–368–5404).

Finding the trailhead: From downtown Louisville, take Interstate 65 south to the Snyder Freeway (Kentucky Highway 841) and go west for 3 miles to exit 6, New Cut Road. Go south on New Cut and continue straight on Manslick Road. In 1.8 miles from the freeway, turn right onto Mitchell Hill Road; after another 1.5 miles, turn left into the parking lot for the Jefferson Forest Welcome Center. The trailhead is on the north side of Mitchell Hill Road at the parking lot entrance. GPS: 38 05.134 N 85 46.081 W. (Don't be confused by a sign on Holsclaw Hill Road for another section of the forest. The welcome center is on Mitchell Hill Road 0.6 mile past Holsclaw Hill Road.)

Parking and trailhead facilities: There's space for eighteen cars, along with rest rooms, water, and vending machines.

Key points:
0.0 Trailhead.
0.3 Limited view of downtown Louisville.
2.0 Jefferson Hill Road.

Jefferson County Forest

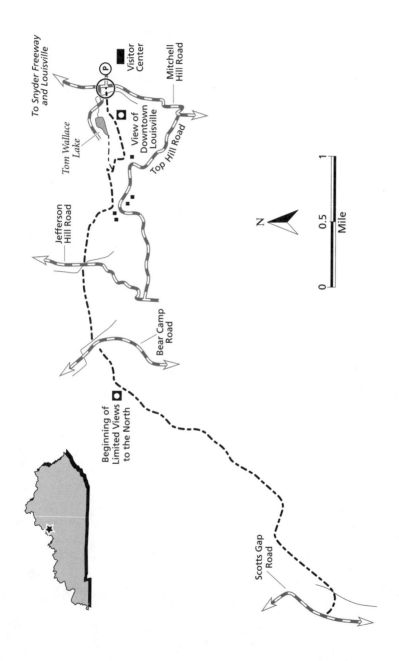

To Snyder Freeway and Louisville

Visitor Center

Mitchell Hill Road

Tom Wallace Lake

View of Downtown Louisville

Top Hill Road

Jefferson Hill Road

Bear Camp Road

Beginning of Limited Views to the North

Scotts Gap Road

N

0   0.5   1
Mile

The hike: Local officials call the Jefferson County Memorial Forest the nation's "largest public urban forest." True, these 5,504 acres of wooded ridges and hollows are in the same county as the state's biggest city. Indeed, from one of the knobs you cross on this hike, you can see the downtown. But otherwise there is nothing at all urban about this hike. You could just as well be a hundred miles from Louisville. In fact, for generations this area of steep hills and winding roads was well isolated from the rest of the county. Cut off by a swamp, it was a place for lumbering, moonshining, and other decidedly noncosmopolitan activities, says Steve Goodwin, the local parks official who oversees the forest. The welcome center—where you can pick up trail maps and other information about the forest—is a renovated two-room schoolhouse built in the early twentieth century when this was still an area very much unto itself. The first forest parcels were acquired for public use in 1946.

This hike, much of it on a ridgetop with partial views north toward the Ohio River and into Indiana, follows a 6.5-mile-long trail running east–west across the main section of the forest. Unfortunately, there is no way to make a loop out of it; you must either retrace your steps or arrange for a shuttle at the western terminus on Scotts Gap Road. The trail crosses two other roads—Jefferson Hill Road at mile 2 and Bearcamp Road at mile 2.8. There are several steep climbs as you go up and down knobs. But the climbs are all of short duration, and the exertion is more than offset by the long segments of flat ridgetop. Be aware that when I took this hike, a number of

Northerly views can be seen from a ridgetop at Jefferson County Memorial Forest.

mileage signs posted along the way were inaccurate. Overnight camping on the trail is not permitted.

The trail—named Siltstone Trail—is well blazed with white diamonds. From Mitchell Hill Road, it heads west into tall hardwoods and evergreens, crosses a small creek on a bridge, and brushes the side of a road leading to Tom Wallace Lake, a popular recreation site. Almost immediately you begin climbing, steeply in places, and at mile 0.3 reach the top of a knob with a view of the downtown's tallest buildings. Like other ridgetop vistas on this hike, this one is partially obstructed by trees, even in winter.

Following the ridgetop, the trail descends gently and then climbs to a saddle, bypassing the next hilltop. From there the trail angles down the north side of the ridge and, at mile 0.9, meets a concrete walk coming from Tom Wallace Lake. Crossing the walkway, you climb west not quite all the way to the appropriately named Top Hill Road; you don't see the road, but you do see the houses perched on it. Walking north—and level—you pass through a beautiful stand of evergreens. Turning west, you leave the ridgetop and descend to Jefferson Hill Road just as it passes over a stream on a small bridge.

After crossing the road and stream, climb west over another knob called Pine Top and descend to cross Bearcamp Road at mile 2.8. You continue west and soon are climbing again, this time to the top of High Knob, the highest point of the hike. Just before reaching the top at mile 3.4, you get the first of numerous views—all limited by trees along the ridge—north to the Ohio River and into Indiana. Those tall smokestacks you see are part of cement works along the river west of Louisville. From High Knob, the rest of the hike is for the most part on top of the ridge and level. At mile 4.3, traveling southwest, you enter an area of extensive tree damage from a 1997 tornado.

After a stint to the northwest, the trail again turns southwest and, at mile 6, starts down the ridge. After reaching the bottom and fording a small stream, you turn northwest, go up a small hill, and cross a power-line clearing. From there you descend to Scotts Gap Road at 6.5 miles. The red-blazed trail you see on the other side of the road makes a 3.5-mile loop through an adjoining forest parcel. Assuming you don't want to add that mileage to your trip, this is where you turn around and begin retracing your steps to the welcome center.

65 Fort Knox

Highlights:	A multitiered waterfall.
Location:	Southwest of Louisville.
Type of hike:	Two short, separate day hikes from the same trailhead: one a loop, one an out-and-back.
Total distance:	4.2 miles.
Difficulty:	Easy.
Best months:	Any month, but especially in spring after a heavy rain when the falls are at their most robust.
Maps:	USGS Fort Knox; trail brochures from the Fort Knox Hunt Control Office (502–624–7311).

Special considerations: This hiking area is sometimes closed for military training and also for hunting. Check beforehand with the Fort Knox Hunt Control Office (closed Tuesday). Also, be aware that the second of these two trails is on a paved surface.

Finding the trailhead: From downtown Louisville, take Interstate 65 south to the Snyder Freeway (Kentucky Highway 841) and go west for 10 miles to the freeway's end at U.S. Highway 31W (Dixie Highway). Turn left onto US 31W and in 10 miles, in the town of West Point, turn left onto a narrow road named the Louisville–Nashville Turnpike. The intersection is marked by a BRIDGES TO THE PAST sign. In 0.7 mile, park in the gravel lot at the end of the road. GPS: 37 58.110 N 85 57.656 W.

Parking and trailhead facilities: You'll find room for about thirty cars and picnic tables, but no other facilities.

Key points:
    0.0   Tioga Falls Trailhead.
    0.9   Base of Tioga Falls.
    2.0   Bridges to the Past Trailhead.
    3.1   Locked gate.
    4.2   Parking lot.

The hike: Fort Knox, famous as the nation's gold depository, is a 170-square-mile army training facility for tank and other armored crews. On a small corner of this huge base are two short trails open to the public, except during special training exercises and some hunting seasons. The two trails share a common parking area and trailhead, and I have paired them as one hike with a total distance of 4.2 miles. In character, however, the two are entirely different kinds of walks.

The first is on a dirt path along a wooded ridge to a multitiered waterfall that is especially impressive after a big rain; this is Tioga Falls Trail, a 2-mile loop. The second is a section of a nineteenth-century turnpike that linked Louisville and Nashville. Unfortunately, the original cobblestones were paved over as part of the development of Fort Knox, so this half of the hike

Fort Knox

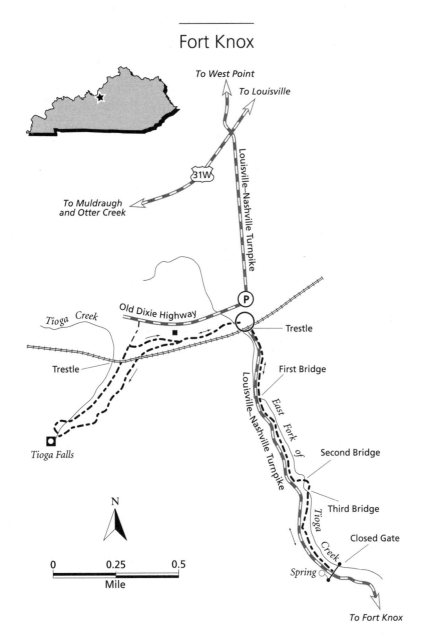

To West Point

To Louisville

31W

To Muldraugh and Otter Creek

Louisville–Nashville Turnpike

P

Old Dixie Highway

Tioga Creek

Trestle

Trestle

First Bridge

Louisville–Nashville Turnpike

East Fork of

Tioga Falls

Second Bridge

Third Bridge

Tioga Creek

Closed Gate

N

Spring

0   0.25   0.5
Mile

To Fort Knox

is on a road. However, you are walking along a pleasant stream flanked by woods and ridges. The road, closed to vehicles and called Bridges to the Past Trail, crosses three pre–Civil War stone bridges said to be among the oldest still standing in the state. The trail ends in 1.1 miles at a locked gate, making the total out-and-back distance of the paved portion 2.2 miles. For each of the two trails, Fort Knox has a pamphlet that explains points of historical interest along the way. The pamphlets, which are helpful, should be available at the trailhead.

The Tioga Falls path, blazed with white paint, leaves the west side of the parking lot and heads west, paralleling railroad tracks above on your left and an old paved road below on your right. As a sign posted on the trail explains, the paved road was the original Dixie Highway, built in 1921 to connect Louisville with what was then Camp Knox. Replaced in 1942 by the current Dixie Highway, the old road, now called Railroad Trestle Road, is blocked off just beyond the hiking area.

You immediately cross the East Fork of Tioga Creek on a bridge and begin climbing a ridgeside. You are going up Muldraugh Hill, on which the developed portion of Fort Knox is located. From here to the falls, you are following old wagon roads. As the interpretive signs make clear, this area was full of farms and dirt roads before the military's acquisition of the land in 1918.

After passing the rear of a contemporary brick house facing old Dixie Highway, you reach the tracks at mile 0.4 and follow them westward for about 20 feet before crossing and turning south. Be careful here, because the tracks are still in use. Originally built in 1873 and operated by various companies, including the Illinois Central, the line is now the Paducah & Louisville Railroad. This crossing spot was once the site of a small railroad station, though there is no sign of it now. Just to the west, the tracks go over Tioga Creek on a 130-foot-high trestle, which you will walk beneath on your way back to the parking lot.

From the tracks, you continue briefly up the wooded ridgeside and then, after a short level stretch that offers a view north to the Ohio River and Indiana shore beyond, descend to the base of Tioga Falls at mile 0.9. Tioga Creek tumbles 130 feet down Muldraugh Hill, and after a heavy rain there are a number of separate gushes at various elevations, making an impressive multitiered cascade. From the falls, the creek flows to meet East Fork, and together they go into the Ohio. The trail pamphlet explains that in the 1800s, to escape malaria, wealthy families from the Deep South summered at a fine two-story hotel just above Tioga Spring. Kentucky, which remained neutral in the Civil War, recognized slavery, and this was as far north as Southerners could come and still be accompanied by their slaves. The hotel is long gone.

After crossing Tioga Creek on rocks at the base of the falls, you turn north, then east, and recross the stream to begin following it north toward old Dixie Highway. You shortly come to the stone walls of an old springhouse; just before these remains, there is a large rock on the creek bank that makes a nice lunch spot. Walking level along the creek, you pass beneath the railroad trestle at mile 1.3; at mile 1.4, turn right—away from the creek bottom—on a faint path. The turn is hard to see and was not marked with a sign when I was there. If you miss it and continue following the creek bottom, you will run into old Dixie Highway in another 0.1 mile.

Going east parallel to old Dixie Highway, the path rises as it circles around the back of the brick house you passed early in the hike. Built in the 1930s as a telephone company facility, it is now private property. Just above the house, the path intersects the first part of the loop. Turn left and you are back at the parking lot at mile 2.

Tioga Creek tumbles down Muldraugh Hill after a good rain, forming a multitiered cascade.

The paved Bridges to the Past portion of the hike starts at the lot's south end beneath another railroad trestle, and climbs steadily but easily up Muldraugh Hill toward Fort Knox proper. This was part of a toll road authorized by the Kentucky legislature in 1829, though construction didn't start for several years. It connected Louisville to Nashville and was well traveled—especially by visitors to Mammoth Cave—before the Louisville & Nashville Railroad was completed in 1859. The railroad ended the road's popularity, though military forces made good use of it during the Civil War. This segment was finally closed to public use in 1919 because of danger from nearby artillery training ranges.

Heading south, you follow the East Fork of Tioga Creek upstream. Initially it's on your right, but at mile 2.3 you cross it on the first of three arch bridges, which are more than 150 years old. If you climb down the creek bank and inspect the south end of the first bridge, you see the year 1945 and the name JOSEF SCHECHTL scratched into mortar between the stones. He was one of a number of German prisoners of war used to repoint the bridges during World War II.

The rock-bottomed stream is lively in spring, and large rock outcroppings above on the far side make this an attractive setting, despite the pavement. You cross the two other bridges in rapid succession at mile 2.8, and at mile 3.1 come to a spring—named Dripping Springs—on the right of the road. Just beyond, a locked metal gate across the road marks the end of the trail and the beginning of Wilson Road, which leads up to the buildings of Fort Knox. On the left side of the road just before the gate is Sieboldt Cave—named for the farmer who once owned the land. In the old days local farmers used the cave as an icebox for their dairy produce. Turn around and you are back at the parking lot at mile 4.2.

66 Otter Creek

Highlights: Overlooks above the Ohio River and Otter
Creek valley.
Location: Southwest of Louisville.
Type of hike: Day hike; loop.
Total distance: 5.3 miles.
Difficulty: Moderate.
Best months: Any month.
Maps: USGS Rock Haven; Otter Creek Park trail map
(office 502–942–3211).

Finding the trailhead: From downtown Louisville, take Interstate 65 south
to the Snyder Freeway (Kentucky Highway 841) and go west for 10 miles to
the freeway's end at U.S. Highway 31W (Dixie Highway). Take US 31W south
for 13.5 miles, turn right onto KY 1638, and in 2.8 miles turn right at the
entrance sign for Otter Creek Park. This is KY 3241, though it's not marked.
In 1.3 miles, after passing the park office on your right, turn right into the
nature center parking lot. The trail starts at the south end of the nature center building. GPS: 37 56.452 N 86 02.910 W. (A small building located just
beyond the nature center at a fork in the park road has maps and other park
information.)

Parking and trailhead facilities: You'll find room for about twenty-five
cars; rest rooms and water are inside the nature center (closed Monday), and
picnic tables outside. The park campground is nearby; the park also has
overnight lodge and cabin accommodations.

Key points:
0.0   Yellow Trailhead.
0.9   Otter Creek Valley Overlook.
2.5   Red Trail junction.
2.7   Ohio River overlook.
3.2   Second river overlook.
3.6   Red and Blue Trails split.
4.0   Side trail to Morgan's Cave.

The hike: Although located two counties away, 2,600-acre Otter Creek Park
is owned by the city of Louisville. It's home to a number of separate camps,
including the YMCA's Camp Piomingo, a summer destination for generations of Louisville youngsters. Located on a ridge above the Ohio River at
the mouth of Otter Creek, the park offers the hiker 18 miles of trails, several leading to commanding views of the river and Indiana shore. This hike
combines parts of three different loop trails to make a wide loop through
the park, including a leg along the edge of the ridge above the river. The
hike involves lots of ups and downs but of moderate grade and short duration. The park has plenty of deer and birds. Be aware that Fort Knox is nearby,
and so any booms you hear are very likely artillery, not thunder.

Otter Creek

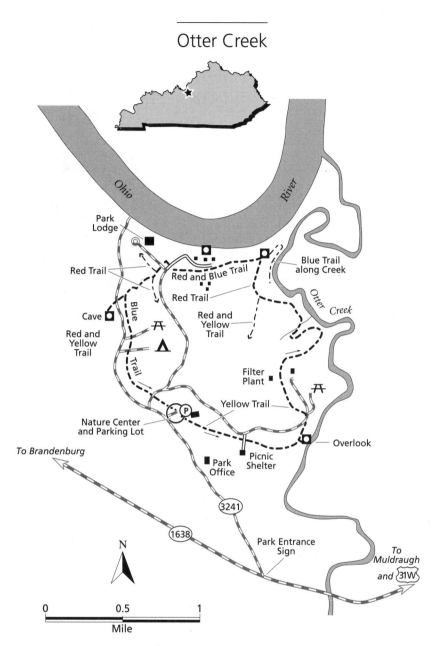

The hike starts on the Yellow Trail loop heading east from the nature center. Just beyond the south end of the building, the path turns left, cuts across a field, and begins following the grass clearing above a buried natural-gas pipeline. The short stretch to the pipeline clearing is faint and a bit hard to follow, but the yellow bands painted on utility poles should keep you on track. Heading southeast and east, the pipeline clearing parallels a paved park road on your left and soon crosses a gravel road leading right to the Pine Grove picnic area. At mile 0.7, after passing through a stand of

The Ohio River flows past the mouth of Otter Creek and a ridge overlooking the valley below.

good-sized hardwoods, the trail leaves the pipeline clearing and follows a path left (northeast) into the woods. This turn is marked by a sign for the Valley Overlook, which you soon reach. The overlook is a small, clear spot on the right of the trail with a view across the Otter Creek valley to the ridges on the other side. The creek is far below, so watch children carefully.

From the overlook, you initially parallel the creek but soon veer to the north, crossing a park road and stream before climbing to a small utility building at mile 1.3. From there you walk on the level ridgeside to another point overlooking the creek valley. Descending at first to the west and then to the northeast, you come down to and cross an Otter Creek tributary at mile 2.1. On the other side, after a short climb, you come to another natural-gas pipeline clearing, which you cross going north. On the far side you enter a pleasant wooded area and climb northward to reach the ridgetop at mile 2.5. Here the Yellow Trail turns left and, combined with the Red Trail, heads southwest back toward the nature center. You, however, turn right and follow the Red Trail alone (blazed with red rectangles) north to an excellent Ohio River overlook at mile 2.7. This is a rock outcropping above a wide bend in the river, and the upstream view is especially good. Just below, Otter Creek flows into the river. From the overlook, it's possible to take the Blue Trail down the ridge to the creek and follow it south to KY 1638. However, in flooded conditions, which are not unheard of along the Ohio, this lengthy stretch of the 8.1-mile-long Blue Trail loop is impassable.

Instead of dropping down to the creek, then, follow the combined Red and Blue Trails west along the ridgetop and reach the first of several park cottages at mile 3. Just beyond this point, a faint side path leads right to another

254

overlook, this one with a good view directly across the river into appealing Indiana farmland.

The combined Red and Blue Trails continue west and, at mile 3.6, cross a gravel road servicing the cottages and immediately afterward a paved road leading 0.3 mile north to the park lodge. (Just in case hunger calls, you should know that the lodge does not have a restaurant.) On the other side of the road, the Red and Blue Trails split, the Red going north to the river and south to the park's center while the Blue continues farther west. Following the Blue (blazed with blue diamonds), you soon come to a bluff above a paved road that connects the center of the park with a riverbank boat ramp. The trail parallels the road south and, at mile 4, comes to a side path that descends to the road and a streambed just below it. Across the streambed is a cave that legend holds was used by John Hunt Morgan and his Confederate raiders during the Civil War. Park personnel say it's not certain that the famous guerrilla was ever on what is now park property, but it's called Morgan's Cave nevertheless. The cavern, which has water running out the opening, is gated shut except for special tours. The round-trip from the Blue Trail to the cave is 0.3 mile.

After running near the top of an old quarry, the Blue Trail continues south above the road. At mile 4.5, where the road curves right, the trail descends to the roadside and follows it briefly before heading up a hillside and crossing an asphalt road that leads to an old picnic area. You shortly cross a second asphalt road, this one to the park campground. Continuing south, you proceed through a flat area full of cedars and pines, and at mile 5.1 cross the main park road. After traversing another pine grove, you are back at the nature center at mile 5.3.

67 Yellowbank Wildlife Management Area

Highlights: Quiet woods and open fields full of wildlife.
Location: West of Brandenburg along the Ohio River.
Type of hike: Day hike; loop.
Total distance: 3.5 miles.
Difficulty: Easy.
Best months: Spring and fall.
Maps: USGS Lodiburg (Ky.) and Rome (Ind./Ky.).

Finding the trailhead: From downtown Louisville, take Interstate 65 south to the Snyder Freeway (Kentucky Highway 841) and go west for 10 miles to the freeway's end at U.S. Highway 31W (Dixie Highway). Take US 31W south for 13.5 miles, turn right onto KY 1638, and, in 8.8 miles, turn right onto KY 448 toward Brandenburg. In another 1.2 miles, turn left onto KY 1051. After 2.3 more miles, turn left onto KY 79; 2.4 miles later, turn right

Yellowbank Wildlife Management Area

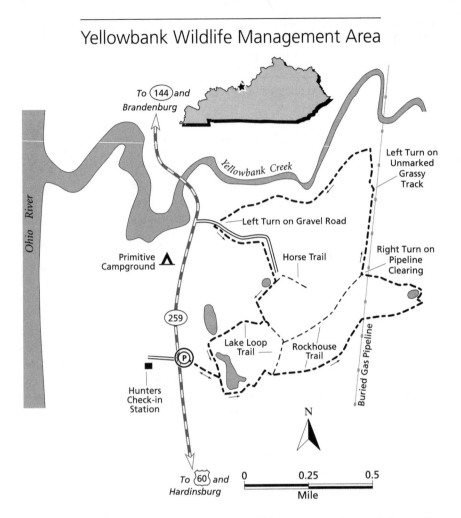

To (144) and Brandenburg

Yellowbank Creek

Ohio River

Left Turn on Unmarked Grassy Track

Left Turn on Gravel Road

Primitive Campground ⚊

Horse Trail

Right Turn on Pipeline Clearing

(259)

Lake Loop Trail

Rockhouse Trail

Buried Gas Pipeline

Hunters Check-in Station

N

To (60) and Hardinsburg

0   0.25   0.5
Mile

onto KY 144. Continue on KY 144—making sure to bear right at Paynesville—for 15 miles to KY 259. Turn right onto KY 259 and, in 7.3 miles—after passing a paved road right to the Yellowbank office (270–547–6856) and crossing Yellowbank Creek—turn left into the small gravel lot marked for trailhead parking. The trail starts on the lot's east side. GPS: 37 58.282 N 86 30.494 W.

Parking and trailhead facilities: You'll find room for about four cars, but no facilities. There's additional parking across KY 259 at the hunters' check-in station, and a primitive campground with pit toilets 0.2 mile north on KY 259.

Key points:
0.0 Lake Loop/Rockhouse Trailhead.
0.4 Bear right onto Rockhouse Trail.
1.2 Right turn onto gas pipeline clearing.

1.5   Left onto grassy, unmarked track.
2.3   Left onto gravel road near KY 259.
3.0   Right onto Lake Loop Trail.

The hike: Located along the Ohio River, 60 highway miles west of Louisville, the state's Yellowbank Wildlife Management Area offers 6,000 acres of bottomlands and ridges covered by a combination of hardwood forest, open fields, and ponds. You can count on seeing lots of songbirds, including warblers, and most likely wild turkeys, quail, and doves. In the bottomlands, if you don't see frogs, you will certainly hear them. What's nice about this spot is that the sounds of nature are the only thing you hear. As you can tell from the lengthy directions above, Yellowbank definitely qualifies as remote. This was principally dairy farming land until 1976, when the state acquired the major hunk of acreage. Most of the farm buildings are now gone, but the old homestead sites are still recognizable.

The wildlife area gets its the name from the creek that runs through the middle and empties into the Ohio River just north of the trailhead. The area is crisscrossed by gravel roads, horse trails, old footpaths, and a wide swath of grass running above a buried Texas Gas natural-gas pipeline There are also two designated hiking loops—Lake Loop, less than a mile in length, and Rockhouse Trail, a little over 2 miles. The following hike combines all of the above, including the pipeline clearing, to make a longer loop that takes you up several ridges as well as down to the creek bottom. There are a number of ups and downs, but with the exception of a steep, brief descent near the end of the hike, all are moderate.

From the parking lot, head southeast on the grass-and-dirt track that serves as the first leg of what is initially the combined Lake Loop/Rockhouse Trail. You pass through fields planted in sunflowers and grasses for wildlife food and habitat, and come to a large pond stocked for fishing. Turn right along the shoreline and, at mile 0.2, go around the south end of the pond on top of the levee. From there you follow a path northeast into the woods for about 150 yards and then start up the hill on an old roadbed. At mile 0.4, the shorter Lake Loop forks to the left and you bear right onto Rockhouse Trail. In some spots the trail is faint and difficult to see, but the way is well marked by blue-and-silver trail emblems attached to trees.

After climbing gently to the northeast among hardwoods that get taller the farther you go, Rockhouse Trail intersects the pipeline clearing at mile 0.8. Crossing the clearing, you continue to the northeast, walking along the top of a small cliff with a ravine on your right. The trail name comes from a rock house in the side of the cliff below. At mile 1, the trail reaches the head of the ravine; if there has been a recent rainfall, you will be treated to the sight of water falling over the cliffside into the hollow below. This is a good spot for lunch.

From the top of the ravine, the trail climbs a short distance to a small wildlife pond, which you round in a counterclockwise direction. At the northwest corner, the trail leaves the pond and climbs northwest into a field that was once the site of a farmhouse. It then follows an old grass roadbed to

The Yellowbank Wildlife Management Area is dotted with small ponds.

intersect the gas pipeline clearing once again, this time at mile 1.2. Here Rockhouse Trail turns southwest on its way to rejoin Lake Loop and return to the parking area. You, however, turn right and take the pipeline clearing as it descends north toward Yellowbank Creek. It will be another 1.8 miles before you are back on a designated hiking trail.

Descending along the clearing, you pass the remnant of a dirt road to your left and a short distance later, at mile 1.5, turn left onto a grassy, unmarked track branching into the woods (GPS: 37 58.822 N 86 29.639 W). This old farm track, which is used by horseback riders, descends north, paralleling the pipeline clearing until it hits level ground and curves west at mile 1.7. After crossing several bottomland fields, the track turns south and climbs partway up a pleasantly wooded ridge. Although it may be hidden by the trees, the creek is just to your right and easily reached at this point. The climb is a short one; before you know it, you are on your way down again. Steve McMillen, state fish and wildlife biologist for the area, recommends this section in early and mid-spring as especially rich in ferns and wildflowers. Passing a small muddy pond on your left, you come down to a metal gate blocking vehicles from the trail, and just beyond the gate, at mile 2.3, you hit an unmarked gravel road. A right on the road would get you to KY 259 in less than 0.1 mile, and from there it's a 0.5-mile walk south along the highway back to your car. This hike, however, turns left onto the gravel road and follows it uphill.

The road is open to vehicles but lightly used. At mile 2.6, at the top of the hill, the road turns right and cuts between two small fields. At mile 2.8, at a sign prohibiting further motorized travel, you come to a fork. To your left is a horse trail heading east—back toward Rockhouse Trail and the pipeline clearing. You, however, bear right onto a grassy roadbed going southwest past a pond to the edge of a field. Continuing south, you reach Lake Loop at mile 3 and turn right, following the trail downhill through an area of rock outcroppings covered with wildflowers in spring. This is the only steep part of the hike.

At mile 3.3, you come down to a wetland. Walk west across the levee at the south end of the wetland, turn left, and follow the trees south. You are soon back at the large pond you passed at the beginning of your hike. Turn right and retrace your steps on the grass-and-dirt road to your car.

Western Kentucky

Western Kentucky offers a wide range of hikes—from a short stroll around Columbus-Belmont State Park to a multiday backpacking trip in Land Between the Lakes. It also offers what you won't find anywhere else in the state: vast cypress-sprouting sloughs that are far closer to the scenery and feel of the Deep South than to the mountains of eastern Kentucky. In fact, from the Mississippi River bottomlands of Fulton County, you can drive to Tupelo in about half the time it takes to get to Pikeville.

Western Kentucky is dominated by water—the Ohio and Mississippi Rivers on the north and west, and Kentucky Lake and Lake Barkley in the middle. Most of the following hikes are on or close to one of them. There is another common denominator. Western Kentucky is, for the most part, low and flat. If you get above 500 feet, you are mountain climbing in this part of the state. The elevation along several of the river-bottom hikes doesn't vary more than a few feet. So ignoring summer heat and mosquitoes—which, of course, you can't ignore—this is pretty easy walking. The one big exception is Hike 79, where the multitude of ups and downs more than makes up for the gentleness of the terrain.

68 Audubon State Park

> **Highlights:** A mature hardwood forest with many songbirds; a small lake with beavers, muskrats, and waterfowl.
> **Location:** The city of Henderson.
> **Type of hike:** Day hike; loop.
> **Total distance:** 3.6 miles.
> **Difficulty:** Easy.
> **Best months:** Spring and fall.
> **Maps:** USGS Evansville South (Ind./Ky.); Audubon State Park *Visitor's Guide* (office 270–826–2247.)

Special considerations: Dogs, even on a leash, are not allowed on this hike.

Finding the trailhead: From the junction of U.S. Highways 60 and 41 on the northern outskirts of Henderson, take US 41 north for 1.7 miles and turn right at the entrance sign for Audubon State Park. In 0.4 mile, turn left at the sign for the nature center and museum, and park in front of the first building, which is the park office. The hike starts a few steps east of the parking lot at the beginning of an old asphalt road closed to traffic. GPS: 37 52.923 N 87 33.449 W.

Parking and trailhead facilities: There are spaces for about twenty cars next to the office, which has rest rooms and information. Additional parking is available by the nearby museum, which offers exhibits on the life and

Audubon State Park

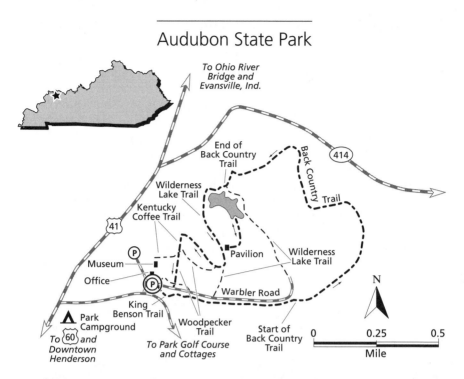

art of John James Audubon as well as a glass bird-observation room (an entrance fee is charged at the museum). The park campground is 0.3 mile west on the park road just off US 41.

Key points:

0.0   Warbler Road.
0.6   Right onto Back Country Trail.
2.1   Shore of Wilderness Lake.
2.7   Lake observation point.

The hike: Naturalist John James Audubon (1785–1851), famous for his realistic paintings of birds, lived in Henderson for nine years, roaming the woods and sketching wildlife. Born in what is now Haiti, the son of a French sea captain and his Creole mistress, Audubon came to Kentucky with a partner to establish a mercantile business. The enterprise proved successful, giving Audubon an opportunity to pursue his true passion. The Ohio River community of Henderson was then—and is now—on a major flyway for migratory songbirds and waterfowl. Only after he left Kentucky did Audubon become famous. But the park—developed in the 1930s by the old Civilian Conservation Corps (CCC) and one of the state's oldest—commemorates an important period in his development. The park museum claims to have the largest collection of Audubon memorabilia and original oil paintings in the world.

For the hiker, the park offers a pleasant ramble through a mature beech and sugar maple forest to a small CCC-made lake lively with beavers and muskrats. The former are nocturnal, but you are likely to see muskrats quietly plying the water. Birds, not surprisingly, are the park's main focus, and late April through early May is the prime time for visiting birders. Park naturalist Sondra Cabell says the park is an especially good place to see rose-breasted grosbeaks, indigo buntings, scarlet tanagers, and other colorful species that, while not rare, are not your everyday robin, either. The park is relatively small—692 acres, with plans to add 80 more—and is now all but surrounded by Henderson sprawl. But the park interior has been left in its natural state, and has a greater away-from-it-all feel than many larger, more remote tracts. It's been at least a hundred years since the park was timbered, and so many of the trees are towering. Half the park—the half you will be hiking through—is a designated nature preserve and strictly regulated. That's why dogs are prohibited; so are bicycles.

The hike starts at the entrance to an old asphalt road that used to take motorists eastward to a CCC-built picnic shelter. The shelter burned down long ago, and the road is now a walkway. Named Warbler Road, it is narrow and sufficiently lined with trees and wildflowers to make the paved surface unobtrusive. If you have children with you, you may want to start on King Benson Trail, an interpretive nature path that branches off into the woods at the beginning of Warbler Road. It parallels the road for less than 0.2 mile before crossing it and looping back to the parking lot. Going east on Warbler Road, you climb a hill—where Wilderness Lake Trail shoots off to your left—and then drop into a trough and go up a second hill. The string of large, private homes you see on the ridge your right are just across the park boundary.

At mile 0.6, you leave Warbler Road and climb the steps on your right that mark the beginning of Back Country Trail. Reaching the top of the ridge, the trail continues east before turning north and descending. At the beginning of the descent, if it's winter and the trees are leafless, you get a good view of the Ohio River to the north. After crossing two small streambeds on bridges, you climb back up the ridgetop near an electronics tower before descending to cross another drainage. After regaining the ridgetop once again, you enjoy a more extended stretch of level walking.

At mile 1.8, the trail curves west, and as you proceed, the noise of US 41 traffic may become noticeable—if not annoying. The highway, which crosses the Ohio just north of Henderson, is a key link to Indiana and the Hoosier city of Evansville. Descending the ridge, you reach the shore of Wilderness Lake at mile 2.1. This is the end of Back Country Trail. To your left, Wilderness Lake Trail goes to the lake's south end and on to Warbler Road. You, however, go straight on Wilderness Lake Trail, and soon cross the earthen dam at the lake's north end.

As you round the lake, watch closely for the telltale wake of a cruising muskrat. Just before the dam, on the left of the trail, is an observation hut. From the dam, the trail climbs up the ridge for a good view of the lake and, proceeding south, comes to a small, dilapidated stone pavilion at mile 2.5. Here Wilderness Lake Trail continues south, but for a nice side trip take the path marked LO (for Lake Overlook). It descends northeast along a finger of the ridge, and at mile 2.7 ends at the lakeshore on an isolated point that makes a good spot to observe beaver, muskrat, and waterfowl activity.

Wilderness Lake is small but teeming with wildlife.

After returning to the pavilion, follow Wilderness Lake Trail uphill to a junction with two short trails—Kentucky Coffee Tree Trail and Woodpecker Trail—that go west to the office/museum area. Either will do. I took Kentucky Coffee Tree, which descends to a ravine at mile 3.3 and then follows the ravine south for a short distance before crossing it on a wooden bridge. Just before the bridge, Woodpecker Trail merges on the left. Just after the bridge, Kentucky Coffee Tree Trail turns right and heads for the museum, and Woodpecker Trail bears left for Warbler Road. Take Woodpecker Trail; you reach Warbler Road at mile 3.5. Turn right and you are back at the parking lot at mile 3.6.

69 Sloughs Wildlife Management Area

      Highlights: Wooded and open marsh with a variety of waterfowl and shorebirds.
      Location: Near the Ohio River, west of Henderson.
      Type of hike: Day hike; loop.
      Total distance: 2.5 miles.
      Difficulty: Easy.
      Best months: Spring.
      Maps: USGS Smith Mills; Sloughs Wildlife Management Area map (office 270–827–2673).

Sloughs Wildlife Management Area

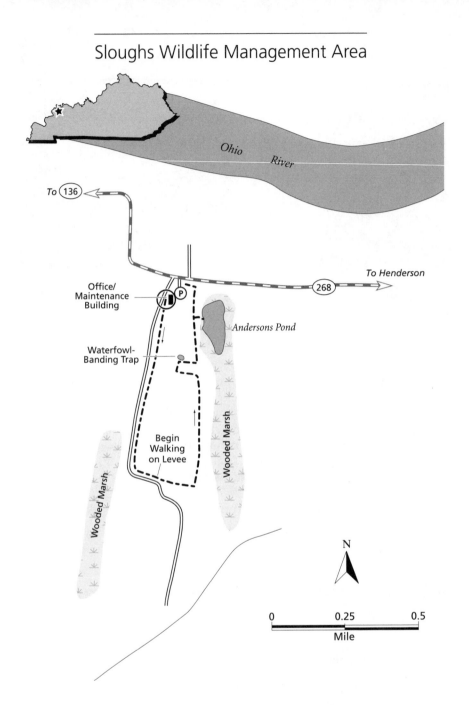

Ohio River

To 136

To Henderson

268

Office/
Maintenance
Building

Andersons Pond

P

Waterfowl-
Banding Trap

Begin
Walking
on Levee

Wooded Marsh

Wooded Marsh

N

0   0.25   0.5
Mile

Special considerations: Sections of this wildlife area, including the part this hike explores, are closed to public access annually from October 31 through March 15. Also, this hike is on a dirt road and levees; this section has no trails.

Finding the trailhead: From downtown Henderson, take U.S. Highway 60 west for 4 miles, turn right onto Kentucky Highway 136, and in 3 miles—in the community of Geneva—turn right onto KY 268. Take KY 268 for 6.5 miles and—after passing several wildlife-viewing stands on the left side of the road—turn left onto the narrow gravel lane marked by a sign for the Sauerheber Unit of the Sloughs Wildlife Management Area. Park near the metal building. The hike starts just west of the building. GPS: 37 51.560 N 87 46.783 W.

Parking and trailhead facilities: There's room for about ten cars, but no facilities. Camping is allowed in the Sloughs Wildlife Area; there are no designated sites—and no drinking water.

Key points:
- 0.0   Metal building.
- 0.9   Dirt road turns east.
- 1.0   Begin following levee to avoid high water.
- 1.2   Turn north.
- 1.9   Waterfowl-banding trap.

The hike: A *slough* is a swamp or marsh, and the state's Sloughs Wildlife Management Area is well named indeed. These 10,600 acres along the Ohio River are oozing with flooded fields and woods. For anyone not familiar with this type of liquid terrain, a visit takes you into an intriguing new world—one where handsome bald cypress trees shoot out of the water and hundreds of shorebirds dart across the muddy flats. Hike 72 offers a similar experience.

The Sloughs area consists of six different tracts spread over northern Henderson and Union Counties. This hike is in the Sauerheber Unit, the most popular part because of the number of migratory birds it attracts. Each winter this 3,000-acre tract, named for a former game warden, draws 15,000 migratory ducks and more than twice that many Canada geese. Because Sauerheber serves as a waterfowl refuge, it's closed to the public in winter, when most of the migrants are in residence. You should voluntarily avoid the summer months; in addition to the heat, the "mosquitoes will absolutely carry you away," says office clerk Connie Morton. But in early spring, after the tract is opened and before the western Kentucky sun begins blazing and the monster insects begin buzzing, the walking is delightful. There are still sandpipers and other shorebirds to see, as well as some geese and ducks that stay year-round. If you're lucky, you may get a glimpse of the pair of bald eagles that make Sauerheber their home.

Sauerheber is completely level and has no trails. You simply go where you want to go, restricted only by the water. The following route, which I took on a sunny morning in late March, is a good one for sampling this swampy area. From the parking lot, walk to the far side of the metal building, which is both office and maintenance barn for Sloughs. Just on the other side of

Swamps line the country road through Sloughs Wildlife Management Area.

the building, you will find a dirt road running parallel to the gravel lane you took in from KY 268. Turn left onto this narrow, little-used road and follow it south between a farm field on your left and woods on your right. Just where the water starts depends on the time of year and how much rainfall there has been. At some point, however, you will notice that the right side of the road is a swamp, and shortly you see cypress trees towering above you.

At mile 0.9, an unpaved boat launch slips into the swamp as the road curves east into the open field. Just after the curve, the elevation drops an imperceptible few feet but enough that, in spring at least, water is likely to be lapping at your feet about this point. The road continues a little less than a mile before dead-ending near Pond Creek, the source of the water around you. But from here on, the road is impassable for much of the year. It may be late May or early June before it dries out completely. So instead of continuing on the road, climb up the earthen levee running parallel to the road and walk on it. The Sauerheber Unit is crisscrossed by a number of these grass-covered embankments; in winter they are used to control the water level for the benefit of the visiting waterfowl. In spring they make a welcome bridge that keeps hikers' feet dry.

The nearby road soon turns south again, but you continue east on top of the levee. At mile 1.2, as you near trees marking the field's eastern boundary, the levee turns north. You turn with it, keeping the woods on your right. There are birds everywhere—shorebirds and mallards in the wet field, large birds in the trees. As I made my way, a kingfisher eyed me warily from a brambly bush growing out of the middle of the levee. At mile 1.7, the levee turns west, and you follow it until it ends in a field. Here you take a path running north and, at mile 1.9, come to a small pond covered by a large wire contraption: a trap used to catch waterfowl so they can be banded for research purposes.

From the trap, walk back east through the field—there are no levees here—to the edge of a soggy forest lining the east side of the field. Turn north and follow the line of trees toward KY 268. At mile 2.4, just before reaching the fence along the highway, turn left onto the grass strip paralleling the road. It quickly takes you to the gravel drive leading to the maintenance building, and you are back at your car at mile 2.5.

Options: For a more traditional hike, the Sloughs Wildlife Management Area's Cape Hills Unit south of the Sauerheber Unit has a 1.2-mile trail (2.4 miles out-and-back) across a wooded ridge. There are no overlooks or special scenic rewards, though you are likely to see deer. The trail follows an old dirt track from near the town of Smith Mills north to a small stream and parking area along Martin-Martin Road. It's an easy walk, with little elevation change. From Sauerheber, take KY 268 west for 1.5 miles and turn south onto KY 136. In 7.4 miles, in Smith Mills, turn left onto Mill Street, and in 0.9 mile bear left at the fork and park at the top of the hill. The unmarked trail starts at the north end of the small parking area (GPS 37 48.754 N 87 45.385 W).

70 Higginson-Henry Wildlife Management Area

Highlights: Pleasant wooded ridgetops and ravines.
Location: South of Morganfield.
Type of hike: Day hike or one-night backpack; loop.
Total distance: 7 miles.
Difficulty: Easy.
Best months: Spring or fall.
Maps: USGS Bordley, Waverly, and Morganfield; Higginson-Henry Wildlife Management Area trail map (office 270–389–3580).

Special considerations: Backpackers planning to camp overnight should contact the Higginson-Henry manager beforehand.

Finding the trailhead: From Morganfield, take Kentucky Highway 56 southeast for 5.3 miles and turn right onto the road marked by a sign for Mauzy Lake. In 0.4 mile, bear right at the fork, and in another 0.3 mile turn left into the gravel parking area. The hike starts at the northwest end of the lot. GPS: 37 37.426 N 87 51.618 W.

Parking and trailhead facilities: There's room for a dozen cars, but no facilities. Camping is allowed around the lake; there are no designated sites—and no drinking water. There is a convenience store 1.3 miles east at the KY 56/141 junction.

Key points:
0.0   Trailhead.
0.4   Right turn onto gravel road.
2.4   Cross KY 758.
3.2   Old fire tower on gravel road.
4.3   Recross KY 758.
6.8   Lakeshore.

The hike: This wildlife area is on land that used to be part of an army training base named Camp Breckinridge. After World War II, the federal government closed the facility and sold off the level acreage to private buyers. The hilly part not suitable for farming was acquired by the state and turned into this 5,424-acre wildlife management area. Shaped in a long, thin rectangle, it stretches across a series of ridges and ravines, all of moderate grade. The area was named for two local sportsmen killed in a boating accident.

This hike uses a variety of paths and forest tracks to follow the rolling terrain across most of the Higginson-Henry area. The ridgetops offer some limited views north and west, but there are no good overlooks or other special points of interest. This is attractive but simple forestland. The bottomlands are full of small, intermittent streams likely to be flowing in spring. There are also lots of wildflowers, turkeys, and deer and, according to the

Higginson-Henry Wildlife Management Area

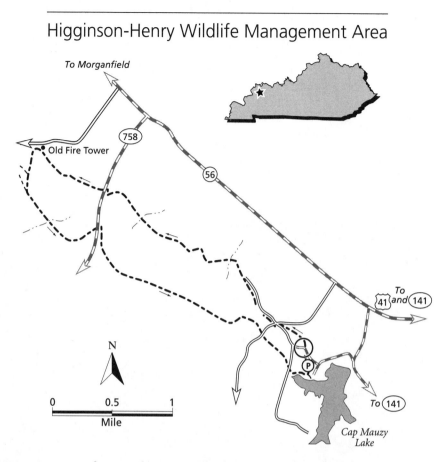

state, some gray foxes and coyotes. The loop starts and ends near Cap Mauzy Lake, an eighty-acre impoundment built by the army for use in training and now a favorite of local anglers. It was named for a former game warden.

This is a popular horseback riding area, and the route has been well trod by four-footed users, making it generally easy to follow. Indeed, some of the trail, especially near the lake, is badly eroded. The farther you get from the lake, the narrower and more pleasant the paths become. The woods are closed to motorized vehicles.

From the parking area, take the trail going northwest that's marked by horseback-riding signs. After passing through a beautiful stand of tall pines, you cross the road just west of the parking area—and just east of the line where the road surface turns from pavement to gravel. After a dip, the trail climbs gently through young hardwoods, passing two old concrete buildings that were once army latrines. At mile 0.4, the trail ends at the gravel road— above the spot where you crossed it just minutes ago. Turn right and follow the road as it heads northwest and rises slightly. Make sure you continue straight on this road at its junction with another gravel road.

At mile 0.9, the road dead-ends in the woods, and you continue on a path to the northwest. Here and at various other high points throughout the hike,

The trail at Higginson-Henry Wildlife Management Area gently climbs through young hardwoods.

you can see north and northeast across the flat farmland extending toward the Ohio River. Also, you occasionally hear a loud hum, which I found impossible to identify. Glen Wells, a veteran Higginson-Henry employee, later explained that the noise is made by the air vent of a large underground Peabody coal mine to the east.

At mile 1.1, after descending the ridge, you cross a small creek lined in spring with wildflowers, and immediately climb up another ridgeside. You repeat this up-and-down sequence several times before reaching KY 758 at mile 2.4. At mile 2, you come into a creek bottomland that may be confusing. There you find two trails and nothing to identify the correct one. Take the trail going straight (west).

Just before KY 758, the trail dead-ends into a path running parallel to the road. Turn right and follow this path for about 30 yards to the road. On the other side, you make an easy climb to the ridgetop and follow it with few interruptions to an old fire tower at mile 3.2. The tower, which anchors an antenna and is not climbable, is just off a gravel road coming from KY 56. The trail supposedly continues across the road and loops through the small part of the wildlife area north of the road. The Higginson-Henry trail map still shows that stretch of the trail, but I sure couldn't find it. So instead of crossing the gravel road, turn and follow the stone-and-dirt path running south—away from the road.

Descending, you come to a fork at mile 3.4 and bear left (the right prong dead-ends in 0.1 mile). Continuing down, you soon come to another trail junction and again bear left. Going southeast, you come into an attractive bottomland near a large field. At mile 4, after crossing a creek, the trail ends and you turn left onto a swath of grass and mud. This cut, made by workers to improve wildlife habitat and retard any fires that might develop, climbs gently and soon joins an old dirt road that reaches KY 758 at mile 4.3.

On the other side, jog right and immediately begin paralleling the road south to a forest track coming from KY 758. Bear left on the track, which climbs southeast to the ridgetop and begins a relatively level stretch. To your left you can see the ridgeline you took on the hike's westward leg.

At mile 6.1, the trail dips into a ravine and then climbs again to cross a gravel road. From there you descend to the lake, crossing a lake-access road before reaching the shore at mile 6.8. A short side trail soon forks right to the water's edge; the main trail turns north, climbing through the pine grove to the parking area at mile 7.

Options: At the eastern end of Higginson-Henry, there is a small tract developed for bird-watching. Called the Lee K. Nelson Wildlife Viewing Area, it's an attractive spot with a mile-long loop trail around a pond. From the Mauzy Lake road, take KY 56 east for 2.1 miles and turn left onto the gravel road. In another 0.4 mile, turn right and park.

71 Mantle Rock

Highlights: A large natural arch.
Location: Near the Ohio River, west of Marion.
Type of hike: Day hike; partial loop.
Total distance: 1.8 miles.
Difficulty: Easy.
Best months: Any month.
Maps: USGS Golconda; Mantle Rock map from The Nature Conservancy's Kentucky Chapter (859–259–9655).

Special considerations: Dogs are not allowed.

Finding the trailhead: From Marion, take U.S. Highway 60 west for 11.3 miles to the town of Salem and turn right onto Kentucky Highway 133. In 13 miles—2 miles after the community of Joy—turn left onto the narrow gravel road next to a historical marker for Mantle Rock. In 0.1 mile, park in the gravel lot. The hike starts at the south end of the lot. GPS: 37 21.608 N 88 25.439 W.

Parking and trailhead facilities: There's room for about ten cars, but no facilities.

Key points:
0.0   Beginning of rough gravel road.
0.2   Gate and information kiosk.
0.4   Mantle Rock.
0.6   Beginning of loop.
1.2   End of loop.

The hike: This short hike takes you to Mantle Rock, a large sandstone arch located in a beautiful stream-crossed bottomland. Despite its brevity, the walk offers scenic rewards—enough, I think, to justify the drive to reach this corner of Kentucky.

Measuring 188 feet in length and 30 feet in height, Mantle Rock is one of the longest arches in the state. It is also part of one of the ugliest chapters in American history: President Andrew Jackson's expulsion of the Cherokee Indians from the eastern United States. In the winter of 1838–39, waiting for improved weather that would allow them to cross the Ohio River, many Cherokees on the forced trek west took shelter in Mantle Rock and nearby rock houses. Those who did not survive the brutal Kentucky winter were among the 2,000 to 4,000 Cherokees who perished in this unfortunate migration, known as the Trail of Tears.

The Cherokees were by no means the first Native Americans to use Mantle Rock. According to The Nature Conservancy, which owns the 190-acre preserve surrounding the arch, people were hunting and gathering food here 10,000 years ago. In addition to history, The Nature Conservancy says the area is significant for a number of plant species found there, including June grass, prickly pear cactus, and a rare kind of goldenrod.

Mantle Rock

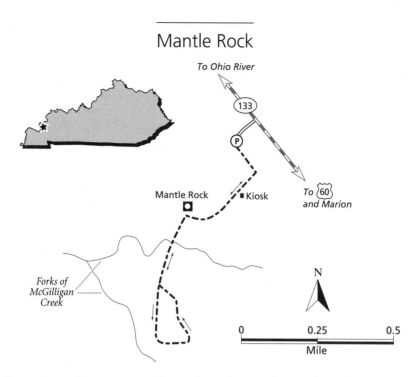

To Ohio River

133

P

Mantle Rock ■ Kiosk

To 60 and Marion

Forks of McGilligan Creek

N

0   0.25   0.5
Mile

From the parking area, walk south on the rough gravel road. It descends gradually through a field, curving first southeast and then southwest before reaching a gate and information kiosk at mile 0.2. Here the road ends, and you take a broad dirt path into a forest of good-sized hardwoods. At mile

At 188 feet in length, Mantle Rock is one of the longest arches in Kentucky.

0.4, immediately after the trail curves west, you see a cliff about 40 feet to the right of the trail and, in front of the cliff, gracefully sloping Mantle Rock. In spring a small, rock-bottomed stream with grassy banks runs along the arch, adding to the pleasantness of the scene. This is a spot to enjoy.

From the arch, the trail goes south, crossing first a small stream and then a larger one, the latter a fork of McGilligan Creek, a tributary of the Ohio. Following an old roadbed covered by moss and lined, at least in spring, with wildflowers, you parallel a cliff and creek bottom on your right and at mile 0.6 come to a sign marking the beginning of the trail's loop portion. Taking the loop's southbound leg, you continue south on the attractive old roadbed. At mile 0.8, the trail turns east and climbs gradually. The flowing water you hear below on your right is another fork of McGilligan Creek.

After passing through a small stand of cedars, you come to a stake marking a left turn and the start of the loop's northbound leg. Now you are on a relatively new path, which was faint and hard to follow when I was there. Thankfully, The Nature Conservancy's liberal use of green-and-yellow trail markers kept me on track as I threaded my way through the trees.

At mile 1.2, you reach the sign marking the start—and end—of the loop segment. From there you retrace your steps past Mantle Rock and reach the parking area at mile 1.8.

72 Ballard Wildlife Management Area

Highlights: A cypress swamp.
Location: West of Paducah.
Type of hike: Day hike; loop.
Total distance: 5.8 miles.
Difficulty: Easy.
Best months: Spring or fall.
Maps: USGS Olmsted (Ill./Ky.); Ballard Wildlife Management Area map (office 270–224–2244).

Special considerations: This area is closed annually from October 15 through March 15, and in addition is subject to Ohio River flooding in spring. The Ballard area has no trails; this hike is entirely on gravel roads.

Finding the trailhead: From Paducah, take U.S. Highway 60 west for 20 miles to La Center and turn right (north) onto Kentucky Highway 358. In 5.5 miles turn left onto KY 473, and in 0.4 mile—at the four-way stop—go straight on KY 1105. In 3.2 miles bear right onto KY 473 (the same KY 473), and in 2.3 miles turn left onto Wildlife Lodge Road, marked by a sign for the Ballard Wildlife Management Area headquarters. At the four-way intersection in 0.7 mile, turn left onto the gravel road, and in another 0.4 mile pull into the dirt parking area on the right side of the road next to the wildlife-viewing platform. GPS: 37 10.639 N 89 01.861 W.

Ballard Wildlife Management Area

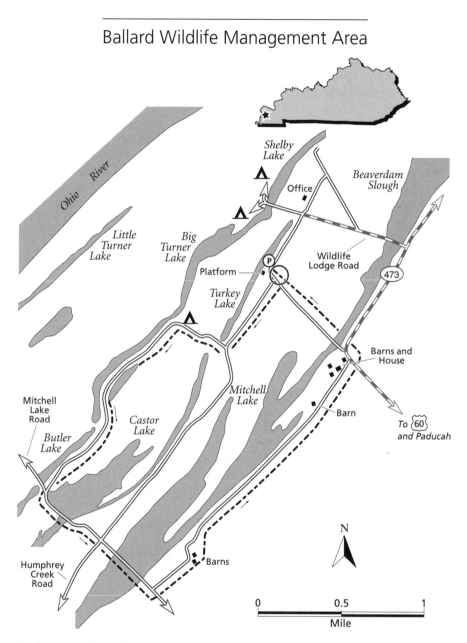

Parking and trailhead facilities: You'll find room for five cars, but no facilities. The wildlife area office, with a rest room and information, is 0.5 mile north—just beyond Wildlife Lodge Road. There are primitive—very primitive—camping areas on Shelby and Big Turner Lakes.

Key points:
- 0.0   Start of hike on gravel road.
- 0.5   Right turn at end of Turkey Lake.
- 2.2   Left onto Mitchell Lake Road.

3.2   Left onto first road south of Mitchell Lake.
5.0   Left onto KY 473, then left again onto gravel road.

The hike: Once a collection of more than twenty farms, the Ballard Wildlife Management Area is now a refuge for migratory waterfowl. Each winter this 8,373-acre, state-owned tract along the Ohio River gets hundreds of thousands of Canada, snow, and blue geese, plus thousands of mallards, wigeons, and other ducks. Bald eagles also nest here. For the migrants' protection, the area is closed from October 15 through March 15. For the hiker, the weeks just after the opening and just before the closing are a wonderful time to visit. While most—though not all—geese and ducks have gone, the cypress-filled lakes, wooded marshes, and open farm fields provide rich visual rewards. With the exception of the similar but smaller Sauerheber tract in Hike 69, this is bottomland scenery you won't find elsewhere.

The Ballard area—which is as flat as a pool table—has no trails, and so the hike is entirely on gravel roads. They get little vehicle traffic, and make fine walking paths—in early spring or fall, that is. In summer, hiking here would be brutal, if not suicidal; the sun would bake you while mosquitoes ate you. I chose the following route because it offers a good mix of lakes, woods, and open fields. The Ballard area is broken up by small bodies of water, all naturally made and regularly flooded by the Ohio. Some, however, are called lakes, some sloughs. What's the difference? None, really. With only a few exceptions, all are only about 5 feet deep, says Ballard manager Charlie Wilkins. Their level is controlled somewhat by a system of levees.

From the parking area, start southeast but immediately turn right onto the gravel road running southwest parallel to thin, shallow Turkey Lake. Indeed, the lake can be almost nonexistent. When I was there, the woods to the left of the road were off limits because of a bald eagle nest. At the time, the wildlife area had two resident pairs of eagles. At mile 0.5, you turn right onto the gravel road going across the south end of Turkey Lake. At mile 0.8, after cutting through a wooded marsh, you come to Big Turner Lake and one of Ballard's primitive camping areas. Big Turner is popular with anglers. In this and the other lakes, the catch includes bass, bluegill, crappie, catfish, and anything else found in the Ohio River.

At the campground, the road turns southwest along Big Turner's cypress-studded shore. On your left, a planted field gives way to a pond before the trail winds into a wooded area. At any point in the woods, take a short detour right and you quickly come to the edge of a handsome cypress swamp. Whether you are at the end of Big Turner Lake or the beginning of Butler Lake may be hard to tell. Whichever, it will be a perfect spot for a rest break.

At mile 2.2, at the end of Butler Lake, you turn left onto Mitchell Lake Road and follow its packed-dirt-and-stone surface southeast, passing Castor Lake on your left. In spring the woods here sparkle with blooming redbud trees. Ignore the first road you cross—Humphrey Creek Road—and continue southeast on Mitchell Lake Road as it cuts through a field and crosses the lower end of Mitchell Lake, another favorite of anglers.

At mile 3.2, you turn left onto a gravel road—the first you come to after crossing the lake—and walk northeast between fields of grass and corn. In

An old barn is near the shore of Mitchell Lake.

spring patches of the ground are covered with a beautiful purple bloom—identified by Charlie Wilkins as a weed named henbit. At a couple of picturesque old barns, the road jogs north, taking you closer to the lake. On a warm day you see dozens of turtles sunning themselves on shoreline logs and deadheads. Even though most of the migratory waterfowl have gone or not yet come, you are also likely to see some ducks and geese plying the water.

At mile 5, just after passing three more barns and a house, the gravel road dead-ends into KY 473 at a hairpin turn. Turn left onto the highway and then left again onto the gravel road going north into the wildlife area's interior. After crossing a slough, the road cuts through a wooded marsh and reaches the parking area at mile 5.8.

73 Columbus-Belmont State Park

Highlights: A Mississippi River bluff with a magnificent view.
Location: Western tip of Kentucky.
Type of hike: Day hike; loop.
Total distance: 1.7 miles.
Difficulty: Easy.
Best months: Any month.
Maps: USGS Arlington; Columbus-Belmont State Park map (office 270–677–2327).

Columbus-Belmont State Park

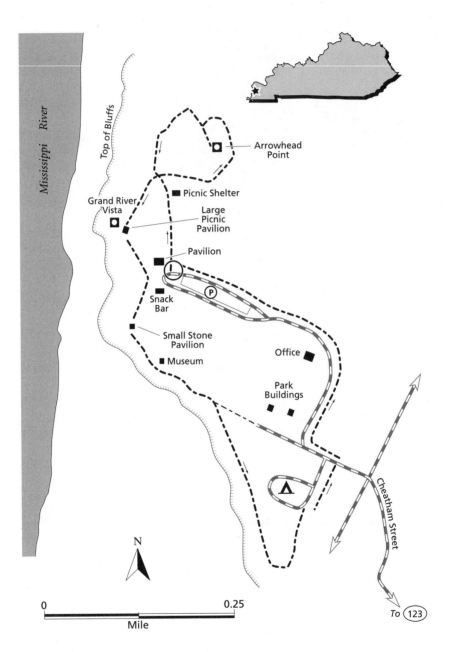

Mississippi River

Top of Bluffs

Arrowhead Point

Grand River Vista

Picnic Shelter

Large Picnic Pavilion

Pavilion

Snack Bar

Small Stone Pavilion

Museum

Office

Park Buildings

Cheatham Street

To 123

N

0   0.25

Mile

Special considerations: A short section of this hike runs along the edge of the park campground and should be bypassed by noncampers, according to the park manager at the time this book was written.

Finding the trailhead: From Bardwell, take Kentucky Highway 123 south for 10 miles to the town of Columbus and turn right onto Cheatham Street. From Clinton, take KY 58 west to Columbus, turn right onto KY 123, and in 0.1 mile turn left onto Cheatham Street. Cheatham becomes Park Road and ends in 0.8 mile at a parking lot for the picnic area. The hike starts at the west end of the lot. GPS: 36 45.932 N 89 06.619 W.

Parking and trailhead facilities: There's room for two dozen cars, along with drinking water, rest rooms, and, in summer, a snack bar. The park campground is 0.4 mile from the picnic area.

Key points:
0.0   Start of hike on asphalt walkway.
0.3   Arrowhead Point.
0.6   View of the Mississippi from pavilion.
1.0   Bluff at campground.

The hike: This little hike, the second shortest in the book, is included because it takes you along a bluff high above the Mississippi River with stupendous upstream and downstream views. It is one of the most dramatic overlooks you will find anywhere in the state. Indeed, that's exactly why the little town of Columbus played a role in the Civil War.

In 1861, disregarding Kentucky's neutral status, Confederate troops fortified these bluffs to stop Union forces from using the Mississippi to penetrate the South. On November 7, 1861, under a little-known brigadier general named Ulysses S. Grant, the Yankees attacked the Confederate camp at the Missouri town of Belmont just across the river from Columbus. The cannon fire from the Kentucky bluff helped turn back the Northern advance. Militarily the battle was inconclusive, but the aggressiveness shown by Grant's troops gave a significant boost both to Union morale and to his career. The next year, after the loss of strategic forts on the Tennessee and Cumberland Rivers, the Confederates abandoned Columbus.

This 156-acre state park was developed in the 1930s to commemorate that battle and preserve the extensive earthworks. It's main attribute, however, is the commanding vista of the Mississippi. The park doesn't have much of a trail system, and so this hike relies on a combination of paths, paved walkways, and Park Road. From the end of the parking lot, where placards tell you about the battle, take the asphalt walkway north to a small picnic shelter and a sign marking the start of the Confederate trenches. With earthen mounds rising up on both sides, you follow a dirt path along the trench floor. The depth gives you an immediate appreciation for just how much work it took Confederate soldiers to construct the fortifications. The trench curves right and then left as it circles northward, climbing gently. At mile 0.3, after jogging south on top of the earthworks, you come to Arrowhead

The bluff high above the Mississippi River provides majestic northerly views.

Point overlooking a section of the trench system, most of it overgrown by vines and bushes when I was there.

From there you head northwest through woods to a modern metal fence, which you follow as it curves south. Taking log stairs, you descend once again into the trench and circle back to the start of the trench loop. There you bear right along the fence and climb steps leading up to the open bluff. Here the metal fence gives way to an older, wooden one more in keeping with the surroundings. Follow the fence as it curves along the edge of the bluff to a large picnic pavilion and a grand view of the Mississippi. If you stay even a few minutes, you are likely to see a barge or two moving goods up or down the river. On display behind the pavilion is a section of a large chain that the Confederates ran across the river to stop Union gunboats.

Continuing along the bluff, you follow the wood fence and then take an asphalt walkway to a small stone pavilion. Here you have the best river view of all. Stay on the walkway as it goes southeast, passing a building that served as a hospital for the Southern troops and is now the park museum (a small fee is charged). Just behind the museum is a redoubt that has been beautifully restored; it's worth a stop.

At mile 0.9, just after passing beneath a utility wire, turn right off the paved walkway onto a narrow, unmarked dirt path that climbs up to the bluff at the edge of the campground. Here you have another good view of the river. If you can't find the little path, just thread your way uphill through the trees, making sure to skirt the eroded, vine-filled gully on your right. Cindy Lynch, the park manager at the time this was written, said the campground is off limits to visitors who aren't registered campers; thus you may have to bypass this next stretch.

At the campground, walk along the edge of the open bluff to the start of another fortification. Follow the trench east to its end near the campground loop road. Taking the road north, you reach the campground entrance at mile 1.3. Turn left and follow Park Road back to the picnic area parking lot.

74 Reelfoot National Wildlife Refuge

Highlights: A quiet cove on the upper reaches of Reelfoot Lake.
Location: Southwest corner of Kentucky, near Hickman.
Type of hike: Day hike; out-and-back.
Total distance: 4.4 miles.
Difficulty: Easy.
Best months: Spring and fall.
Maps: USGS Bondurant and Samburg (Tenn.); Reelfoot National Wildlife Refuge pamphlet (office 901-538-2481).

Special considerations: The refuge is closed annually from November 15 through March 15, and there is a two-day deer hunt in the first week of November. Also, this hike is on a gravel-and-dirt road, not a trail.

Finding the trailhead: From Hickman, take Kentucky Highway 94 west for 4.5 miles and turn left onto KY 311. In 1.6 miles, turn right onto KY 1282, making sure to follow the sign for the Long Point Unit of the Reelfoot National Wildlife Refuge and not the refuge's visitor center, which is 6 miles south in Tennessee. After 2.5 miles on KY 1282, turn left onto the gravel road marked by a sign for the refuge. In 0.5 mile, park on the left of the road next to the wildlife-viewing platform. The hike starts at the platform. GPS: 36 30.881 N 89 19.237 W.

Parking and trailhead facilities: You'll find room for about ten cars, but no facilities.

Key points:
0.3 Left turn at the T.
2.0 Road ends.
2.2 Turn around at blind.

The hike: In late 1811 and early 1812, the most severe series of earthquakes ever recorded in North America rocked the Mississippi River area where Kentucky, Missouri, and Tennessee meet. Known by the name of the Missouri town just north of the river, the New Madrid quakes literally changed the geography, rerouting streams and creating Reelfoot Lake. Named for a Chickasaw chief born with a deformed foot, this long, shallow lake—5 feet deep on average—is mainly in Tennessee. But its upper reaches stretch into Kentucky, as does part of the 10,428-acre federal wildlife refuge established in

Reelfoot National Wildlife Refuge

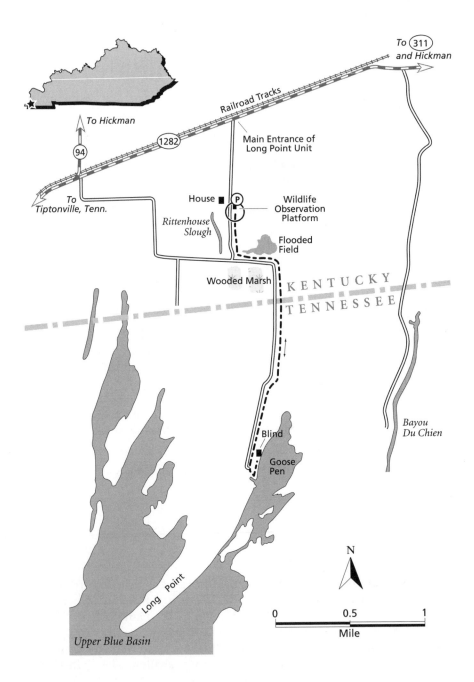

To (311) and Hickman

Railroad Tracks

To Hickman

1282

94

Main Entrance of Long Point Unit

To Tiptonville, Tenn.

House ■ (P)

Rittenhouse Slough

Wildlife Observation Platform

Flooded Field

Wooded Marsh

KENTUCKY

TENNESSEE

Bayou Du Chien

Blind

Goose Pen

Long Point

N

0   0.5   1

Mile

Upper Blue Basin

1941 around the northern shoreline. The refuge's Long Point Unit—named for a thin strip of land jutting into the lake's Upper Blue Basin—is accessible by car only from Kentucky.

This hike crosses the Long Point Unit, starting in marshland on the Kentucky side and ending in Tennessee at a scenic cove full of water lilies, bald cypress trees, and waterfowl. Long Point has no trails; except for a short stretch at the lakeside, this hike is on a gravel-and-dirt road. Though little used, the narrow road is open to vehicles—meaning, of course, that you could drive to the lake. You would, however, miss a lovely walk—lovely, that is, in the cool of spring or fall. There is absolutely no shade to ward off the summer sun.

From the wildlife platform, follow the road south, passing a field on your left that in spring looks more like a pond. The principal purpose of the refuge is to provide food and habitat for waterfowl on the Mississippi Flyway, and levees allow the water level to be manipulated. In winter the refuge is a sanctuary mainly for Canada geese and mallards. That's why the facility is closed for that part of the year. Bald eagles and marsh birds are also visitors. When I took the hike in late March, the field was flooded and waterfowl were still using it. So were some carp; the large fish were visible as they smacked their way through the shallow water. On the right side of the road, the ditch sprouting cypress trees is called Rittenhouse Slough.

At mile 0.3, the road comes to a T and you turn left. (A right would take you 1.4 miles across open fields and swamp to the intersection of KY 94 and KY 1282 on the refuge's western boundary.) Going east, the road skirts a wooded marsh on your right and, at mile 0.6, turns south once again. At mile 0.8, you cross the unmarked Kentucky–Tennessee line as the road contin-

Water lilies dot a quiet inlet in Reelfoot National Wildlife Refuge.

ues south through dry fields planted with corn or other crops. It's a quiet stretch, good for bird-watching—or just thinking.

At mile 2, as the road bends left, a sign prohibits further vehicle travel. The lake, dotted with cypresses and covered by water lilies and families of ducks, is just beyond. Going southeast, you quickly reach the grassy shore— a great place to watch nature. This secluded body of water, which is connected by a couple of ditches to the lake's Upper Blue Basin, is known locally as Goose Pen. That's because years ago it was fenced off to make a home for crippled geese. Now, from time to time, refuge workers use it to trap ducks for banding. The bands allow researchers to track migration. Following the shoreline north, you come to a small hut at mile 2.2. This is the blind where workers operate the large net that traps the waterfowl. North of the blind, the open shore is replaced by forest. Turn around and retrace your steps to your car.

Options: For a shadier walk, take the tree-lined dirt road running down the Long Point Unit's eastern boundary. The road starts on KY 1282, 1.2 miles east of the main entrance road, and goes south along a bayou before ending in 2.7 miles in a field. The road is attractive but lacks the scenic climax of the other hike.

75 Honker Lake

Highlights:	The wooded shoreline of Lake Barkley and a small lake that attracts waterfowl.
Location:	Land Between the Lakes National Recreation Area.
Type of hike:	Day hike; loop.
Total distance:	4.5 miles.
Difficulty:	Easy.
Best months:	Spring and fall.
Maps:	USGS Mont; Land Between the Lakes "Hike & Bike Trail Map" (office 270–924–2000).

Special considerations: Ticks are a problem here; take appropriate precautions.

Finding the trailhead: From Interstate 24 or U.S. Highway 62, southeast of Calvert City, take Kentucky Highway 453 south into Land Between the Lakes (LBL), where the highway loses its numerical designation and becomes the Trace. The LBL's North Welcome Station, which has maps and other information, is 5 miles south of US 62. From the welcome station, continue south on the Trace and, in 8.8 miles, turn left onto Silver Trail Road. In 3 miles, park in front of the Nature Station. The trail starts on the parking lot's north side. GPS: 36 54.093 N 88 02.214 W.

Parking and trailhead facilities: There are spaces for about forty-five cars. Rest rooms and vending machines are available at the Nature Station, an

Honker Lake

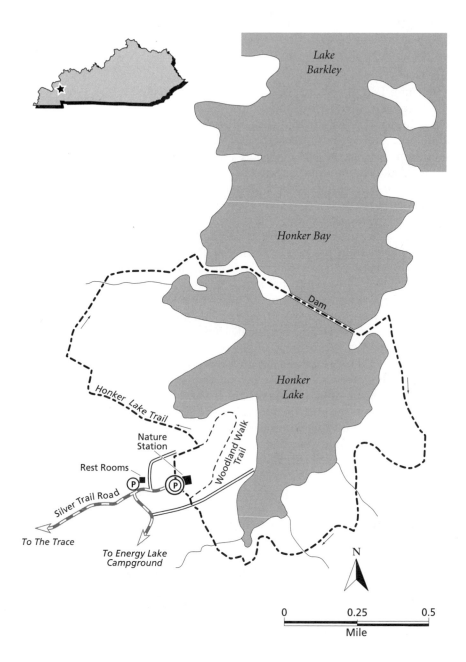

Lake
Barkley

Honker Bay

Dam

Honker
Lake

Honker Lake Trail

Nature
Station

Woodland Walk
Trail

Rest Rooms

P

P

Silver Trail Road

To The Trace

To Energy Lake
Campground

N

0   0.25   0.5
Mile

environmental education facility with displays and a live animals building (entrance fee charged). More rest rooms and additional parking are also found a short walk west on Silver Trail Road.

Key points:
0.0   Beginning of Honker Lake Trail.
1.6   Shoreline between Honker Lake and Lake Barkley.
1.9   Honker Lake dam.
4.1   Bridge across Long Creek.

The hike: Land Between the Lakes (LBL) was created in the 1960s by the federal government to turn the remote hill country between two large man-made reservoirs—Kentucky Lake and Lake Barkley—into a multiuse recreation area that would attract people from across the country. Shaped in a long, thin rectangle, this 170,000-acre tract stretches from Kentucky into Tennessee and has more than 300 miles of shoreline. In addition to a multitude of boat-launch facilities and campgrounds, it offers 200 miles of paths and rustic roads for hikers, bikers, off-highway vehicles, and horses. Initially managed by the Tennessee Valley Authority but now under the USDA Forest Service, LBL is a rustic place with few amenities for visitors. Make sure you buy whatever food you need before you come. Also, be aware that LBL is notorious for its robust crop of ticks from April through autumn; hikers are advised to wear long pants and apply tick repellant.

For backpacking in LBL, see the next two hikes—76 and 77. This hike is for visitors who don't have the time or inclination for an overnight but want to see a pleasant stretch of lakefront. Honker Lake—the name comes from the sound made by Canada geese—was created by damming off an inlet of Lake Barkley. It's a reservoir within a reservoir. The purpose was to create a separate body of water whose level could be better controlled to accommodate geese and ducks. Honker Lake is a refuge for both migrant and resident waterfowl, and the surrounding shore is set aside as an environmental education area with special restrictions, including no camping. The Honker Lake Trail is open all year, but the lake itself is closed to boats during the winter because of its refuge function.

From the parking lot, descend north on wood-and-gravel steps to a dirt path and—just before reaching a gravel road—turn right. Shortly, Woodland Walk Trail branches right to begin a mile-long loop around the nature station, and you turn left onto Honker Lake Trail. Entering the woods, the trail goes northwest into a stand of tall hardwoods and climbs gradually up a hill, reaching the top at mile 0.6. After a level stretch, the trail, which is marked by posts with white-and-brown emblems, curves north and descends to cross a small stream at mile 1.4. Turning east, you come to an old gravel track; you can turn right onto this or continue on the path. Either way, at mile 1.6 you reach a thin strip of land running between Honker Lake on your right and an inlet of Lake Barkley—named Honker Bay—on your left. On both bodies of water, you are likely to see waterfowl and wading birds. Tall pines and the sound of croaking frogs contribute to the scene's attractiveness.

286

Lake Barkley is visible from the Honker Lake Trail.

Continuing east, you climb to the top of a small hill and descend to cross the narrow dam separating Honker Lake from its big brother. When Lake Barkley is at a high level, it can overcome this thin barrier, temporarily eliminating Honker's separate identity. The dam is a favorite of anglers, so you're apt to have company here. Reaching the dam's eastern end at mile 2.1, you curve northeast on gravel before turning into the woods and going south. After angling away from the lakeshore to avoid a low-lying wet area, the trail turns northwest toward the lake and then roughly follows the shoreline south, in the process crossing two small streams on bridges.

As you circle the lake's southern tip, you might hear the loud honking of geese. They like to congregate on a grassy field just across the lake. Curving north, you cross a small stream and then take a long wooden bridge over Long Creek. This is a scenic part of the hike, and a good place for a rest stop.

From the bridge, the trail winds north and crosses a gravel road leading to the lake. On the far side of the road, you meet the other end of Woodland Walk Trail. Following the signs for the Nature Station, you climb first northeast and then northwest. After passing the Nature Station's outdoor animal cages, you reach the building and parking lot at mile 4.5.

76 North–South Trail

<table>
<tr><td align="right">Highlights:</td><td>Quiet coves and ridgetops along Kentucky Lake.</td></tr>
<tr><td align="right">Location:</td><td>Land Between the Lakes National Recreation Area.</td></tr>
<tr><td align="right">Type of hike:</td><td>One- to three-night backpack; shuttle (one-way).</td></tr>
<tr><td align="right">Total distance:</td><td>About 31 miles.</td></tr>
<tr><td align="right">Difficulty:</td><td>Moderate.</td></tr>
<tr><td align="right">Best months:</td><td>Spring and fall.</td></tr>
<tr><td align="right">Maps:</td><td>USGS Birmingham Point, Mont, Fairdealing, and Fenton; Land Between the Lakes "Hike & Bike Trail Map" (office 270-924-2000).</td></tr>
<tr><td align="right">Permits and fees:</td><td>A $10 permit is required for backcountry camping in LBL. Permits (good for twelve months starting March 1) can be purchased at Golden Pond Visitor Center (open all year from 9:00 A.M. to 5:00 P.M.) and North Welcome Station (open March through November from 9:00 A.M. to 5:00 P.M.).</td></tr>
</table>

Finding the trailhead: From Interstate 24 or U.S. Highway 62, southeast of Calvert City, take Kentucky Highway 453 south into Land Between the Lakes (LBL), where the highway loses its numerical designation and becomes the Trace. The LBL's North Welcome Station, which has maps and other information, is 5 miles south of US 62. From the welcome station, continue south on the Trace for 18.3 miles to the Golden Pond Visitor Center entrance on your left. Take the entrance drive 0.2 mile and park in front of the building. The trail starts on the west side of the Trace across from the visitor center entrance. GPS: 36 46.631 N 88 03.938 W.

Parking and trailhead facilities: You'll find spaces for fifty cars, as well as rest rooms, drinking water, vending machines, a telephone, maps, and other information.

Key points:
0.0   North–South Trailhead.
3.9   Shore of Vickers Bay.
8.4   LBL Road 141 near Rhodes Bay.
10.0 Higgins Bay.
13.3 LBL Road 140 near Sugar Bay boat launch.
16.2 LBL Road 139.
18.0 Hatchery Hollow.
22.5 LBL Road 114.
25.1 Pisgah Bay boat-launch area.
27.6 LBL Road 110 near Hillman Ferry Campground.
29.1 Beach at Moss Creek area.

The hike: North–South Trail runs the length of LBL—from the South Welcome Station in Tennessee to the North Welcome Station in Kentucky. (For background information on LBL, see Hike 75.) This hike follows the trail's northern half, starting at Golden Pond Visitor Center about 10 miles above

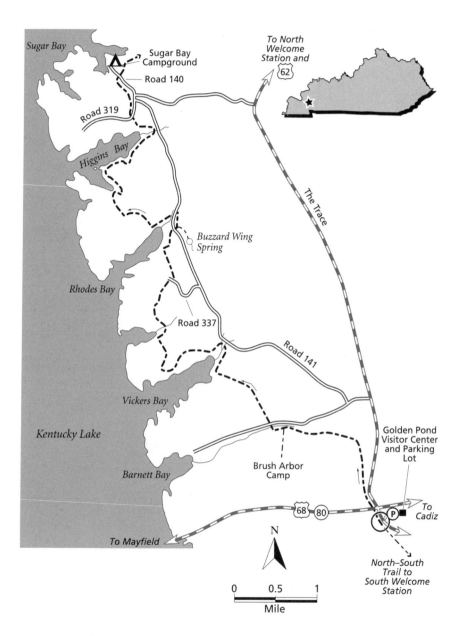

Sugar Bay

Sugar Bay
Campground

To North
Welcome
Station and
62

Road 140

Road 319

Higgins Bay

The Trace

Buzzard Wing
Spring

Rhodes Bay

Road 337

Road 141

Vickers Bay

Golden Pond
Visitor Center
and Parking
Lot

Kentucky Lake

Brush Arbor
Camp

Barnett Bay

68 80

To
Cadiz

P

To Mayfield

N

North–South
Trail to
South Welcome
Station

0   0.5   1
Mile

North–South Trail, Map 2

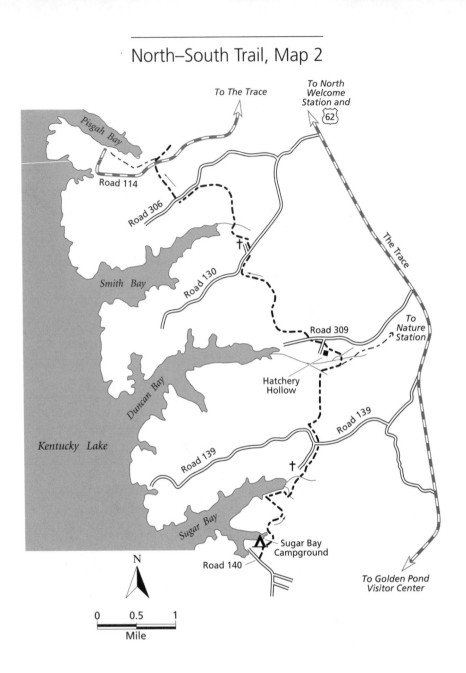

To The Trace

To North
Welcome
Station and
62

Pisgah Bay

Road 114

Road 306

Smith Bay

Road 130

The Trace

Road 309

To
Nature
Station

Hatchery
Hollow

Duncan Bay

Kentucky Lake

Road 139

Road 139

Sugar Bay

Sugar Bay
Campground

Road 140

To Golden Pond
Visitor Center

N

0   0.5   1
Mile

North–South Trail, Map 3

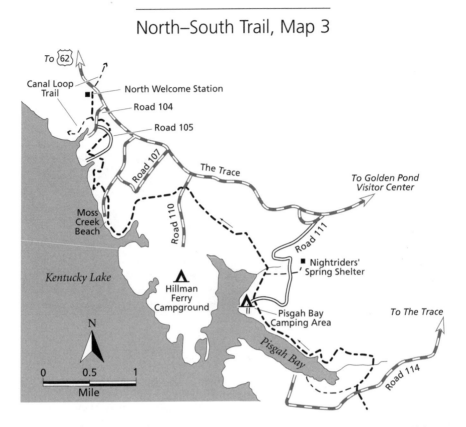

the Tennessee line. According to LBL distance figures, the entire trail is 60 miles long, and this northern part 31.2 miles. Based on my pedometer, GPS, and map readings, I believe the actual mileage is less than that. But since LBL personnel insist their figures have been verified by odometer-equipped vehicles, those are what I will use.

Whatever its exact length, the trail is a lovely backpacking route along Kentucky Lake, with a good mix of shoreline stretches and ridgetop bluffs. There's also a good deal of bottomland walking along small streams that feed into the lake. Kentucky Lake, an impoundment of the Tennessee River, is the largest man-made reservoir east of the Mississippi in length and surface area. (Lake Cumberland is larger in water volume.) Kentucky Lake drains some 40,000 square miles and covers 160,300 acres. It's relatively deep and has the blue of a natural lake instead of the soupy green of many lesser reservoirs. It also has lots of barge traffic; the Tennessee River is a major commercial route to and from the Ohio River. Completed in 1944 for the purpose of flood control, navigation, and hydropower generation, the lake is operated by the Tennessee Valley Authority.

There is no way to make a loop out of North–South Trail. As the name implies, this is a linear experience. Unfortunately, LBL has not yet spawned—at least as of this writing—a shuttle service to help hikers out, and LBL personnel say the nearest taxi is in Murray or Paducah, a good 25 to 30 miles

Early morning fog rises off Kentucky Lake as two anglers try their luck.

away. This means that if you want to do the entire northern half of the trail, you need two cars.

Making life easy for backpackers, North–South Trail is lined with attractive, level camping spots. LBL allows camping just about everywhere—except inside cemetery boundaries, within 200 yards of the Trace and other major roads, and in certain posted sites, such as the environmental education area at Honker Lake. Warm-month backpackers, however, will have to contend with ticks. The critters are prevalent enough that the North Welcome Station sells a repellent to spray on clothing. That's one reason—heat and mosquitoes are two more—I recommend spring and fall hiking. The LBL "Hike & Bike Trail Map" shows several sites with drinking water, but backpackers shouldn't count on this. At Hatchery Hollow, for example, the faucet was inoperable when I was there. All water from the lake, streams, and springs must of course be treated.

North–South Trail's northern half is divided into four sections. For northbound hikers, the first is 8.7 miles long. It starts at Golden Pond Visitor Center, which is named for what was once a settlement on LBL. Like other communities, it was eliminated and its residents resettled when the recreation area was developed in the 1960s.

The official trailhead is south of the parking area, but instead of spending time looking for it, simply take the entrance drive 0.2 mile west to the Trace. There you will find North–South Trail running along the west side of the road. Cross the road, turn right, and follow the shoulder for 0.2 mile to the underpass beneath US 68/KY 80. A short distance on the other side, the trail angles away from the Trace and into the woods. Here and throughout, the North–South is well marked by white plastic stakes. (Side trails are blazed with yellow marks.) However, be careful about mileage signs you see along the way. LBL has had trouble with pranksters changing the distance figures. Also, several years ago the trail's section boundaries were changed, and some of the old signs remain in place.

Going north and then west, you descend into sizable pines and hardwoods. At mile 2.3, after crossing several small streambeds on wooden bridges, you come to a large bottomland field and a side trail that leads south 0.5 mile to Brush Arbor Camp—an overnight shelter and spring. Continuing west, you follow a rock-bottomed creekbed for a short distance before crossing first it and then an unmarked dirt road. There are numerous good camping spots in this attractive area. After climbing several hills, you descend at mile 3.9 to the shore of Vickers Bay, the first in a series of secluded Kentucky Lake inlets that the trail passes on its way north.

Crossing two creeks, you move counterclockwise around the head of Vickers Bay and then mount a series of ridges rimming the bay's north side. There are numerous ups and downs in this stretch, none of them strenuous but in the aggregate enough to qualify as a workout. Turning north, you reach a small, unnamed bay. Again going counterclockwise, you cross a stream in the bottomland at the head of the bay and then climb steeply northward to the top of a ridge. At mile 7.1, the trail turns right onto a dirt road, LBL Road 337, and follows it for 0.4 mile before turning left off the road. Continuing along the ridgetop, you come to a bluff overlooking Rhodes Bay before descending to just above the water's edge. Following the Rhodes Bay shoreline northeast, you cross a stream and, at mile 8.4, come to LBL Road 141, which marks the end of the trail's first section. A small trickle of water named Buzzard Wing Spring is 0.1 mile south on the east side of the road. The spring is designated a backcountry campsite, and has a fire ring and a small flat spot, but is uninviting.

The second section of the trail is 9.6 miles in length, according to the LBL mileage. Turning left (northeast) onto Road 141, you follow it briefly before turning left off it and fording a small stream. Taking a series of old farm tracks, you then mount the ridgetop and descend north to the shore of a finger of Higgins Bay, another quiet lakeside spot. Following the level lakeshore, you pass a strange sight—a tiny island covered by a graveyard. The numerous graveyards you see along the trail are testament to the days when farms and small communities dotted the LBL countryside and the now-inundated Tennessee River banks.

After crossing several streambeds at the top of Higgins Bay, you go north over a knob and come down to LBL Road 319 at mile 12.4. Turn right onto this dirt road and go north for a short distance before turning left into the woods and crossing gravel LBL Road 140 at mile 13.3. The Sugar Bay boat launch and backcountry campground—with portable toilets and picnic tables but no drinking water—is just a few steps north on the road. This would be a good turnaround point for anyone wanting to make this an out-and-back hike.

Going northeast, you climb several ridges as you skirt a large inlet off Sugar Bay and then the end of the bay itself. At mile 15.6, the trail dead-ends into an old dirt road, marked when I was there by a sign incorrectly identifying it as Road 139. To your left is a cemetery; you turn right and follow the dirt track up to the top of the ridge. There you run into a gravel road, which is the real Road 139. It's also known as County Line Road because it roughly follows the line between Lyon and Trigg Counties. Turn left onto Road 139 and take it for 0.3 mile to a sign directing you to branch right onto an old dirt track.

After a level stretch, you descend into a bottomland where you skirt a large farm field and, after crossing a creek, come to a side trail leading right 4.8 miles to the Nature Station on Lake Barkley (see Hike 75). North–South Trail, after crossing a large creek on a substantial wooden bridge, curves left (west) and at mile 18 comes to Hatchery Hollow, marking the end of the trail's second section.

Hatchery Hollow is so named because the building there, now mainly a storage facility, was once the base of TVA efforts to reintroduce bald eagles into the area. At this writing LBL has seventeen eagle nests. Duncan Bay, which is just to the west, is considered one of the best eagle-viewing sites in northern LBL. The Hatchery Hollow mileage sign says there is drinking water 0.1 mile to your left—an imprecise reference to the faucet on the side of the hatchery building. I had trouble finding the faucet, and when I finally did, there was no handle to turn on the water.

From the mileage sign, the trail crosses first the driveway to the old hatchery building and then gravel LBL Road 309. Winding northward, you climb to the top of the ridge and a view of Duncan Bay. At mile 19.7, the trail makes a right turn onto gravel LBL Road 130, followed in short order by a left turn onto a gravel road that dead-ends into the Gray family cemetery. Here you turn right onto a path and descend into the bottomland at the tip of Smith Bay, another inlet said to be good for viewing eagles.

After crossing the Smith Bay drainage, you climb a hill and turn left onto dirt LBL Road 306. In 0.4 mile, you leave the road, following a path that descends northwest to cross an asphalt road at mile 22.5. This is LBL Road 114, which marks the end of the third section. A side trail left leads about 1 mile to a boat-launch and camping area that is said to have drinking water. On the other side of the road, North–South Trail follows a dirt track northeast along a field. After crossing an especially attractive stream, the trail turns west and comes to the end of thin Pisgah Bay. Running along a rocky beach littered with mollusk shells, this stretch is one of the most delightful of the hike. Just before reaching the Pisgah Point boat-launch and camping area, the trail turns away from the lake and climbs north to cross gravel Road 111 at mile 25.3.

The trail then descends to another arm of Pisgah Bay. Just before crossing a stream at the end of the bay, a side trail branches right to Nightriders' Spring, a small overnight shelter 0.6 mile away. From here the North–South climbs out of the bottomland, crosses a ridge, and enters an area marred by the repeated appearance of a scraggly power-line clearing. At mile 27.6, you cross paved LBL Road 110, which goes south to Hillman Ferry, one of the few developed campgrounds in LBL; it has drinking water, vending machines, showers, and a pay phone.

Winding southwest, the trail approaches but never crosses paved LBL Road 107. Just before the road, you drop south and follow a small, unnamed inlet to reach the rocky shoreline of Kentucky Lake at mile 28.9. This is the first time on the hike that you've been on the main body of the lake. It's also the only time, so if you want to take a dip in the lake itself, this is the place to do it. It's called the Moss Creek Day Use Area. The residential development you see across the lake is near the town of Benton.

After a brief stretch along the beach, the trail veers right onto a paved road that climbs north to a bluff. Looking northwest, you can see the 8,422-foot-long dam that creates the lake. To the left is Kentucky Dam Village State Resort Park. The road then dips, and you leave it to turn left onto a path that climbs once again above the water. After turning away from the lake to circle a couple of ravines, you descend and cross gravel LBL Road 105 near a boat-launch ramp at the end of a small inlet. Then, climbing to another bluff, you follow the ridgetop northeast and again cross Road 105. After skirting the power-line clearing, you descend and cross a paved road, LBL Road 104, near the head of another small inlet. Turning north, you pass the end of Canal Loop Trail on your left (see Hike 77) and, after crossing the power-line clearing and a wooded area, come to an asphalt walkway. Cutting across a picnic area, you reach North Welcome Station—with drinking water, rest rooms, and vending machines—at mile 31.2.

Options: To shorten this into an out-and-back hike and eliminate the need for a shuttle, simply stop at any of the shore points along the trail. The Sugar Bay area at LBL Road 140—mile 13.3 when walking north from Golden Pond Visitor Center—makes a good overnight spot if you want a semideveloped campground with tables and portable toilets (but no drinking water).

77 Canal Loop

Highlights:	Sections of shoreline along upper Kentucky Lake and Lake Barkley and the canal that connects them.
Location:	Land Between the Lakes National Recreation Area.
Type of hike:	Day hike or one-night backpack; loop.
Total distance:	About 12 miles.
Difficulty:	Easy.
Best months:	Spring and fall.
Maps:	USGS Birmingham Point; Land Between the Lakes "Hike & Bike Trail Map" (office 270–924–2000).
Permits and fees:	A $10 permit is required for backcountry camping in LBL. Permits (good for twelve months starting March 1) can be purchased at Golden Pond Visitor Center (open all year from 9:00 A.M. to 5:00 P.M.) and North Welcome Station (open March through November 9:00 A.M. to 5:00 P.M.).

Special considerations: On weekends, especially in nice weather, this trail is highly popular with mountain bikers. For the sake of your mental health and possibly physical well-being, you should avoid these high-use days. Also, ticks are a problem here; take appropriate precautions.

Finding the trailhead: From Interstate 24 or U.S. Highway 62, southeast of Calvert City, take Kentucky Highway 453 south into Land Between the Lakes (LBL), where the highway loses its numerical designation and becomes the Trace. The LBL's North Welcome Station, which has maps and other information, is 5 miles south of US 62. The hike starts at the parking lot. GPS: 36 58.272 N 88 11.925 W.

Parking and trailhead facilities: You'll find spaces for eighty cars, along with rest rooms, drinking water, vending machines, a telephone, maps, and other information.

Key points:
0.0 Canal Loop Trailhead.
0.5 Shore of Lake Barkley inlet.
2.1 C connector.
2.8 LBL Road 102 at Nickell Branch boat-launch area.
6.0 B connector.
6.5 A connector.
8.2 Microwave tower.
8.9 Kentucky Lake Drive.
10.8 D connector.

The hike: The northbound Tennessee River and the westbound Cumberland River come side by side in northern Tennessee and flow together through Kentucky to the Ohio River. In the mid-1960s, two decades after the Tennessee was dammed to make Kentucky Lake, the Corps of Engineers

Canal Loop

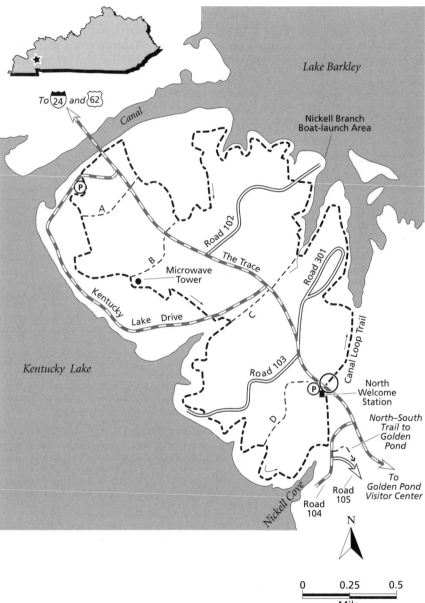

Lake Barkley

Nickell Branch
Boat-launch Area

To 24 and 62

Canal

P

A

Road 102

The Trace

B

Microwave
Tower

Road 301

Kentucky

Lake Drive

C

Canal Loop Trail

Road 103

Kentucky Lake

P

North
Welcome
Station

North–South
Trail to
Golden
Pond

D

To
Golden Pond
Visitor Center

Nickell Cove

Road
105

Road
104

N

0   0.25   0.5
Mile

finished damming the Cumberland just a few miles to the east. The result was Lake Barkley, named for the U.S. senator from Kentucky who was vice president under Harry Truman.

Lake Barkley isn't nearly as big as its neighboring reservoir—nor, to my mind, as blue and appealing. Still, with 1,000 miles of shoreline, it's a sizable body of water with scores of secluded inlets. This hike takes you along the northern shoreline of both lakes—and to the edge of the canal that connects the two. Though not as heavily used by commercial barges, the Cumberland River gets its share, and watching towboat captains pilot their cumbersome craft from one lake into the other through the canal is intriguing. The people who operate the two lakes try to ensure that the water levels are the same—354 to 359 feet, depending on the time of year.

This hike is a good compromise itinerary for backpackers who want to experience LBL but don't have time for the longer North–South Trail (see Hike 76). But be aware that there is a difference between the two. While the northern half of the North–South is open to mountain bikes (the southern half is not), the trail's length and isolation keep two-wheel traffic to a trickle. But Canal Loop is easily accessed, and four connector trails that cut across it allow bikers to tailor the length of their trip to their endurance. The result is that unlike the North–South, Canal Loop is heavily used by bikers. The trail erosion you see in the early portions near the welcome station is a testament to this. This hike will be more appealing if you don't attempt it on a high-volume weekend.

According to LBL, the entire loop—which this hike follows—measures 11.8 miles. (The loop plus all four connectors is said to total 14.3 miles.) While I doubt that the trail is actually this long, I am using the LBL figure because (as with Hike 76) LBL personnel say it has been verified by odometer-equipped vehicles.

As with North–South Trail, LBL regulations allow backcountry camping just about anywhere along the trail. The lakeshore segments offer the most pleasant spots. You pass no water source other than the two lakes and a limited number of streams, all of which must be treated before using.

This is a loop and so, of course, you can go either way. I traveled counterclockwise, and these directions assume that approach. The trail is well marked by blue metal strips. From the welcome station parking lot, cross the Trace and, at the CANAL LOOP TRAIL sign on the shoulder, head north into the thin woods. Descending gently on a well-worn mud path, you parallel a small streambed and reach the tip of a Lake Barkley inlet at mile 0.5.

Veering west, you climb to a gravel road and then curve back down to follow the inlet north toward the main lake body. Near the north end of the inlet, the trail climbs west across the little peninsula and turns south to follow the shoreline on the other side, away from the lake. The trees here are taller, the trail in better shape, and the area more secluded than the initial stretch.

At mile 2.1, just after the trail crosses a stream, C connector (0.6 mile in length) splits off to your left. It rejoins the main trail on the south side of the loop near Kentucky Lake. Like the other connectors, it's marked with yellow strips. The main trail winds north along the inlet and at mile 2.8, after

The Canal Loop Trail passes a number of small inlets and bays off Lake Barkley, including this one near the Nickell Branch Recreation Area.

turning west and climbing, crosses gravel LBL Road 102. The Nickell Branch boat-launch and camping area is just to your right.

From the road, the trail curves southwest and crosses an ugly power-line clearing before turning north and again reaching the lake. From a small inlet, you quickly follow the shoreline around to the main lake body. This is one of the most pleasant stretches of the hike. From bluffs above the water, you have a view north of the dam and the Lake Barkley end of the canal. Hopefully a barge will be coming out of or going into the canal so you can watch the captain maneuver the behemoth.

The trail continues winding along the shoreline to mile 4.7. There, near the canal entrance, it climbs up a ridge and goes first west and then south as it circles a large field in the canal bottomland. This is the least scenic part of the hike. After dipping down to cross an old road and power-line clearing, the trail rises and dips a second time. Here, at mile 6, B connector (0.5 mile in length) branches left. At mile 6.5, after winding north close to the Trace, you pass A connector (0.5 mile in length), and shortly afterward come to the edge of the canal.

Turning left, you pass under the Trace at mile 6.9 and, in rapid succession, cross paved Kentucky Lake Drive, circle a parking area, and veer northwest back toward the road. Instead of recrossing it, however, you turn south and skirt a low-lying area on your right. After passing the other end of A connector, you climb and follow the ridgetop southeast to the other end of B connector at mile 8.2. Just beyond B, you circle a tall microwave tower, which you no doubt began seeing miles earlier. From the tower, you descend gradually through a wooded area to Kentucky Lake Drive at mile 8.9. Shortly after crossing the road, you pass the other end of C. At the edge of a power-line clearing, the trail turns south and follows a streambed to an inlet of Kentucky Lake. From the inlet, you climb to a bluff overlooking the lake. You then descend and circle another inlet before climbing once again to a bluff. The trail is especially pleasant here as it follows the main Kentucky Lake shoreline from high above.

Briefly the trail runs along a dirt-and-gravel road, and then leaves it to begin circling a number of small shoreline inlets and drainages, a process that involves several climbs and descents. At mile 10.8, you pass the south end of D connector, which goes north 0.9 mile to North Welcome Station. After descending to the bottom of another ravine, the trail follows Nickell Cove north and crosses a drainage feeding into the cove. On the other side of the bridge, Canal Loop Trail runs into North–South Trail. Turn left and follow the path across a power-line clearing and wooded area to an asphalt walkway at the edge of a picnic area. North Welcome Station is on the far side of the picnic area at mile 11.8.

78 Lake Barkley State Resort Park

Highlights: Lake Barkley's shore and woods.
Location: Just east of Land Between the Lakes.
Type of hike: Day hike; loop.
Total distance: 5 miles.
Difficulty: Easy.
Best months: Any month.
Maps: USGS Canton; Lake Barkley State Resort Park *Visitor's Guide* (office 270-924-1131).

Special considerations: A portion of this loop is on paved park roads.

Finding the trailhead: From Land Between the Lakes National Recreation Area, take U.S. Highway 68/Kentucky Highway 80 east for 2.5 miles and turn left onto KY 1489. In 2 miles, where KY 1489 turns right, continue straight on the park road. Following signs for the lodge, turn left in 0.6 mile, right in another 0.6 mile, and right again in 0.4 mile. Just before the main lodge building, take the ramp down to the parking area. The trail starts just east of the parking lot—near the playground at the end of the east wing of the lodge complex. GPS: 36 50.933 N 87 55.804 W. (From Cadiz, the nearest town of any size, take US 68/KY 80 west and turn right onto KY 1489. The lodge is 8 miles from Cadiz.)

Parking and trailhead facilities: You'll find a large lot with all but unlimited parking, along with overnight rooms, a restaurant, vending machines, rest rooms, and drinking water.

Lake Barkley State Resort Park

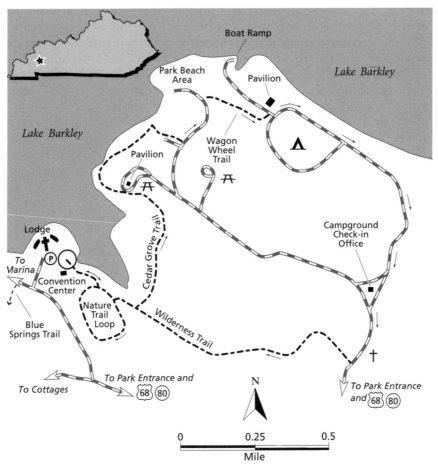

Key points:
- 0.0 Trailhead.
- 0.1 Left at fork.
- 0.2 Left at fork.
- 0.4 Left onto Cedar Grove Trail.
- 1.3 Beginning of lakeshore stretch.
- 1.8 Left onto park road.
- 2.0 Right onto Wagon Wheel Trail.
- 2.3 Right onto campground road.
- 3.5 Right onto Wilderness Trail.
- 4.5 Beginning of small nature trail loop.

The hike: With 3,700 acres, this is the largest park in the state system. It's also one of the most popular. As the "resort" part of the name suggests, it has plenty of amenities, including a handsome wood-and-glass lodge over-looking Lake Barkley. So despite the name of one of the park trails—Wilderness Trail—this is not a place for rugged, backcountry hiking. If you want that, go west a few miles to Land Between the Lakes. What this well-maintained park does offer is a stroll through lakeside woods with wildflowers and deer.

Although there are plans to rectify this shortcoming, as of this writing there is no way to loop through the park entirely on footpaths. With one exception (see Options), the trails are all relatively short, out-and-back affairs. So this hike, which makes a circle though a large hunk of the park forest, includes about a mile of road walking. It's a park road—narrow, surrounded by trees, and as pleasant as a road can be.

By the way, if you are from outside Kentucky and wondering why everything in this part of the state seems to be named Barkley, here's the reason. Alben W. Barkley, a Kentucky politician who went on to be a national player, was from nearby Paducah. Before being elected vice president with Harry Truman in 1948, Barkley served more than two decades in the U.S. Senate; half that time he was the Senate's Democratic leader. After failing to receive his party's 1952 presidential nomination, he won a new Senate term two years later, and died two years after that at age seventy-eight.

From the parking lot, walk down to the playground at the end of the east lodge wing. As you near the lakeshore, you will find a common trailhead for three trails: Lena Madesin Phillips, Cedar Grove, and Wilderness Trails. Following the path south, you quickly come to a fork marking the entrance to Phillips Trail, a short nature loop best saved for the end of the hike. Bear left and you come just as quickly to a second fork; to your right is the other end of the Phillips loop, but you go left. At mile 0.4, after crossing a creekbed likely to be dry, you come to a third fork. To your right is Wilderness Trail, which you will take on the return leg. To your left is Cedar Grove Trail, which you take now.

Appropriately named, the trail meanders north through a pleasant stand of tall cedars, climbing gently from the lakeside bottomland partway up the ridge. Where the cedars give way to hardwood trees, the trail turns left and begins to descend. This turn was unmarked when I took the hike—and easily missed, at least by me. If you go too far, as I did, you will run into the park road.

The trail descends through hardwoods into a drainage area and then climbs to the grass lawn in front of a picnic pavilion just off the park road. At the pavilion, you immediately turn left and descend a short distance through the woods to the lakeshore at mile 1.3. Here, just a few feet off the trail, you will find a secluded rest spot on the rocky "beach." Trail signs give directions for bypassing this segment in high-water conditions.

The trail follows the shore for only a short distance before veering away from the water and rising slightly. Just before you reach the start of the park's beachfront area, a plastic stake directs you southeast to a short, paved drive, which dead-ends into the park's beachfront road at mile 1.8. Turn left onto the road and follow it for 0.2 mile to the start of Wagon Wheel Trail on the right shoulder.

Wagon Wheel Trail climbs easily and, at mile 2.3, ends at an asphalt road. To your left is a boat ramp; to your right the park campground. Turn right

An isolated spot along the shoreline makes a nice place for lunch.

and then immediately left and follow the campground loop road eastward along the ridgetop overlooking the lake. This is the beginning of the road stretch. Park officials had plans to develop a campground trail that would eliminate most of this road walk. Check at the lodge to see if it's a reality yet. Even if it's not, you can walk part of the way on the lightly wooded strip along the road's lake side.

The road climbs and, at mile 3.3, shortly after passing the campground check-in station, intersects the main park road. Turn left onto this road and, at mile 3.5, just after a small cemetery with gravestones dating to the 1800s, turn right onto Wilderness Trail. This attractive, moss-covered path initially goes northwest on the ridgetop but soon descends into a ravine. Here you follow—on your left—a small streambed full of ferns and wildflowers. At mile 4.3, after finding yourself once again among cedar trees, you meet Cedar Grove Trail.

Turning left and retracing your steps, you come to one end of Phillips Trail. This interpretive loop, named in memory of a woman active in the business world, includes a wooden suspension bridge that jiggles when you walk over it—a feature certain to please children. A pamphlet—available at the lodge and at the beginning of the loop—explains points of interest. At mile 4.9, you exit the other end of the loop, and at mile 5 are back at the trailhead near the lodge.

Options: Blue Springs Trail, which starts south of the lodge, makes a loop of about 1.5 miles when combined with a short park road. I did not take this trail, but the park says the lakeshore portion is a good place to see deer and geese.

79 Pennyrile Forest

Highlights:	Small streams and waterfalls in isolated hollows.
Location:	Northwest of Hopkinsville.
Type of hike:	Day hike or one-night backpack; shuttle (one-way).
Total distance:	13.5 miles.
Difficulty:	Strenuous.
Best months:	Spring.
Maps:	USGS Dawson Springs and Dawson Springs SW; Kentucky Division of Forestry map of Pennyrile Nature Trail (available at Madisonville forestry office, 270-824-7527; Pennyrile Forest State Resort Park, 270-797-3421; and Pennyrile State Forest headquarters, 270-797-3241).

Special considerations: Plans to enlarge the state park golf course (now in the early stage) could alter the first 1.5 miles of this hike.

Finding the trailhead: From Hopkinsville, take Kentucky Highway 109 north for 20 miles and turn left onto KY 398. In 1.7 miles, turn right at the main entrance to the Pennyrile Forest State Resort Park; 0.5 mile later, park by the lodge. (From the Western Kentucky Parkway, take the Dawson Springs exit, go south for 8 miles on KY 109, and turn right onto KY 398.) From the lodge parking lot, walk a few steps north and turn left onto the road to the park golf course. The trailhead is less than 0.1 mile on your right. GPS: 37 04.395 N 87 39.854 W.

Parking and trailhead facilities: There are spaces for about seventy-five cars, as well as overnight rooms, a restaurant, a telephone, rest rooms, and drinking water in the lodge. The park campground is off KY 398 just south of the lodge entrance.

Key points:
- 1.5   Forest Road 20.
- 6.1   Clifty Shores Road.
- 7.9   Lake point.
- 12.0   Lakewood Drive.
- 13.1   Old Hospital Road.

The hike: In the late 1990s, doing much of the work on his own time, state forester Richard Hane set about to develop a hiking trail through the northern half of the 14,468-acre Pennyrile State Forest, the largest forest owned by Kentucky. The result is the beautiful and strenuous Pennyrile Nature Trail, which this hike follows. Though he cautions that the figure has not been verified by on-the-ground "wheeling," Hane puts the trail's length at 13.5 miles based on map and GPS measurements. My own measurements indicated that it's somewhat less, but 13.5 is the mileage you see on the trail markers—and the one used here.

Pennyrile Forest

To Dawson Springs

Tradewater River

Lakewood Drive

Old Hospital Road

No Outlet Road

Outwood Hospital

Lake Beshear

Lakeshore Point

Hopkins Park Road

Clifty Shores Road

109

Clifty Creek

To Hopkinsville

20

Indian Bluffs Trail

State Forest Boundary

398

Park Golf Course

Park Campground

Lodge

Pennyrile Lake

To Hopkinsville via 91

N

0   0.5   1
Mile

Running from the Pennyrile Forest State Resort Park to the town of Dawson Springs, the trail winds through numerous bottomlands that early in the year are flowing with attractive streams and dotted with small, picturesque waterfalls. That's why I say spring is the best time to visit. Between these low-lying areas, the trail climbs constantly. For much of the way, you are on the ridge above the east shore of Lake Beshear—a 760-acre reservoir with a wiggly, natural-looking shoreline that belies its man-made status.

None of these ups and down is in itself a killer. But all together they take their toll by the second half of the hike, especially if you are carrying a backpack. Also, this is a new trail, and on some of the sloping ridgesides, a path has yet to take hold, making it tough on ankles. Be aware as well that unless stepped-up use has eliminated the brambles I encountered, you will be happier in long pants. But don't be put off by these cautionary notes. This is one of the best backpacking trails in the state—certainly in the western half.

Hane calls his creation a nature trail, but it's a nature trail for adults. Unlike the elementary interpretive material you find on so many nature trails, the plaques posted along this one are sophisticated explanations of the processes—both natural and human—that have gone into creating the forest you see today.

I suggest walking south to north because the park is one of the state's nicest, and makes a good place to leave your car. How you get back to it, however, will be a problem if you don't have a second car to stash at the trail's northern terminus. Dawson Springs has no taxi or, as this is written, any other kind of shuttle possibilities. Check with the Madisonville forestry office or state park to see if any have since developed. The trails ends at the south end of Dawson Springs; the spot has parking room for about six cars, but no facilities. The town center with stores, restaurants, and telephones is another 1.5 miles north on KY 109. The KY 398 turnoff to the state park is 5 miles south on KY 109.

Backcountry camping is prohibited in the state park, but only the first 0.5 mile of the trail is in the park. Beyond that you are in the state forest, where camping is allowed. There are no permit requirements or designated sites; all water must be treated. Plans to enlarge the park's nearby golf course could eventually move the park boundary northward, possibly affecting the trail's first 1.5 miles.

Pennyrile Nature Trail starts together with Indian Bluffs Trail, a short path that leads to the golf course. From the trailhead on the north side of the golf course road, you climb up the ridge along a rock outcropping. After Indian Bluffs Trail splits off to the south at mile 0.2, you descend and cross a stream. You then return to the ridgeside for a flat stretch through a pleasant stand of tall pine trees.

As an interpretive plaque you see later in the hike explains, what is now Pennyrile Forest was hardscrabble farming country until the 1930s, when a New Deal resettlement program bought out the homesteaders. To help restore the land, the fields and pastures were planted with millions of pines. The bottomlands and slopes never farmed remain in hardwoods.

In this early stretch, as throughout the hike, the trail is marked every 40 to 60 feet or so with black-and-white PNT signs attached to trees. Without these, you would lose your way where leaves cover the new, lightly trod path. At mile 1.5, the trail crosses FR 20 and follows an old dirt road along a creek into an appealing bottomland, with a waterfall on your right. This stream flows into a branch of Clifty Creek, which you cross and follow toward Lake Beshear in a valley lined with rock outcroppings. This can be a wet section, and your boots may get a bit soggy. You pass a beaver pond on your left shortly before the trail begins a steep climb up the ridgeside.

Near the top of the ridge, you pass one of the old homesites. After a view of the lily-covered end of Lake Beshear down below, you descend and follow a dry drainage away from the lake. Again climbing the ridge, you walk over several old gas-well pipes before descending to cross a creek at mile 4.1. On the other side, the trail goes up a rock-strewn area and follows the level ridgetop north with views of the lake below on your left. Turning, you follow a ravine southeast and, after crossing the stream in another appealing bottomland, begin winding your way northeast. At mile 6.1, shortly after passing another delightful falls on the left of the trail, you cross gravel Clifty Shores Road just west of KY 109, marking the end of the hike's first—and easier—half.

The trail now takes a meandering, up-and-down route northwestward, back toward Lake Beshear. After reaching the end of a small inlet, you follow the shoreline from above on the ridge. At mile 7.9, the trail descends on an old roadbed to a point of land sticking out into the lake. This point, covered with grass and wildflowers, makes a great place for lunch or a rest. You can easily walk down to the water's edge, which is lined with large, flat rocks.

From the point, retrace your steps about 300 feet up the hill and turn left (southeast). Following a stream on your left, you walk along the steep slope above the stream before crossing it and climbing north. Here the trail begins a series of lengthy swings toward KY 109 as it circles streambeds and ravines draining into the lake. One of these eastward legs takes you close to the entrance to Outwood, a state facility for the mentally retarded.

At mile 11.2, on the last of these spokes, just before hitting paved No Outlet Road, the trail turns abruptly left (west) and descends into a lovely ravine lined with fern-covered rocks. On the left of the trail you pass an overlook above a waterfall—another good rest spot, though be careful of the drop-off if small children are with you. After climbing back up the ridge and turning north, you cross first No Outlet Road and then, at mile 12, Lakewood Drive.

Continuing north, you cross KY 109 and a power-line clearing before following an old dirt road into a ravine and coming to a dilapidated asphalt road. This is Old Hospital Road, which you take to your left. The road curves south and quickly brings you, at mile 13.5, to the Tradewater River and a pedestrian bridge. On the other side is KY 109 and the trail's end.

Appendix A: For More Information

FEDERAL GOVERNMENT

Big South Fork National River and
Recreation Area
Kentucky Visitors Center
H.C. 69, P.O. Box 1
Stearns, KY 42647-0001
(606) 376-5073

Cumberland Gap National
Historical Park
Box 1848
Middlesboro, KY 40965
(606) 248-2817

Daniel Boone National Forest
Forest Supervisor's Office
1700 Bypass Road
Winchester, KY 40391
(859) 745-3100

   Morehead District Office
   2375 KY 801 South
   Morehead, KY 40351
   (606) 784-6428

   Stanton District Office
   705 West College Avenue
   Stanton, KY 40380
   (606) 663-2852

   London District Office
   761 South Laurel Road
   London, KY 40744
   (606) 864-4163

   Somerset District Office
   135 Realty Lane
   Somerset, KY 42501
   (606) 679-2010

   Stearns District Office
   US 27 North, P.O. Box 429
   Whitley City, KY 42653
   (606) 376-5323

   Redbird District Office
   H.C. 68, Box 65
   Big Creek, KY 40914
   (606) 598-2192

Fort Knox
Hunt Control Office
Fort Knox, KY 40121
(502) 624-7311

Land Between the Lakes National
Recreation Area
100 Van Morgan Drive
Golden Pond, KY 42211
(270) 924-2000

Mammoth Cave National Park
Mammoth Cave, KY 42259
(270) 758-2251

Reelfoot National Wildlife Refuge
4343 Highway 157
Union City, TN 38261
(901) 538-2481

U.S. ARMY CORPS OF ENGINEERS

Nashville District
(for Barkley, Cumberland, Dale
Hollow, Laurel, and Martins
Fork Lakes)
P.O. Box 1070
Nashville, TN 37202
(615) 736-7161

Huntington District
(for Dewey, Fishtrap, Grayson,
Paintsville, and Yatesville Lakes)
502 8th Street
Huntington, WV 25701
(304) 529-5452

Louisville District
(for Barren, Buckhorn, Carr Fork,
  Cave Run, Green River, Nolin,
  Rough River, and Taylorsville
  Lakes)
P.O. Box 59
Louisville, KY 40201-0059
(502) 582-5736

KENTUCKY GOVERNMENT

Kentucky Department of Fish and
  Wildlife Resources
1 Game Farm Road
Frankfort, KY 40601
(502) 564-4336
(800) 858-1549

Kentucky Department of Parks
Capital Plaza Tower
500 Metro Street, Suite 1100
Frankfort, KY 40601-1974
(800) 255-PARK

Kentucky Division of Forestry
627 Comanche Trail
Frankfort, KY 40601
(502) 564-4496

Kentucky Geological Survey
Room 228, Mining and Minerals
  Resources Building
University of Kentucky
Lexington, KY 40506-0107
(859) 257-5500

Kentucky State Nature Preserves
  Commission
801 Schenkel Lane
Frankfort, KY 40601
(502) 573-2886

Kentucky Tourism Cabinet
Capital Plaza Tower
500 Metro Street, 22nd Floor
Frankfort, KY 40601
(800) 225-TRIP

Lilley Cornett Woods
H.C. 63, Box 2710
Skyline KY 41851
(606) 633-5828

LOCAL GOVERNMENTS

Lexington-Fayette County Parks
  and Recreation Department
545 North Upper Street
Lexington, KY 40508
(859) 288-2900

Metropolitan Parks Department
(for Louisville and Jefferson
  County)
1297 Trevilian Way
Louisville, KY 40213
(502) 456-8100

PRIVATE ORGANIZATIONS

Bernheim Arboretum and Research
  Forest
P.O. Box 130
Clermont, KY 40110
(502) 955-8512

Clyde E. Buckley Wildlife
  Sanctuary
1305 Germany Road
Frankfort, KY 40601
(859) 873-5711

Nature Conservancy, Kentucky
  Chapter
642 West Main Street
Lexington, KY 40508-2018
(859) 259-9655

Shaker Village of Pleasant Hill
3501 Lexington Road
Harrodsburg, KY 40330
(800) 734-5611

Sierra Club, Cumberland Chapter
259 West Short Street
Lexington, KY 40507
(859) 255-7946

Appendix B: Further Reading

HISTORY

Aron, Stephen. *How the West Was Lost: The Transformation of Kentucky from Daniel Boone to Henry Clay*. Baltimore: Johns Hopkins University Press, 1996.

Caudill, Harry M. *Night Comes to the Cumberlands: A Biography of a Depressed Area*. Boston: Little, Brown, 1962.

Clark, Thomas D. *A History of Kentucky*. Ashland: Jesse Stuart Foundation, 1992. (Originally published New York: Prentice-Hall, 1937.)

Coleman, J. Winston, Jr., editor. *Kentucky: A Pictorial History*. Lexington: University Press of Kentucky, 1971.

Harrison, Lowell H., and James C. Klotter. *A New History of Kentucky*. Lexington: University Press of Kentucky, 1997.

HIKING AND OUTDOORS

Berry, Wendell. *The Unforeseen Wilderness: Kentucky's Red River Gorge*. San Francisco: North Point Press, 1991.

Bluegrass Group of the Sierra Club. *Hiking the Red: A Complete Trail Guide to Kentucky's Red River Gorge Including Natural Bridge State Park*. Louisville: Harmony House, 2000.

Deaver, Brenda G., Jo Anna Smith, and Howard Ray Duncan. *Hiking the Big South Fork*, 3rd ed. Knoxville: University of Tennessee Press, 1999.

Manning, Russ. *100 Trails of the Big South Fork*. Seattle: The Mountaineers Books, 2000.

Manning, Russ. *The Historic Cumberland Plateau: An Explorer's Guide*. Knoxville: University of Tennessee Press, 1999.

Ruchhoft, Robert H. *Kentucky's Land of the Arches*. Cincinnati: Pucelle Press, 1986.

Sides, Stanley D. *Guide to the Surface Trails of Mammoth Cave National Park*. St. Louis: Cave Books, 1995.

Appendix C: A Hiker's Checklist

Always make and check your own checklist!

If you've ever hiked into the backcountry and discovered that you've forgotten an essential, you know that it's a good idea to make a checklist and check the items off as you pack so you won't forget the things you want and need. Here are some ideas:

Clothing
- [ ] Dependable rain parka
- [ ] Rain pants
- [ ] Windbreaker
- [ ] Thermal underwear
- [ ] Shorts
- [ ] Long pants or sweatpants
- [ ] Wood cap or balaclava
- [ ] Hat
- [ ] Wool shirt or sweater
- [ ] Jacket or parka
- [ ] Extra socks
- [ ] Underwear
- [ ] Lightweight shirts
- [ ] T-shirts
- [ ] Bandanna(s)
- [ ] Mittens or gloves
- [ ] Belt

Footwear
- [ ] Sturdy, comfortable boots
- [ ] Lightweight camp shoes

Bedding
- [ ] Sleeping bag
- [ ] Foam pad or air mattress
- [ ] Groundsheet (plastic or nylon)
- [ ] Dependable tent

Hauling
- [ ] Backpack and/or day pack

Cooking
- [ ] 1-quart container (plastic)
- [ ] 1-gallon water container for camp use (collapsible)
- [ ] Backpack stove and extra fuel
- [ ] Funnel
- [ ] Aluminum foil
- [ ] Cooking pots
- [ ] Bowls/plates
- [ ] Utensils (spoons, forks, small spatula, knife)
- [ ] Pot scrubber
- [ ] Matches in waterproof container

Food and Drink
- [ ] Cereal
- [ ] Bread
- [ ] Crackers
- [ ] Cheese
- [ ] Trail mix
- [ ] Margarine
- [ ] Powdered soups
- [ ] Salt/pepper
- [ ] Main-course meals
- [ ] Snacks
- [ ] Hot chocolate
- [ ] Tea
- [ ] Powdered milk
- [ ] Drink mixes

Photography
- [ ] Camera and film
- [ ] Filters
- [ ] Lens brush/paper

Miscellaneous
- [ ] Sunglasses
- [ ] Map and compass
- [ ] Toilet paper
- [ ] Pocketknife
- [ ] Sunscreen
- [ ] Good insect repellent
- [ ] Lip balm
- [ ] Flashlight with good batteries and spare bulb
- [ ] Candle(s)
- [ ] First-aid kit
- [ ] Your FalconGuide
- [ ] Survival kit
- [ ] Small garden trowel or shovel
- [ ] Water filter or purification tablets
- [ ] Plastic bags (for trash)
- [ ] Soap
- [ ] Towel
- [ ] Toothbrush
- [ ] Fishing license
- [ ] Fishing rod, reel, lures, flies, etc.
- [ ] Binoculars
- [ ] Waterproof covering for pack
- [ ] Watch
- [ ] Sewing kit

About the Author

Michael H. Brown is a Kentucky native and for twenty-eight years was a reporter for the *Louisville Courier-Journal,* the last seventeen as Washington correspondent. He and his wife, Margaret, have five children and currently live in Arlington, Virginia. In addition to Kentucky, the couple's hiking experience includes long-distance backpacking trips in New England, Washington State, France, Spain, and Italy. The Browns also cycle, and have pedaled across the United States.